THE CHRISTIAN STATE

The Christian State

AUGUSTINE J. OSGNIACH, O.S.B., Ph.D.

PROFESSOR OF PHILOSOPHY, ST. MARTIN'S COLLEGE,
LACEY, WASHINGTON

Author of
Analysis of Objects

THE BRUCE PUBLISHING COMPANY
MILWAUKEE

Imprimi potest: ✠ Lambertus Burton, O.S.B., Abbas S. Martini
Nihil obstat: D. A. Hanly, P.A., Censor librorum
Imprimatur: ✠ Geraldus Shaughnessy, S.M., S.T.D., Episcopus Seattlensis

15 Januarii, 1943

THIS BOOK IS DEDICATED
TO
CHRIST THE KING
OF
ALL AGES, NATIONS, RACES
AND TONGUES

CONTENTS

vii

FOREWORD

THE champions of the *philosophia perennis,* the Aristotelian-Thomists, always at work on every far-flung frontier, assimilating to eternal principles without fear or quibble all the facts from all the particular sciences as rapidly as they are discovered, have naturally been especially preoccupied of late with social, economic, and political problems. The monumental sociological study of *The Framework of a Christian State* by the Irish Jesuit, Father Cahill, the rich fruits of heroic action and historical contemplation embodied in Don Luigi Sturzo's *Church and State,* the lifelong investigations of "distributive justice" by the greatest economist in the United States, Monsignor John A. Ryan, the two profoundly practical commentaries on the epoch-making labor-capital encyclicals of Pope Leo XIII and Pope Pius XI, by Oswald Von Nell-Breuning, S.J. (*Reorganization of Social Economy*) and Joseph Husslein, S.J. (*The Christian Social Manifesto*), and the first installments in *The Thomist* (July, 1941) of what promises to be the most mature and searching analysis yet made of the concept of democracy, by Professor Mortimer J. Adler, of the University of Chicago, and Father Walter Farrell, O.P., these are examples taken almost at random from a rich body of up-to-the-minute research which, if it were studied by the self-styled naturalistic professors of the social sciences and by our politicians adrift in chaos, would cure them of at least the most perilous of their diseases of the soul.

Nobody knows better than I, however, that our idolatrous "humanistic" worshipers of unreal abstractions are little likely to make the slightest sustained effort to study these calmly objective works which combine the wisdom of a spacious past with an encyclopedic observation of the present. I can never forget how, in my own agnostic-socialistic days, I glanced at the works of Hilaire Belloc and John A. Ryan only to close them almost immediately, easily confirmed in my deep-rooted delusion that anything of Catholic vintage must of necessity be reactionary and more or less befogged by superstition. In the field of the social sciences it was the erudite and irresistibly charitable philosophy of history of the eminent convert, Christopher Dawson, which, from the human point of view, awoke me from my dogmatic slumbers. Of that faith which comes not to conflict with but to crown reason I will not speak here, for facts and reason alone would suffice to impel any man who is really emancipated from his complexes to join me in my allegiance to the Catholic social scientists.

When I consider how apparently hopeless my own case may well have seemed to those who knew the truth, I cannot despair that more and more of those who still think as I did will discover that all forms of what is called humanism find their inevitable apotheosis in some liturgical hatred which hypostatizes and deifies some such unreality, some such mere *ens rationis* as the proletariat, the Aryan race, or the liberalistic "will" of a mythical Rousseauistic "democracy," that most so-called altruism is but a myopic, self-deceived, hedonistic egoism, and that evolutionary progress is a pseudo-scientific delusion that will sooner or later invariably lead to despair and to nihilism in the strictest sense of the word, a nihilism which combines epistemological skepticism, aesthetic and moral relativism, and metaphysical tychism (the glorification of a mathematical "chance" with a capital C).

So let all Aristotelian-Thomists redouble their prayers and their works. They must make their prayers into works and their works into perpetual prayers. They will, I know, redouble their studies of social dilemmas, confident that the time will come, unless the end of the world is hard at hand, that more and more of the superstitious, "naturalistic," rationalizers, even those as timorously arrogant as I was, will somehow, in God's good time, be brought to talk and write less, and to listen and read more.

What moment therefore, in our Dark Age, could be more opportune for the appearance of this book by this Benedictine, Dr. Osgniach, this contemporary member of that ancient order which really, more than any other influence, humanized in the love of God the barbarians of the earlier Dark Ages while the noisy public figures who throng the more sensational pages of literary and propagandist histories only make the confusion worse confounded? Father Osgniach has chosen the strictly philosophical approach to the analysis of the Christian state. This is well, for contemporary Catholic thought is much better provided with historical, sociological, anthropological, economic, and political science investigations in the light of which the deepest implications in the works of St. Thomas Aquinas, St. Robert Bellarmine, and Suarez may be clarified. Father Osgniach's work is *sui generis*. No contemporary philosopher has faced more fairly and unflinchingly all the solutions offered for all the painful problems of today from that of sovereignty to that of private property, and from that of private property to that of legalized sterilization. He steers his untroubled way through a perfect archipelago of sophisms, slogans, and panaceas, and his work abounds in such healing paragraphs, climaxes of long-sustained, close reasoning, and rich marshaling of facts as the following two (on p. 163 and p. 183) which I quote, trusting that they will allure readers, even as perverse as I have been, to venture on into the text with a hope, long dulled by the futilities of pragmatists and others, now at last renewed.

"In order to provide in a worthy manner for his moral and material wants man needs civil society. But for a society to exist and tend to its end, a power is required to direct it to that end, and with it the right to ordain whatever is demanded by the common good. In other words, it is necessary that authority have the right to command and the subjects the duty to obey. This right and this duty do not depend on human will; they are the demands of the moral natural law, the basis of all positive right. We have this ultimate explanation in God. Hence the alternative: We must admit that either God, the Creator of man and

of nature, has the right to command and to enact laws as a
necessary presupposition of all social life; or we must take refuge
in relativism and statal arbitrariness. The first alternative has
the support of the vast majority of men of all races and nations
and times, from today to the remotest times of which history
has any record; the second has the support only of recent innovators who are trying out their experiments, reckless of the cost
to morality, unity, and to the liberty of human actions. The
top-heavy burden of unjust laws contradictory in themselves and
piling up by the thousands and the hundreds of thousands is
beginning to bear fruit which, unless something is done soon
by way of remedy, must end in social chaos and disaster. For
this we owe our thanks to the materialists and atheists of the
past two centuries who merely carried to extremes the tenets of
the protestant revolt against the laws of nature, of Christ, and
of God."

"Whoever repudiates the true teaching of the origin of man,
of his social nature, and of his ultimate end or goal, deprives
himself of all necessary weapons to resist statal despotism, which
robs him of his true dignity as a man and renders him a slave
of the State motivated only by servile fear. But every human being is a proper personality, having a divine origin and a sublime
end in virtue of which he becomes a sharer of time and of eternity. Therefore, it is a strictly philosophical axiom that while
the State is created for time, the individual is created for eternity; that the State is not an end in itself but only a means
toward an end. Hence the State is not a master but a servant
bound to treat the individual as a free and responsible person,
as a creature endowed with immortality. Only thus can the individual vindicate his personal dignity and the proper place
which belongs to him in the natural order and in his social
relations. In all other hypotheses, it is not only extreme temerity
but an impossibility even to remind the State of its duties or to
insist on an adequate cooperation from the State in order that
the individual may attain his ultimate goal and his full moral
and spiritual development. In relation to his ultimate goal man

takes up an entirely special position. In this regard it is no
longer the individual that must serve the State but the latter
is bound to serve the individual because the State is made for
time only, while the individual is created for eternity. If we
deny a transcendental goal to the individual, he will remain
inexorably only a cog in the machinery of the State, and the
goal of the individual will always be subjected to the collective
goal of the majority, which goal can be only temporal, or lasting only as long as a particular group or society exists. Hence
it is that notwithstanding the illusion of progress we are gradually reverting to barbarism."

> HERBERT ELLSWORTH CORY
> *Department of Liberal Arts*
> *University of Washington, Seattle, Wash.*

AUTHOR'S PREFACE

NEVER before in the history of the world have the difficulties of political and social problems been felt so keenly as they are today. Society is shaken to its very foundations. Everywhere there is chaos and commotion, a despair without a hope; political, moral, and intellectual darkness reigns ominously over the earth. The bestial love of every man for himself, of every class and nation for itself, together with falsehood and injustice, have engulfed kingdoms, republics, and empires in a devastating and universal war. Human society which for the past three centuries has been tossing in the delirium of a hundred fevers, has at last gone mad. Trembling on the brink of dissolution, society is rushing into the ruthless grasp of militarism, and is worshiping idolatrously the irresponsible absolutism of the State. New dictators, profiting by the overthrow of all systems and of all laws, have reduced entire nations to want, to massacre, and to ruin. Right has been identified with, and supplanted by, might. Small nations have no longer the right to live; the just claims of minorities are denied. Suppressed, too, are the rights of the various groups in the international society and the laws which make international society possible at all. Personal liberty and human dignity have become empty phrases. The natural rights and duties of the individual and of the family, of such vital importance to the structure and the protection of society, are utterly disregarded. The family, as it was formerly, has almost disappeared; matrimony is destroyed by adultery, and progeny seems to many a curse. The Christian teaching of the divine origin of authority and of natural right has been relegated to oblivion. In vain have the Popes for more than sixty years warned the world of the catastrophe now threatening to overwhelm us. The cry of *"Crucify Him"* has been uttered by all nations; there is blood on the hands of all.

How shall we explain this strange phenomenon? What is the cause of the world's chaos? What has produced this dark disorder in men's minds and morals? Doctrinaries have lied to society. Modern pride has rejected the truths of the ancient philosophy of reason, Insatiable greed has repudiated all idea of right and law. Modern thought has diabolically explained away almost everything that former generations held most sacred and most certain. It has denied God, creation, the distinction of matter and spirit, objective truth, the difference between good and evil. It has rejected the basic traditional principles of thought and being. The State, it is claimed, is not a natural institution arising from man's social and political nature, but merely the creature of brute force and the purely artificial and arbitrary determination of man. Law for Hobbes is but the brute force of the Leviathan: for Rousseau it is merely the changing mood of the mob. For some of our contemporary thinkers there is no law but personal whim. If there is no objective truth, there is no objective norm of right and wrong, there is no law, no obligation, no system of rights and duties. The political theories of Hobbes and Rousseau, of Hegel and others, contain germinally all the characteristic features of the modern totalitarian regimes: the dictatorship of a party in the name of the community; the use of propaganda and appeals to mass emotion, as well as of violence and terrorism; the conception of revolutionary justice as a social weapon; and above all the attempt to enforce a uniform ideology on the whole people and the proscription and persecution of every other form of political thought. Clearly, philosophy has sinned against reason and, in consequence, against nature. In hearkening to this teaching, society renounced the principle of life with which its divine Author had endowed it, and it is now paying the penalty of its apostasy: the whole human race lies prostrate under an anathema. No one who accepts "modern" philosophy and morals has any right to complain.

What Leo XIII said of his times may even more emphatically be applied to our own. "If any one," the great Pontiff writes in the Encyclical *Aeterni Patris*, "look carefully at the bitterness of our times, and if he further consider earnestly the causes of those things that are done in public and in private, he will discover with certainty the prolific source of evils we greatly fear. The cause he will find to consist in this — evil teaching about things human and divine has come from the schools of philosophers; it has crept into all the departments of the State; and it has been received with the common applause of very many. Now, it has been implanted in man by nature to follow reason as the guide of his actions, and, therefore, if the understanding go wrong in anything, the will easily follows. Hence it comes about that wicked opinions, whose seat is in the understanding, flow into human actions and make them bad likewise. On the other hand, if the mind of man be healthy and strongly grounded in solid and true principles, he will assuredly be the source of great blessing, to the individuals and the common weal."

To emerge from the dark abyss into which modern thought has plunged us, it is imperative that we return to the old philosophical principles and reiterate the Christian doctrine of the social and political order. Only a careful analysis and application of the Christian program of reconstruction can save us, on the one hand, from the obsolete optimism of false Utopias, and on the other, from barbarism and despair. Only Christian philosophy can consistently uphold the principles of personal worth and responsibility, which always and everywhere have been the lifeblood of liberty. Without these principles, genuine democracy is impossible; the State becomes a system of organized robbery; the common good of all is sacrificed to the material prosperity of the few; and the law of nations is reduced to the law of the destruction of the weak. The purpose of this work, therefore, is not the presentation of a new philosophy of the State; rather it is an attempt to show how the present-day problems can best be solved in the light of Christian philosophy.

A critical analysis of the modern statal theories will uncover and confirm their inherent weaknesses and aberrations. This is the laudable ideal which induced us to make this humble contribution to the great and necessary work of social and political reconstruction.

If, therefore, this labor of love for the truth shall have contributed even a small part to the progress and welfare of humanity, as all true philosophy should, the author will feel amply rewarded.

It is a pleasure to acknowledge a debt of gratitude to Dr. Herbert E. Cory of the Department of Liberal Arts in the University of Washington, for his brilliant and generous Foreword. My special thanks are due to the Right Rev. Monsignor D. A. Hanly, P.A., and to Professors Mr. Michael J. Contris, and the Rev. Leonard Feeney, O.S.B., for their valuable criticism and for many a suggestion toward clarity of thought and expression. Without their assistance several grave defects would not have been removed. A word of appreciation is also due to my confrere the Rev. Albert Erkens, O.S.B., of St. Martin's Abbey, who has been kind enough to read the manuscript.

A. J. O.

St. Martin's Abbey
Lacey, Washington
July 21, 1941
XXV Anniversary of My Ordination
to the Holy Priesthood.

CHAPTER I

THE NATURAL BASIS OF SOCIETY AND THE STATE

THE problem of the origin of society has far-reaching consequences. Upon one's solution of this problem depends his understanding of the ends and functions of the State. If the origin is determined in the light of State absolutism or totalitarianism, the State becomes an end in itself and man becomes but a means to that end. Again, if the origin is determined in the light of liberalism, the individual becomes supreme and the State subservient, for the liberal denies to law or persons any independent authority. But if the origin of society is sought in the social nature of man, then the end of man becomes the end of the State. This implies a whole series of inalienable rights proper to every human being. It is upon the solid foundation of man's social nature that Christian thought builds a system of social and political philosophy, which determines realistically the nature, purpose, and functions of the State and presents in their true light the relations between the State and its members.

SOCIETY

No being exists in complete isolation from its fellows. Everywhere we behold unity in multiplicity and multiplicity in unity; in each degree of existence we find number and union. Interrelation is evident even among most rudimentary forms of the inorganic world; it is on a somewhat higher level in the vegetable kingdom; it appears more striking among animals; it shines forth in splendor and grandeur in man, the king of creation. "Isolation," in the words of Lacordaire, "is the negation of life, since life is spontaneous movement, and movement supposes relations. It is, moreover, the negation of order, harmony, and beauty, for none of these things can be conceived without the double idea of plurality and unity."[1] We may then, define society as a union of intelligent beings for their mutual perfection.

A thing is natural when it is in conformity with the real constitution of a being. Now the societal state is evidently in conformity with the constitution of man, since he has always and everywhere lived in society. Hence man is naturally social. This is so because the societal state corresponds to man's needs and societal impulse, an impulse so strong and characteristic that it may be regarded as a true instinct. Finally society is a necessary phenomenon, since outside of it man cannot attain his end. Society, for him, is the primary and supreme condition of existence and development.

THE STATE

As a social animal man is impelled to seek some form of human society, but as a political animal he is moved by nature toward that specific kind of society, known as political or civil, the State. By the State is generally meant a stable union of families cooperating under the direction of civil authority, for a common purpose. More precisely, the State is a natural and sovereign society; natural because its specific form is an ordinance of God who made man social by nature; sovereign because it alone can provide all the means to accomplish the statal purpose. Whether the State is ancient or modern, great or small, prosperous or decadent, it is always a natural and sovereign society.

The problem concerning the natural basis of society and of the State is vitally important, not only because of its intrinsic value, but also because of the intellectual confusion and manifold errors prevailing on this point. Instead of shedding light on the problem, non-Christian philosophies have been instrumental only in exercising a dark and sinister influence on the social order. Though originating from contrary principles, such

---

[1] Lacordaire, *Conferences on God* (New York: O'Shea, 1871), p. 227.

erroneous theories agree in their main conclusion, namely, the emancipation of the creature from the Creator, a complete negation of all law which is not of a mechanical character or enacted by the will of a majority. They make it impossible to form a clear idea of the statal purpose, and of the particular statal relations to the individual, to the family, and to other social groups. Hence a critical examination of the various non-Christian philosophies of the State will unquestionably place in clearer relief the profound wisdom of the traditional solution, a solution ever ancient and ever new.

PART I

ERRONEOUS THEORIES OF THE STATE

We shall deal here with the contractualist theories of Hobbes and Rousseau, the former of which gives rise to State absolutism, and the latter to democratic absolutism. This is followed by a consideration of the more recent Spencerian view which regards society as an organism, and which leads logically both to collectivism and liberalism, although these two seem mutually exclusive. Finally, we shall consider anarchism and communism, the former of which regards the State as a parasitic organism harmful to the common good, and the latter as a product of class struggle, a machine of oppression and exploitation.

1. THE THEORIES OF SOCIAL CONTRACT

a) *Hobbes*

The first great modern exponent of a theory of social contract was Thomas Hobbes. To understand the nature of the State we must, he claims, study the primitive times when there was no civil society, and when the instinct of self-preservation reigned supreme. In this primitive state every man had a natural right to whatever was conducive to his happiness; all men had natural rights to all things. This necessarily created a conflict, and a state of universal and continuous warfare became the natural state of man. To put an end to this reign of anarchy, and thereby to avert common disaster, men agreed by a free contract to found a commonwealth for the establishment of peace.

Arguing from this, Hobbes holds that for the preservation of society everyone must willingly surrender himself, soul and body, to his fellow man in order to be handed over in due time to the governing power. This surrender must be complete, placing at the disposal of the sovereign all resources necessary for the maintenance of social peace. Naturally men will not surrender their rights, unless they are compensated in the form of security. This security can be realized only by investing the sovereign with a power sufficiently strong to paralyze individual forces. The more absolute the power of the State the better will it be able to fulfill the goal for which it was instituted. Thus, the sovereign's fullest power over property, over opinion, and even over religion is justified.

Such according to Hobbes is the character and origin of the State. Before the compact every man possessed all rights to all things, and no action was good or bad, just or unjust in itself. With the compact all rights and duties, as well as the distinction between right and wrong, came into existence. For Hobbes statal laws represent the collective conscience which must direct every man's conduct. All rights, all the forces and means of defense are embodied in the sovereign, who can compel the collectivity to respect the social peace. On the other hand, the collectivity having surrendered all rights loses its independence and becomes an amorphous mass burdened only with duties.

No theory of monarchic absolutism could be more complete than that of Hobbes. A detailed confutation seems unnecessary, since the theory is gratuitous in its principles and absurd in its conclusions. Hobbes' assumption of a state of war in primitive society, of the instinct of self-defense, and of a complete subjection, etc., might serve to conceal the whims and caprices of a tyrant, but it cannot explain the State.

b) Rousseau

Though starting from different principles, Rousseau has many points of contact with Hobbes. The Genevan philosopher also begins with a primitive state of nature, but his view is optimistic. "Rousseau, an optimist, saw nothing but good in man's original nature: to the pessimist mind of Hobbes all was evil there."[2] In fact the former regards as good every impulse of nature, whereas "every evil was born of conventionalism, formalism, artificiality."[3] Instead of a state of war, Rousseau imagines a state of nature where life evolves without struggle and pain and is blessed with peace and happiness. Man was naturally good, essentially free, and sufficient unto himself. But unfortunately discord, fraud, quarrels, and wars arose. This state of affairs and the consequent necessity for self-defense led eventually to a contract, and the natural man was transformed into the citizen. Thus, civil society originates from a free contract whereby man surrenders all rights to a common authority constituted by the majority. By virtue of this contract every individual agrees to abide by *the general will*, and in obeying *the general will* every individual is merely obeying himself. Accordingly, government exists by virtue of a tacit agreement with each individual governed, and authority is binding only as long as the community so decrees. Civil authority is but the merger of all rights and wills in the one supreme right and will of the community. The main feature of Rousseau's doctrine is that the government is vested, not in *a* sovereign (as with Hobbes), but in the sovereign *general will*, which is one and indivisible, inerrant and omnicompetent.

Long ago Aristotle pointed out that specific qualities of a thing must be rooted in the very nature of that thing. Thus, for instance, the essential and specific faculties of man arise from one single source which may be called the substance of man, the human *ego*. True philosophy through the centuries has re-

---

[2] Joseph Rickaby, S.J., *Moral Philosophy* (London: Longmans, Green and Co., 1918), p. 301.

[3] *Ibid.*, *Political and Moral Essays* (New York: Benziger, 1902), p. 86.

affirmed this basic axiom. Whatever is accidental and phenomenal in things is in a process of constant flux, but what is essential and specific persists unchanged.

Man has always been a member of the family or of the State.
This truth has been verified by history, manifested by experience,
and confirmed by the most thorough research. A universal fact,
such as this, attested everywhere and at all times, cannot be
explained as a fortuitous and accidental occurrence, as Rousseau,
Hobbes, and other contractualists would maintain. Hence its
constant and true cause must be sought in human nature itself.

2. THE THEORY OF SOCIAL ORGANISM

In opposition to Rousseau, who saw in the State a purely conventional institution, Herbert Spencer would explain the State
as the product of a blind evolutionary process taking place according to the immutable laws of nature. Everything in the universe is regarded as the result of a slow and progressive evolution. Under this same law of evolution individuals are brought
together to form social organisms. Political organization is the
last link in the great evolutionary chain: First man, then marriage, then family, then tribe, and finally the State. Spencer
would describe the State as an organism, not essentially different
from the organic life of individual man, having organs of nutrition, circulation, co-ordination, and reproduction.

Primitive man, as Spencer represents him, was in a state of
savagery, and only after a long period of evolution did he acquire a fitness for social life. Primitive groups exhibited neither
stability nor order. They lived originally in a state of promiscuity; the women were in common; individual marriage was unknown. Hence, according to Spencer, *human life* is an ulterior
development of *subhuman life*, and the monogamic form of
sexual relations marks a high stage of evolution. Thus the State
comes into existence after a long series of progressive develop-
ments. The only true conception of the State is the evolutionary
concept which Spencer claims is admitted by the great majority.

It is clear that "the theory of the social organism reduces the individual to a mere unit in an aggregate; that it is simply a restatement of the old-world materialism. We see that materialism, no less than pantheism, implies the denial of human personality: the individual is no more than an atom lost in the social whole, he being to society just what the cell is to the organic body, his rights in regard to the State no more than those of the cell in regard to the organism. Spencer would no doubt protest against such a conclusion as unfair; still logic is inexorable. If we are assured that progress consists in the aggregation and concentration of units which were at first isolated, that social life in the course of its development passes through the same phases as the life of the individual, then must we not conclude that the absorption of the individual by the State is the goal of political evolution? . . . If then, the individual stands to society as the cell to the whole organism, social progress will be measured in inverse proportion to the development of individual liberty. Thus we see how ill-suited are Spencer's conceptions of liberalism and of society as an organism."[4] We shall have occasion later to examine more fully the theory of the social organism.

According to Spencer the State evolved in that the family and the individual evolved. As noted he held that originally man had no family life but lived in a condition of absolute sexual promiscuity, and that originally man was unfit to live in society because evolving as he was from the lower animals he lacked the necessary moral, intellectual, and cultural capacity. We can best refute Spencer's theory that the State is the product of evolution by refuting his theory that the family evolved from promiscuity and that the individual developed from the lower animals — in intellect and will as well as in body.

a) Promiscuity Hypothesis Unscientific

The alleged promiscuity of the primitive races lacks decisive proof; and the conclusions which Spencer drew were unwar-

[4] Désiré Cardinal Mercier, A Manual of Modern Scholastic Philosophy (London: Kegan, Trench, Truber, 1919), Vol. II, p. 334.

ranted. The philosopher of evolution merely registered certain abuses practiced in some places in regard to marriage. Had he positively *demonstrated* that among primitive races the institution of marriage did not exist, his conclusions might have logically followed from his principles. The mere fact of certain abuses among the primitives does not disprove the existence of marrriage and, therefore, of family life, any more than modern aberrations disproves its sanctity.

That promiscuity was the original state of man is disproved both by history and the most accurate research. The results of the latest discoveries have established the fact that there is no race, however primitive, among whom promiscuity prevails. Devas says, "To suppose that the whole human race for a considerable time were without regular marriage is physiologically impossible. They could never have survived it."[5] E. Westermarck avers that the promiscuity hypothesis is essentially unscientific and without foundation. "The hypothesis of a primitive stage of promiscuity not only lacks all foundation in fact, but is utterly opposed to the most probable inference we are able to make as regards the early condition of man."[6] The most prominent sociologists of today unanimously maintain that family life has been known from the earliest times and is the original and the spontaneous human nucleus. Family life did not evolve from sexual promiscuity but was always present as the basis of the State. The Spencerian origin of the State is utterly false because its primary postulate, the evolution of the family from original promiscuity, is totally at variance with the truth.

b) Man Essentially Different From the Lower Animals

In Spencerian as well as Darwinian thought, man does not differ essentially from brute animals. "The difference in mind between man and the higher animals, great as it is, certainly is

---

[5] C. S. Devas, *Studies of Family Life* (London, 1908), p. 101.
[6] E. Westermarck, *The History of Human Marriage* (London: Macmillan and Co., 1925), Vol. I, p. 38.

one of degree and not of kind."[7] "Intelligence," according to
Spencer, "has neither distinct grades nor is it constituted by
faculties that are truly independent, but its highest manifesta-
tions are the effects of a complication that has arisen by insen-
sible steps out of the simplest elements."[8] Hence a rational action is simply an instinctive response which has survived in a
struggle with other instinctive responses aroused by a situation.
Spencer, moreover, denies freedom of the will and consequently
all morality in the traditional sense of the term. Man, he states,
is quite as free as the moon in motion, neither more nor less.
For the philosopher of evolution, reason and instinct, will, mind,
and life are one.

The above statements are very significant, so significant that
were they confirmed by reality and by fact they would shake the
whole ethicojuridical edifice. Unfortunately for the evolutionists,
evidence in this case, as in so many others, is conspicuously ab-
sent. The motives which induced Spencer to adhere to a rigid
evolutionism are stated in his *Principles of Biology.* No one, he
says, has ever witnessed the creation of a single species. He denies the creation of the world on the ground that such a theory
transcends man's experience. Nothing, he assures us, can be admitted as true or real that has not been first subjected to a
severe and minute analysis. Strangely, the first one to violate
this axiom is Spencer himself. He triumphantly proclaims that
the evolution of one species from another cannot be contested,
although he has been unable to see and check the truth of his
own principle. At the same time he regards the creationist
theory of the species as a mere supposition.

Again, from the fact that superior beings possess a higher
degree of perfection and finality than inferior beings, Spencer
infers that the higher species must have slowly developed from

---

[7] Charles Darwin, *The Descent of Man* (New York: D. Appleton and
Company, 1903), p. 128.
[8] Herbert Spencer, *The Principles of Psychology* (New York: D. Appleton
and Co., 1903), p. 388.

the lower species, under the impulse of a mechanical law of adaptation. That there are grades of perfection in things is an obvious fact. The universe is hierarchically arranged or graded not only by quantitative differences (mechanistic theory) but also according to internal perfection. Thus, for instance, man is superior to the brute beast and the latter superior to the plant. We also distinguish between stages of perfection within the same being, for instance the human organism arising from a primitive cell gradually develops into a complete organism. Under these aspects man is a *microcosm,* for all the perfections of reality as a whole meet in him as in a wonderful alloy. In common with the inorganic world he possesses physical and chemical properties; with the plants, biological activities; with the animal, sensory consciousness and instinct. But he is essentially distinct from the brute animal by reason of his intelligence; points of affinity or resemblance between various species is no cause for overlooking the differences, or for concluding that the higher species have developed from the lower.

If Spencer had restricted his theory to physical evolution, there would be no essential contradiction with the Christian viewpoint, even though the physical evolution of man is still but pure hypothesis without any conclusive scientific proof. But Spencer extended evolution to man's intellectual and volitional faculties. In other words, he holds that originally man was just like the brute animals in every respect and only by the slow and gradual progress of evolution did he develop from subhuman to human level. For Spencer man is identical with the brute animal in kind and different only in degree. Such a contention is utterly fallacious and entirely contradictory of all established proof. Prehistory of the remotest ages has discovered bright traces of culture, art, and progress. Anthropology has absolutely no evidence of a prehistoric subhuman. There are physical but no intellectual differences between the earliest human fossil and modern man.

"If savage," writes Max Müller, "means people without a settled form of government, without laws and without a religion,

then, go where you like, you will not find such a race."[9] Nor
has ethnology been more propitious to Spencerian evolution. In
vain have all the continents been traversed, from the forests of
South America to the farthest parts of Greenland; from the
Eskimos to the Hottentots; from the Hindoos to the savage
tribes of Africa; the answer has always been the same: among
all human races, no vestiges of subhuman man have been found.
All the numerous and insistent attempts to prove the animal
descent of man, as Spencer conceives it, have failed, because it
is impossible to obliterate the differences not of degree but of
kind which separate man essentially from the brute.

To corroborate the confutation of the Spencerian and evolutionist error which admits of only a distinction of degree between man and brute, we can point out other essential differences. In the brute the dominant characteristics are the impulses
of self-preservation and self-reproduction. In this it finds both
the gratification of instincts and the realization of a specific end.
Man likewise, in so far as he possesses vegetative and sensory
life in common with the brute, participates in the same impulses
which, however, must be controlled and regulated by reason.
The struggle for life is undoubtedly the great moving force impelling man to work in the shops, fields, commerce, and industry.
Yet man's actions are being actuated and ennobled by higher
motives. Reason completes and perfects man in such a way as
to elevate him essentially above the animal level.

It has also been contended that man has made greater progress
than the brute solely because of the faculty of speech. But the
hypothesis that the faculty of speech engendered intelligence is
absolutely gratuitous and contradicted by experience. It is contrary to established facts to say that speech slowly produces
reason. It is an attested fact that as soon as speech becomes something more than a mere sound it presupposes reason of which
it is an external manifestation. In the absence of a faculty
capable of forming universal ideas, and of ascending from the
particular to the general it is impossible to have language in the

---

[9] Max Müller, *Nineteenth Century*, Jan., 1885, p. 114.

strict sense of the word. Intellect is a spiritual faculty which forms ideas, judges, reasons, and perceives the logical relations between ends and means, cause and effect. It is true that human intelligence in its functions depends on sensory perceptions from the content of which it extracts its proper object or concept, but it is not limited to these sensory objects. From the concrete and the particular the intellect ascends to suprasensible relations, to the concept of being in general, to the ideas of substance and cause. If the brute lacks the faculty of speech, this is due not so much to the absence of vocal organs as to the absence of thought. Absence of the faculty of speech implies absence of intelligence.

Furthermore, the intellect has the power of self-reflection, it can throw itself in upon itself, an activity which transcends all the conditions of space and time. Only the intellect is able to turn, so to say, upon itself, take stock of its own nature, observe what passes within it, and carry on with its very self a sort of conversation about it all. The human intellect alone discovers the natural laws governing the world, and alone can use these laws in a thousand ways, furthering man's progress. On the other hand, notwithstanding the wonderful finality in the animal kingdom, as in bees, spiders, etc., everything is stationary. If in some rare cases animals exhibit adaptations to new exigencies, and succeed in a certain measure to improve their activities, this is not an indication of real progress. Man alone shows indications of progress; he has devised clothing for his covering, built homes for his protection, railroads and airplanes for rapid transit, he has invented wireless and radio for the transmission of his thoughts, and numberless other devices for his need and comfort.

According to the Spencerian theory of evolution, the atom is a thing destitute of life; and yet human intelligence in his view is nothing but a happy combination of atomic forces due to cerebral secretion. How can a combination of lifeless atoms engender first vegetative, then sensory, and finally intellectual life? How can evolutionism explain man's love for order and truth, the impulse that prompts him to do good, and the feeling of remorse? How can a blind juxtaposition of atoms accomplish such wonderful and radical transformations?

The evolutionist theory is self-contradictory: on the one hand, it cannot deny that man in virtue of his intellectual powers controls the physical forces, such as light, heat, steam, and electricity; on the other hand, it stubbornly persists in maintaining that there are no laws other than physical and biological. Obviously, evolutionism fails to explain both the origin of civil society and the origin of man.

In the light of evolutionism, liberty, peace, right, and morality are but hypocritical veils concealing a brutal and dominant egotism and a savage spirit of destruction and death. It is, of course, true that the human race fell short of preserving the original status assigned to it by the Creator, and of keeping intact the immense patrimony of culture and civilization. Yet the true history of mankind cannot be identified with the records of violence, brutality, and barbarism, for the phenomena of crime and degeneration are not necessary attributes of man.

The Christian conception of the universe helps us to solve all difficulties. It alone places in full light the finality and subordination of all things to God. It alone teaches the true position and excellence of man, in the words of the Scripture, "Let him have dominion." This furnishes the key to the understanding of all material progress achieved by man.

Man's prerogative is to extend his dominion over the external world, over the forces of nature and the treasures contained therein. Had Spencer taken this point of departure as his basic principle, he would have clearly perceived man's relations to the entire universe: that man in the same way as the inorganic world is subject to physicochemical laws; that like the plants he is controlled by biological laws; that he shares sensory life with the irrational animal; and that by his intellectual and volitional activities he so transcends the animal life as to stand out supreme as the lord and master of all creation. Spencer would have understood that man alone possesses the faculty of articulate speech because he alone is endowed with intelligence;

that by means of intelligence and speech he has achieved marvels in the field of art, of letters, of mechanics, and of science; that by his will, or rational appetite, he is prompted to love justice, to pursue virtue, to search after truth and order, and to aspire to a happy and immortal life; that man is a free and responsible being. The philosopher of evolution would have also realized that man's activities must be harmoniously co-ordinated because they emanate from a unique source, the human soul; that the human soul is not a pure spirit, but that though intrinsically independent in its entity and in its higher activities, the soul is extrinsically dependent on the body even in its spiritual activities, in so far as all human knowledge begins in sense perception; and that nothing is more erroneous than to identify, as the materialists do, the external conditions of knowledge and volition with their intrinsic and specific nature. Finally, he would have been convinced that the intimate union of soul and body, so intimate as to form a single principle of operation, explains better than any other theory how in man very often the lowest and most vulgar instincts stand side by side with the noblest ideals; that man is by nature fitted to create the family and to live in society, for in no other way can his material and spiritual needs be satisfied. The Spencerian hypothesis, far from explaining the nature and origin of civil society, negates every philosophical system and bankrupts all political science. A cruder conception of the State could hardly be imagined, nor one more disastrous in its logical consequences.

3. THE THEORY OF SOCIAL ANARCHY

The anarchist theory regards the State as an institution detrimental to culture and progress, as a parasitic organism harmful to the common good. Every association from the family to civil society is not a natural effect but the product of free conventions. Hence anarchy proposes to do away with all existing forms of government and to effect a society which will exercise all its functions without any controlling or directive authority. It claims that the essential prerogative of every man is to develop all his faculties, to satisfy all his passions, and freely to enact his own laws. Man is the best judge of his own capacities, hence humanity will be most benefited in and through the self-realization of the individual. The individual is to be the center and determining power of everything. This doctrine finds its culmination in Nietzsche's *superman*.

Communism is just as individualistic as anarchy in its attempt to abolish the State. Both Marx and Engels regard the State as a product of class struggle, as a means whereby an economically superior class becomes politically dominant, a machine of oppression and exploitation. The State, however, is not condemned by them to an immediate decapitation but to a slow death. It is a necessary transitional phase to a communistic Utopia where all statal mechanism will be eliminated.

It is important to distinguish the old from the more recent current of socialistic thought. The former favors a rather individualistic character wishing to retain private ownership without any change in the existing economic conditions. The latter, communistic in tendency, advocates control and free disposal of produce and consumption by free autonomous groups. Both insist on the abolition of all law and statal power.

The maintenance of private ownership based on an equal distribution of goods is defended by W. Godwin. However, according to him, in cases of extreme necessity every member must freely surrender to another what is necessary for the satisfaction of his neighbor's urgent needs. Godwin was sure that human nature of its own inherent virtue would maintain sufficient order without law. The abolition of civil society and its replacement by an assembly of egoists is insisted on by Max Stirner. According to him, the highest degree of self-realization can be attained only when men are moved to action by a spirit of egoism and apart from civil laws. P. J. Proudhon would abolish all political parties and civil authority in order to achieve full liberty for the individual, but at the same time he would preserve the economic order. By means of a people's bank he would make it possible for everyone to borrow without interest. Contemporary anarchy regards the existence of the State as the root of all social evil. All necessities, such as food, clothing, lodging, and the means of production, should be controlled by free autonomous groups who would substitute for the State while essentially differing from it. The leaders of the school, such as M. Bakounine and Most, take as their guiding principle the fact that every individual is entitled to the necessities of life according to the amount of labor he expends, and that a just reward for labor is and shall continue to be the cornerstone of civil society. According to them the appraisement of the quantity and quality of labor is a function not of the State but of autonomous social groups.

a) Absurdities of Anarchy

It is not difficult to see that the theory of social anarchy abounds in contradictions, is false in its principles, and is absurd in its consequences. Man, as facts clearly show, is neither free from passions nor essentially good. Without unity and subordination no order is possible; without authority no organization is conceivable. Anarchy overlooks the fact that the State is not an artificial but a natural institution, in the same way as is the family. As it is impossible to abolish speech because it is natural to man, so it is impossible to abolish civil society because this too is natural to man. It is absurd to suppose that many individuals could constitute a permanent union and could peaceably attend to their respective needs in the absence of civil authority. It is hard, if not impossible, to see how diverse and very often contrary tendencies could be harmoniously blended without a statal power, especially when we realize how hard it is for existing forms of government to repress theft, crime, and disorder even with the exercise of coercive power. In an anarchist society every individual will struggle for the realization of his tendencies and diversified needs; but such an attempt for self-realization on the part of many individuals will necessarily interfere with the rights of others, the inevitable result being a bitter and universal fratricidal war.

The hope entertained by the anarchist that the individual well-being alone will constitute a secure foundation for the autonomous groups of the future is vain and illusory. It fails to take into account the profound differences in human individuals that are being continually verified by the history of the human race. It is an evident fact that wealth flourishes side by side with abject poverty, that vice and injustice often triumph over virtue and honesty, that human passions far from being a source of harmony and order are the prolific sources of discord and division. Nothing that depends on mere human whims and fancies can be stable and permanent. If social anarchy were to prevail, might would conquer right, egoism and jealousy, hatred and vengeance would triumph over virtue and brotherly love. There would be conspiracies against the family, the individual, and private ownership by popular upheavals, class hatred, and revolutions. Unless one prefers a state of permanent warfare among men, he must admit the necessity of a principle of order, a civil authority. History proves that the greatest violences were perpetrated in times of anarchy when governments became powerless to control class struggles and social disorders.

Again, the anarchist theory militates against all social order, for it does not hesitate to make use of the most violent means to bring about the realization of its dreams. Even in an anarchist society there is no room for unlimited and absolute liberty; hence, in the settlement of disputes, either an appeal will have to be made to one having a right to settle disputes, which is the same as civil authority, or everything will have to be abandoned to blind egoism, might, and violence. The suppression of the State would, in fact, be a declaration of war of every man against every other man, and would create a pseudo-State much more tyrannical than the previous one. It is clear, therefore, that as the civil authority is the positive pole of social order, anarchy is the negative.

It is asserted that the aim of anarchy is only the abolition of civil power and not the abolition of the rights necessary to regulate individual and social relations. If, however, social order is but an artificial product and not an exigency of nature, human rights would be compromised to such an extent as to be reduced to a mere subjective law of the individual. But a purely subjective norm, prescinded from an objective foundation, cannot be a source of rights; right in this case would be confused with might. An essential characteristic of right is duty or obligatoriness, for the exercise of a right by one individual implies an obligation in others to respect that right. Right, therefore, cannot be conceived without a corresponding obligation; but for the anarchist there is no such thing as obligation. No individual man, as such, has the right to exact obedience from another individual; and no individual is bound to obey, unless the right of commanding be fully justified. But anarchy, granting to each individual a complete autonomy, frees man from all obligation; hence, man would become powerless to exercise his rights as the obligation on the part of others to respect his rights would be lacking.

b) *Impracticability of Anarchy*

To these objections others of a practical nature may be added. Anarchy would substitute a new social order for the existing one by confiscating private property. Such a procedure would not only be highly criminal but would entail disastrous consequences in the economic field in general and in the sphere of production and consumption in particular. It is quite apparent that in a society without laws and authority, it would be simply impossible for autonomous groups to arrive at a peaceful and just distribution of consumptive goods. For in virtue of the absolute equality which anarchy advocates, no one will of his own accord accept onerous, unhealthy, and humiliating tasks. Everyone will claim for himself the most fertile fields, the most commodious houses, and the most profitable industries. This universal demand for the best and the finest will unquestionably engender rivalry and bitter struggle. Russia since the reign of its communism began furnishes glaring examples. Thus anarchy instead of building up only tears down and destroys every vestige of progress and civilization.

Social differences, economic injustices, misery, and other evils afflicting the existing social order have, no doubt, contributed much to the spread of anarchistic and socialistic ideas; but the main cause of these must be sought in the modern atheistic and materialistic concept of life. When we hear our modern educators proclaim in the name of science that duty is but a product of custom and environment; that obligation does not differ from utility or pleasure; when they advocate relativism in the field of knowledge and agnosticism in the sphere of religion, anarchy and chaos can be the only logical consequence. In order to save the human race from utter disaster, it is imperative to engage all our resources, social reforms, press, education of the people, State legislation, and the Church in the struggle against this most pernicious of modern heresies. All must contribute their share to the task of social reconstruction.

Our refutation of anarchy will be incomplete, unless we consider its ultimate cause, namely, the materialistic conception of history. This is the false principle that has engendered class hatred and raised aloft the standard of rebellion with its motto: "No God, no country." Anarchy is an apostasy from Christianity, in fact "once given that there is no God, it immediately becomes unjust and impossible for anyone to exact obedience and submission from anyone else. If there is no God, there can be no master. The anarchist conclusion is logical."[10]

PART II

CHRISTIAN PHILOSOPHY OF STATE

We are concerned here, in the first place, with the family, which forms the cell of the social organism. The family is a natural institution necessary for man, because the individual left to himself in an isolated state could not acquire the means

---

[10] *Catholic Encyclopedia*, Vol. 1, p. 453.

necessary for his own physical, moral, and intellectual needs, or for the attainment of his own happiness. The State is a necessary and natural institution, because the family alone is incapable of providing everything for the full development of life, and because the State is needed for the co-ordination of social activities unto the common good, and for the maintenance of peace and order.

1. The Family a Natural and Necessary Society

For an adequate understanding of the nature of the State, it is necessary to consider the family, for the State consists of a group of families. The family is a natural institution having the bond of matrimony for its real foundation. Like the State, the family is regulated by special laws and has its own proper end. According to Aristotle and St. Thomas, the family is a natural society with the specific purposes of providing for the daily wants of life.

The family is a natural society, because both as regards its origin and its special functions it finds its full justification in human nature. It is found everywhere, among modern as well as ancient peoples, without distinction of race or culture. Moreover, the family in its habitual consequences harmonizes with the specific end which characterizes human nature. Contrary to what occurs in the animal kingdom, the family is by nature a stable and constant association corresponding to the peculiar end which distinguishes it from any other human society. A careful study of the two sexes shows that one is made to be the natural integration and complement of the other, and that marriage binds man and woman into a union so close and so intimate as to constitute a unique principle for the propagation and conservation of the species and for the physical, moral, and intellectual development of the partners and of their offspring. The very nature of the component parts of the family compels, as it were, the married couple to love each other, to bear with, and mutually to help one another, and shows in a forceful manner that here there is no question of a transitory institution. A further consideration of the sacrifices inherent in the physical and moral education of the child confirms the logical and practical necessity of the stable union of the spouses.

Consideration of the proper end of society will lead to the same conclusion. From the viewpoint of the finality or economy which reigns in the universe, the powerful instinct that urges the union of the two sexes cannot be explained unless we simultaneously admit that the family has for its purpose the propagation of the species. The human race would be doomed to annihilation if births did not exceed deaths, or if life did not constantly reproduce itself upon the ruins of the past and of death. Hence the natural term or finality which prompts the union of the two sexes cannot be other than the preservation of the human species.

But it is not enough to bring children into this world; provision must also be made for their rearing and education. The purpose implied in the union of the two sexes would not be fully realized if it were limited to the generative act. Even in animals themselves, the impulse to care for and defend their offspring is always conjoined with the sexual instinct, at least as long as their needs persist. Now what has been said of the animal may for stronger reasons be applied to man. From birth the animal is provided with a covering against the inclemencies of the weather; whereas man is left relatively destitute. The former receives from nature means for self-defense; man is forced to manufacture them; the animal finds readily in nature the proper nourishment; not so man. Again, the animal is endowed by nature with a most perfect art which guides it either to build a nest or to dig a hole. Man, on the other hand, acquires art only by the slow process of learning, endeavor, and sacrifice. Man more than any other living being is in need of domestic society. The irrational animal nourishes its offsprings for a short time and abandons it when the offspring becomes sufficient unto itself. Having attained its instinctive development, the offspring no longer recognizes its parent and vice versa. The offspring of man, on the other hand, is the most helpless of all creatures at the time of its birth and for years after. For a long time he must rely absolutely on the help of others; a thousand dangers surround its cradle, and his infancy has innumerable needs. Nature gave to man none of the perfect equipment for self-preservation and defense given to other animals. The sacred fire which nature has instilled into a mother's breast is something sublime. The mother, so feeble, is yet able to bear all sorrows and undergo all sacrifices for the preservation of her offspring. The parents, animated by a divine magnetism, will see to it that the tender infant is preserved and developed along physical, intellectual, and moral lines. In order to assure for the offspring a proper future, prolonged parental efforts are necessary.

In addition to material needs, there are also spiritual needs which are all-important and which must be satisfied. Parents must provide for the education of their offspring with zeal, foresight, and sacrifice, since education is the basis of better life, social and civil. Character thus developed by education, becomes worthy of man, and will enable him to fulfill in a rational manner all those ends which are inherent in his nature. The family, therefore, is the first and most elementary form of society founded in the very nature of man.

2. THE STATE A NATURAL AND NECESSARY SOCIETY

But, if the family is the primary foundation of civil society, the State, consisting as it does of a group of families, must in its turn be a necessary institution based on human nature. It is absurd to suppose that man should be naturally bound to attain an end without possessing necessary means to accomplish it. But man has many needs which cannot be satisfied either by individual endeavors or by domestic society. Even the life of a plain laborer or of an humble artisan has so many diversified needs that the family alone cannot competently satisfy them. If the family alone had to provide directly all the needs of life such as food, clothing, lodging, implements of labor, etc., its lot would not be a happy one. As everyone knows the family by itself is not capable of providing everything for the full development of life, and, therefore, the State is a necessary and natural society.

a) Social Consideration

Again, the various pursuits of art, science, philosophy, and culture require means which ordinarily are beyond private initiative and necessitate the existence of a large civil society called the State. This larger association of individuals is required in order to effect a harmonious whole wherein all social activities become co-ordinated for the common good. This social co-ordination brings about the division of labor which enables some to devote all their energies to the cultivation of the soil, others to the handling of machinery, and still others to the pursuit of letters, arts, commerce, and industry. In this manner progress is rendered possible, and all that is necessary for the satisfaction not only of actual but also of future needs can be produced. With the intensification of progress and culture, man by living in human society is urged on to enlarge the sphere of his activities especially in the domain of the good, the true, and the beautiful.

Consequently the general conclusion follows that man does not exist in the universe as an isolated atom, but as an integral part of a unified whole, a member of the family that has a common origin and a common end. Again, we cannot ignore the law written in our very nature, which all instinctively obey and which manifests itself in a thousand different ways, namely, the *law of solidarity*. This law binds all beings together, and in a sense makes all things, good and evil, joys and sorrows, affronts and honors, common to all. Now what does all this mean? It means that there exists among men a mysterious union by reason of which all goods become so to speak common to them, and the more common the closer are the ties by which men are bound one to another. Nature itself requires this, and requires it because no individual is isolated; all are members of one great family; all are sharers in a common nature.

b) Maintenance of Peace and Common Well-Being

The necessary axiom that man is by nature a social being explains the existence of the State, the various rights to command, and the duty to obey. The social impulse of man is not limited to the family but finds in the State a fuller development. Without the State humanity would be doomed to extinction, and would lapse into barbarism and anarchy. Social as well as individual rights, peace and internal prosperity, would be seriously compromised, if there were no centralized authority to spur on the indolent, to keep in check the forward, and compel all to respect the social order. In the absence of this centralized power the fundamental basis of all culture and progress would be wanting, because instead of order and social peace there would be a war of every man against every other man. Besides the defense of the juridical order and internal peace, provision must also be made for the protection of the citizens against external enemies. For this, neither the individual nor the family is sufficient; only the State possesses the adequate means to assure this protection. To sum up in the words of Cardinal Manning: "When God made man, He made society; society springs out of the creation of man, because from man comes the family, and from the family comes the people, and from the people comes the State. The whole civil order of the world is nothing but the growth of that society which lay in the first man, as the tree lies in the seed. Therefore, in our very nature is the society of mankind."[11]

3. NATURE OF THE STATE

a) The Essential Elements of the State

The term State generally expresses two distinct ideas. It may indicate an organized and independent society; or denote authority, that is, the sovereign power, the unifying energy of civil society. We shall limit ourselves here to the first meaning.

---

[11] H. E. Manning, *The Fourfold Sovereignty of God* (New York: Benziger), p. 61.

A plurality of men and families constitutes the material cause or element of civil society. No matter how small or how large in numbers the members of a State may be, they form the material element of the statal organism. For the perfection and development of the political society, the constituent elements must reside in a stable and fixed territory. This requirement though not essential is, nevertheless, necessary for the perfection of the statal entity. Thus a nomadic people possessing a juridical code, a legal system, a ruling sovereignty, would constitute a State, however imperfect and undeveloped, and not merely an amorphous prestatal conglomeration. Another element, no less important, is unity and cohesion under the same authority and with the same organization. Social authority is a moral power which compels and directs the social elements toward the attainment of the common well-being. This authority in its specific functions is supreme and independent. It is in virtue of this independence that the State is distinguished from a corporate town, province, family, or from any other social organization. Finally, the State demands a spiritual element which must inspire both rulers and subjects, namely, the idea of a common end constituting the collective consciousness. The external projection of the State is the articulate disposition of parts in such a way as to form an organic whole. The organic conception of the State is a true conception if contained within the proper limits of analogy.

b) Society, an Organism Only Analogically

Society is not, as Rousseau and Hobbes claim, an assembly of individuals bound together by public compulsion, or, as Beccaria imagines, an aggregate of atoms tending mechanically to the same end. It is rather a true organism whose structure is analogous to that of a living body. As an organism consists of heterogeneous parts, each endowed with its proper physical structure and with specific energies or functions, and as these parts are blended together into one being, and cooperate in the common welfare of the whole, in like manner society which is constituted of many individual persons differing from one another in character, intellectual abilities, and physical potentialities, points to the welfare of the entire social body.

Moreover, as a living body is animated by a soul which unites the various members and cements them into an individual physical substance and regulates all the vital functions; so, in society there must be a unitive principle, namely, authority, whose purpose is to bind together the component members into a moral unity and to regulate their social functions. Justly then, contemporary philosophy rejects any atomistic statal theory which divides society into as many independent monads and as many equal atoms as there are individuals. Obviously, such a theory would operate only to disrupt the State by undermining the existence or action of civil authority.

However, it must be noted that between a living organism and a social organism there is only analogy and not identity, for analogy implies partial identity and partial difference. Logically there is no justification to push our comparison beyond the limits of resemblance implied in the analogy. We must not overlook the differences which *de facto* intervene between the two terms. The wide differences between living organism and social organism will not permit attributing to the latter what is specifically proper only to the former.

A living organism is an *unum per se,* a physical substantial unit; in this case heterogeneous parts constitute a true unitary being. Since these heterogeneous parts are subordinated to one another according to the gradation of specific energies assigned to them by nature, they must also, under the impulse of an internal law of harmony, *necessarily* cooperate in the well-being of the whole. Society on the contrary is a moral organism, an accidental whole, an aggregate of complete individuals, each having a principle of life, specific activities, and a proper end, and preserving unaltered even in society the quality of personality. Man living in human society does not lose that physical unity which distinguishes him from all other men and from the central authority itself. Man remains an independent principle of intellective and volitional actions, capable of influencing the social body not by an intrinsic determination but by a free choice of will.

c) Society As a System of Relations

For a better grasp of the inner nature and the ontological value of this social organism, it must be borne in mind that this social reality resolves itself into a vast texture of interrelations among the constituent parts. These mutual interrelations among the members of the social body have no independent existence, do not stand on their own feet; but are dependent on and rooted in the individuals. Friendship, for instance, considered concretely is a reality inhering in certain human individuals from whom it is distinguished and from whom it cannot be separated. Human imagination may indeed feature friendship as an abstraction which does not and cannot exist in and by itself, but friendship cannot be found anywhere save in particular friends.

A social relation is, according to the accurate phrase of Scholastic philosophy, an *ens entis,* a dependent entity, an accidental and not a substantial reality inasmuch as it can exist only in virtue of inherence. For instance, man in so far as he is a companion, a subject, or a citizen is something more than a mere human individual. This additional *something* is but a modification or perfection of his being, whereby he is referred to something else. However, the social relation is a real relation. We say a *real relation* in order to distinguish it from a *logical relation* which is a product of the mind. Of this kind are the relations perceived between a species and a genus, and the relations perceived among the various ideas in consciousness; such are called logical because they are based *immediately* on ideas and not on reality. Then there are relations which are independent of the thinking subject, relations whose terms exist in concrete reality. These relations are not, as Kant contends, merely subjective categories imposed by the mind on objects, for the mind itself is forced to recognize them. Of this kind are the relations of causality, of finality, of paternity, of quantity, of quality, such are not arbitrary constructions of the mind, but exist in reality, that is to say, they are objective.

In order to fathom more thoroughly the nature of political society, let us see whether we are justified in ascribing to it the notion of personality in its strict and proper meaning. Certain defenders of the Sociological Theory, base the moral and juridical personality of the State upon a concept of personality which is univocally applied both to an individual human being (as Peter or Paul) and to a collective entity (as Church or State). In justification of this, they appeal to the fact that the social organism possesses a collective consciousness, a general will, and a common purpose. Society according to them is a moral person distinct from its members and is both a principle of action and a subject of attributions, in other words, it has all the characteristics of personality.

To this we reply that a collective consciousness and will prescinded from the particular human persons is a pure abstraction. Collective consciousness depends both for its existence and its activity on the individuals composing it. Those who assert that any collectivity of wills or thought is sufficient to constitute a person arbitrarily mutilate the concept of personality. The true ontological concept of personality denotes an incommunicable substance complete in itself and endowed with intellect and will. Hence society is not a person nor is it a *real* being distinct from the individuals constituting it.

d) Necessity of Civil Society

Against the erroneous theories which threaten the very foundation of modern society, it will not be superfluous to reaffirm that man is by nature ordained to live in society, that a well-regulated social life cannot exist without law. Juridical order is, therefore, an exigency implied in the very social and rational nature of men. The State is essentially a permanent aggregation of human beings cooperating for a common purpose which is the maintenance of social order and the general welfare. This conception is surely superior to the materialistic theories of the State. Both in its concrete determinations and in its constituent parts the State cannot be surrendered to changing whims and fancies; it is an exigency of human nature, a part and parcel of the moral order and not an artificial product. The law of sociability is as natural to man as the law of gravitation is to physical forces. Everywhere and always we find man living in civil society. The characteristics of universality and permanence are a clear indication that political organization is a property of human nature and an ordinance of God. Only in society can man lead a life worthy of his high calling and attain the object of his aspiration, moral, intellectual, and physical development. The State also demands authority and law as an absolute condition of progress, civilization, and culture. Although God did not create the State directly, He willed it in that the need of reciprocal defense, languages, customs, and the social impulse induces men at all times and in all places to establish the State.

Therefore, the State cannot be regarded as an artificial, arbitrary, or contingent event. Civil society must exist since it is the indispensable condition of man's existence and of the realization of his end. Aristotle wisely remarked that man outside civil society would be either a beast or a god. This is as true today as it was then; it shows the anarchist tendencies to be absurd and destructive of social life. The State regarded as an organism in the sense of being derived from nature and constituting an integral part of the moral order is independent of the human will. Since the State entails an end exacted by the moral order, it follows that obedience to laws and to legitimate authority is something intrinsically good. This enables us to understand the supreme sacrifice of life made for the defense and safety of the fatherland.

Political society must be regarded neither as a contractual agreement to provide the necessities of life, nor as a mere means of social defense against the machinations of anarchy. Against our thesis of the natural necessity of the State, it is also claimed that civil society is a consequence of the fall of man by sin. St.

Augustine seems to advocate the above conception. A few remarks, however, will clarify the Augustinian position. In the first place, it is certain that St. Augustine does not regard the State as an institution intrinsically bad; he points out only that the origin of the various States is almost always accompanied by wars, rapine, and all sorts of violence. He contrasts this situation with that of the Christian Church, whose origin and external projection form the kingdom of peace. This interpretation is confirmed by another passage wherein the holy doctor regards the State as an exigence of human nature, having its foundation in the family.[12] St. Augustine speaks, indeed, of the social contract[13] and affirms that "it is of general agreement of human society to render obedience to kings." However, the term pact or agreement in the same book of Confessions often denotes law or decree. Thus divine law is called the eternal pact of salvation.[14] From this nothing positive can be inferred in favor of the contractualist theory.

Those theologians who have regarded the State as the result of original sin could not have implied that civil society would have been a superfluous institution on the ground that in the state of original justice every one would have spontaneously complied with his duty. The authority of St. Thomas suffices to show the weakness of this opinion. "Man is by nature a social animal. Hence men in the state of innocence would have lived in society. The very nature of society demands that authority be entrusted to someone who will direct it to its end, the common good."[15] The basic cause of the State must be sought not in the fall of man but rather in human nature. Hence all the attacks directed against the traditional doctrine of the State fall to the ground, and the old Aristotelian solution stands forth in all its pristine force. While in all other theories the solution of the problem of the State remains an enigma, in the light of sound philosophy it becomes clear and strictly scientific.

---

[12] St. Augustine, *De Civitate Dei* (Lipsiae: Teubner, 1928). Bk. XIX, c. 16.
[13] St. Augustine, *Confessions* (New York: G. P. Putnam's Sons, 1932), 13, c. 8.
[14] *Ibid.,* 1, c. 18.
[15] St. Thomas, *Summa Theologica,* I, q. 96, a. 4.

SELECT READINGS

Brennan, R. E., O.P., *Thomistic Psychology* (New York: The Macmillan Co., 1941).

Catholic Encyclopedia, art. "Society."

Encyclopedia of the Social Sciences, art. "Society."

Haas, F. J., *Man and Society* (New York: Century Co., 1930), Ch. I.

O'Toole, G. B., *The Case Against Evolution* (New York: The Macmillan Co., 1925).

Ross, E. J., *A Survey of Sociology* (Milwaukee: The Bruce Publishing Co., 1932), Ch. III.

Ryan-Boland, *Catholic Principles of Politics* (New York: The Macmillan Co., 1940), Ch. III.

Willigan-O'Connor, *Sociology* (New York: The Macmillan Co., 1940), Part II.

CHAPTER II

THE ULTIMATE ORIGIN AND BASIS
OF CIVIL AUTHORITY

THE problem of the origin of civil authority may be treated as a question of historical fact and development, or of philosophical source and basis. Civil power here does not mean the ability or sheer might of the well-organized State to coerce subjects into compliance with laws, but rather the legitimate authority to rule and to direct all the pertinent activities of civil society unto the common good. We are seeking, therefore, the final basis for the right to rule, a basis which must be moral, for otherwise there can be no question of such a right or of the legitimacy of civil power.

Woodrow Wilson regarded the origin of civil authority as a question "of fact, to be settled, not by conjecture, but by history."[1] Wilson was wrong in this for he, as do most modern naturalists, failed to discriminate between the specific characteristics of authority and its historical origin, between its essence and purpose and its phenomenal occurrences and circumstances. Civil authority always manifests itself in the same manner because its essential characteristics are inseparable from each concrete situation. Hence, it is of far greater importance to establish the philosophical ground common to all forms of civil authority, whether ancient or modern, great or small, than to investigate the historical facts and occurrences accompanying the rise of civil power. The philosophical question is also of greater importance for another reason. Modern naturalism, under diverse forms and tendencies but always with the same catastrophic results, is building a new social order having no other basis than

---

[1] W. Wilson, *State* (Boston: Heath, 1898), p. 1.

historical foundation, custom, or cultural development. The basic moral principles of the social order having been discarded, the most sacred personal and family rights are being disregarded and trampled upon.

In the light of true philosophy the State typifies a human end embodied in the moral order. From this it logically follows that obedience to civil laws and submission to political authority are a moral exigency or need. If obedience and submission to civil authority were devoid of a moral basis, the State would be but a protective system — against the ravages of anarchy, and civil authority would be but a result of custom and, more frequently, of violence and might. As man cannot live without society he cannot live without authority. Authority is the alternative of chaos.

PART I

ERRONEOUS THEORIES OF CIVIL POWER

The purpose of this section is a critical analysis of various naturalistic and contractual theories concerning the origin of civil power. By naturalism we understand that theory which purports to reduce man and all human affairs to the purely phenomenal order of a universe devoid of all intrinsic rationality and robbed of all relationship to anything transcendental to itself or even to any reality transcendent to bare sense experience. In the light of this naturalistic postulate, Spencer and other writers contend that civil authority is begotten by violence. For Bluntschli the ultimate basis of civil power is the caprice and despotism of the majorities; for Lasson it is political will. Others make custom and tradition the ultimate source of authority. Hobbes identifies civil power with the will of the sovereign, which is absolute and unlimited; and Rousseau holds that authority comes from the people in whose name only can it be validly exercised.

1. NATURALISTIC THEORIES

a) *Various Viewpoints*

Some contend that civil power has its justification not in a system of rights but in a positive fact. Spencer, for instance, says: "It is unquestionably true that Government is begotten of aggression and by aggression."[2] Some see the specific characteristic of social authority in coercion or compulsion. "Dynamic law," according to F. De Luca, "is the originating principle of social phenomena."[3] "Society" he continues "is an aggregate of a group of forces; it is the battlefield upon which these forces struggle for pre-eminence and control."[4] A struggle for power, or rather a struggle for existence, where the weak are victimized by the stronger, constitutes the ordinary and constant process both in the workings of nature and in the sphere of human ideals. A. Gumplowicz holds that civil authority originates in the overpowering of one tribe by another. "As in the society of buffaloes and elephants," writes A. Groppali, "the plundering hordes are guided by a leader, so the primitive human communities during recurring conflicts submit themselves to the authority of the more cunning and stronger. Afterwards, either because of the law of inertia, or because of the continuation of warfare, the leader also retains his authority in time of peace; thus we have the first form of government embodied in a leader or in the military class which surrounds him."[5] G. Jellinek comes very close to this materialistic conception of civil authority by regarding the State, in its origin, not as a juridical institution, but as a historicosocial formation followed by a system of laws.

Contrasting the modern with the ancient conception of the State, Bluntschli contends that as medieval science derived the

---

[2] Herbert Spencer, *Social Statics* (New York: D. Appleton and Co., 1903), p. 334.

[3] De Luca, *La Dinamica delle Forze Sociali* (Napoli, 1906), p. 62.

[4] *Ibid.*, p. 69.

[5] A. Groppali, *Filosofia del Diritto* (Milano, 1906), p. 267.

State and civil authority from God, modern science must limit itself to nature, which according to the materialists is abstracted from the idea of God. While the concept of God, he remarks, can satisfy the religious sentiment, it is altogether outside the sphere of political science. Although Bluntschli insists that private and personal rights should not be subordinated to public or common rights, yet by repudiating the divine origin of authority he strikes out the sole guarantee against governmental arbitrariness and caprice. Accordingly, in his view the ultimate norm of civil authority will be the caprice and despotism of the majorities, and the only point of direction will be the right of the stronger. The end of the State in his theory is not so much the common well-being, as a progressive self-development of the nation. He is quite vague as to in what this self-realization consists. An unlimited evolution of popular culture is a very relative concept lending itself to abuse and serving as a subterfuge for the arbitrariness of certain factions and of the majorities and for the violation of any right, however sacred.

Lasson teaches that there are no rights apart from the State; that the purpose of the State consists in providing security and maintenance of the juridical order; and that the subjective right itself is derived from the political will. He is very confident that the governmental will, though actuated by egoistic motives, will not deviate from the right direction. According to circumstances of time and place, the State will know how to limit its own activities. It is even claimed that this political will is the most effectual guarantee of popular liberties and the most powerful stronghold of social well-being. Unfortunately, such an ardent optimism is not supported either by experience or history, since it is well known that the most barbarous and unjust laws have, from time to time, been sanctioned by the will of the rulers. As a matter of fact, it is quite obvious that men in power are not always faithful to their high mission, and that their actions frequently are not inspired by the principles of justice and equity. Rulers, like all other human beings, are fallible and too often the victims of egotism and passion. Moreover, political will is but a fiction of the imagination, for the State as such no more than a province or a township can have a will properly so called. Concretely, political will is but the collective will of individual subjects vested with social authority; consequently according to circumstances it may be either the will of a popular majority, or of a king, or of a president, or of an absolute despot. Political will, therefore, cannot be regarded as an infallible criterion of the common good.

Nor can it be maintained that moral juridical principles gradually emanated from the State, since it remains to be shown how the State itself acquired these principles. As has already been stated, the so-called general will and the so-called popular soul as such have no existence in themselves but actually exist only in the soul and will of the individual man. Consequently the State cannot possess, much less communicate to others, what it has not. It communicates to others only what it has gradually received from the individuals constituting it. A State, which arises in virtue of a mechanical principle and whose members have no notion of political authority, no notion of the necessity of obedience due to constituted power, is incapable of explaining the nature of authority. The State cannot be the supreme source either of the ethicojuridical principles or of the social order.

That which discriminates and specifies the State is its ethical or moral character. Since the members constituting society are moral beings, their interrelations and the end toward which the State tends must also be of a moral order. The State necessarily presupposes a ruler or superior enjoying the right to exact obedience. Whoever denies moral obligation denies this ruler, and must consistently proclaim the triumph of might over right. To exist and to exercise its functions, the State demands a juridical system. But a juridical system having for its scope the regulation of social relations presupposes a moral order of which it is an integral part. Hence the content of positive law must have either a direct relation with the moral order or an indirect relation as in the case of morally indifferent actions. In both cases it imposes an obligation in conscience, finding a justification for this in the nature of political society.

Knowledge and selection of what is useful and necessary to the social welfare is the supreme task and art of the lawgiver. The primary function of the State is the maintenance of adequate living conditions. The State has the equally important duty of protecting and fostering those things which are calculated to enrich the social life, and which are a clear indication of culture and progress. This explains why many actions intrinsically indifferent become, as soon as they are enjoined by law, obligatory on the part of the subjects. In order to explain political obligation, Bosanquet identified the State "with the Real Will of the Individual."[6] However, this identification leaves the problem unsolved. The question here is: why must the individual obey legitimate authority and respect the moral order, even against his own will and inclinations? Intrinsic motives such as good will and a spirit of sacrifice, or external forces such as coercion and police power cannot be the answer. There can be no effective and lasting observance of the law without the moral factor and without a social life resting upon moral motives. Fear and self-interest, convention, and culture may counsel and even compel, but they cannot oblige a citizen to perform certain actions or to refrain from others. Utility and coercion, when not regulated by a superior law, contribute more to the destruction than to the consolidation of the State.

To avoid these difficulties, some theorists appeal to tradition and custom. But custom, no matter how deeply rooted in tradition and social consciousness, is subject to continuous change and to atrophy or abrogation. Experience shows that the most ancient and well-established customs are at times suddenly and violently overthrown. But civil power or authority is a constant and a universal factor. There is no society, however primitive, without a ruler whose task is to co-ordinate and direct the diverse human activities toward the common good. If civil author-

---

[6] Bosanquet, *The Philosophical Theory of the State* (London: Macmillan and Co., Ltd., 1899), p. 154.

ity had been engendered by custom, the effect would by far exceed the cause because one is changeable and the other is constant — which is absurd. Consequently custom cannot be regarded as the ultimate source of civil authority without contradicting the most elementary principles of logic and experience. Nothing could prevent the laws introduced and consecrated by one custom from being supplanted by a contrary custom. Moreover, if obedience to legitimate authority were simply a product of custom and association and not a requirement of human nature, civil power could not engender moral obligation.

It is true that custom can introduce new laws and abolish existing ones; but the inference that custom is the ultimate source of rights is unwarranted. In order to create a law, custom must possess the following requirements: It must, in the first place, be general. In other words, it must be recognized by all, or at least by the majority of the people. It must, moreover, be stable and reasonably regarded as necessary and legitimate. The mere fact of its long duration is not a sufficient justification. For instance, many nations victims of long oppression have never ceased to strive for their respective independence. Slavery triumphed for centuries among the Romans and Oriental nations, but this fact did not give the owners a true right over the slaves; nor did it engender a moral obligation in the victims of oppression. Custom may give rise to a right, it may modify or abolish a law, only when it is preceded by general juridical principles and when it is recognized as reasonable and as an exigency demanded by the common good.

b) Inconsistencies of Naturalism

From a naturalistic viewpoint, no law, however absurd it may be, can ever be unjust. Granting the principle that everything is relative, that there is no absolute measure to evaluate the content of a law, it follows that the only thing left is the legislative will of the State. When naturalism speaks of just and unjust laws, of a conservative, reactionary, or tyrannical State, it violates the rules of consistency. In order to talk of unjust laws, one must admit that beside and beyond the positive law there is an ethico-juridical order which cannot be the product of the human will, and which constitutes the cornerstone of all legislation. Naturalism does not and cannot recognize this higher order. Once more our conclusion must be that civil power is founded in the social nature of man. Without a superior order a strict duty or obligation is impossible; for an *immanent obligation,* namely, an obligation which is recognized within oneself, supposes a *transcendent ruler,* namely, a superior being distinct from human reason and will. To discover a true law or a true obligation is to find oneself in the presence of a higher intelligence or will, in the presence of God Himself. Without knowing God, I may *know* my duty but I cannot account for it.

By political authority is understood the moral power of command supported by the physical coercion (if need be) which the State exercises over its members. It thus limits their liberty and imposes upon them an obligation binding in conscience. These characteristics constitute the essence of all authority worthy of the name. The naturalistic or empirical theories are incapable of arriving at such a true philosophical notion of civil authority, because they reject *a priori* a transcendental source of obligation independent of the human will. In so doing they render all authority impossible. Since all men are equal as to essence and nature, how can anyone limit the liberty of another unless he himself has the authority to do so from a higher source and ultimately from God Himself?

Naturalism asserts that the State apart from the moral order has a right to enact and promulgate laws and that its subjects have the duty to obey. This is mere assumption with no reference to a source for such right and duty. It is obvious that the State does not exist *ab aeterno* but in time, and that it does not antedate but follows the existence of the individual. Therefore, the origin of the State and the origin of political power must be explained. To say that the State has simply arrogated this right leaves the problem unsolved, for this presupposes the State as a juridical institution already possessing the right of enacting obligatory laws. Nor can it derive this right from its subjects. If this were the case, the subjects might, if they so desired, revoke the right they had previously surrendered. Naturalism cannot even appeal to the well-known maxim that promises must be kept, for in so doing, it would go beyond the data of experience and contrary to its principles it would recognize something of a transcendental, general, and necessary nature. It would abandon the field of pure experience and enter into the sphere of morality; it would desert relative truths and embrace absolute truths. This is equivalent to a complete surrender of the naturalistic position. But the cry *Non serviam* is older than the earth. Only one who believes in the existence of a personal God can speak of an ethicojuridical order embracing all times and all peoples.

On the other hand, if general and necessary standards form the basis of political society, the case is entirely different. In the light of such principles (principles abstracted from human caprice, custom, or self-interest), it becomes a sacred duty to keep promises, not to steal, not to kill, not to bear false witness, and to give to everyone his due. Such principles also explain the true nature of civil authority and the obligatory force of juridical norms. In all other theories which ignore these general principles one cannot speak of enduring social relations, for every citizen is free according to his caprice, interest, or passion to obey or to rebel against authority. Naturalism can call such conduct unworthy, but it may not criticize such conduct as contrary to one's duty and be consistent with its own principles. If no other standard but physical force, self-interest, and custom be recognized in social relations, it would be preposterous to appeal to the notion of duty. But once we admit the principle that civil society is a necessary institution, having its ultimate justification in nature and in the Author of nature, we immediately infer that whatever is requisite for its existence and for its rational development must likewise be necessary. Thus we can explain and justify the statal right to command whatever is demanded by the social good and the duty of the subjects to obey. On the same grounds civil power cannot command anything contrary to the moral law. A legislator promulgating an immoral law would oppose and attack the supreme principles of justice upon which human society rests. Likewise, a judge applying such a law to particular cases and the citizen compelled to comply with it violate the dictates of their own conscience. For a law to impose an obligation, it not only must come from competent authority but it also must agree with moral principles.

c) Devastating Consequences of Naturalism

The denial by naturalism of the existence of a higher order (or to put it bluntly — the denial of God) logically results in atheistic and materialistic systems of government. To convince ourselves of this, it is enough to realize that in order to insure its observance all law requires a sanction. As the positive law loses its efficacy by the abolition of penal sanctions, so the ethico-juridical order loses its obligatory force by the elimination of all after-death sanctions. Communism, for instance, denies a transcendental sanction to the social order. The same political philosophy advocates and effects the abolition of all personal rights, whether property, speech, religious, or political. It strives ruthlessly to uproot Christianity, to destroy individuality, and to erect a totalitarian state of omnipotent power over every phase and factor of human life and human beings. Furthermore, if right and duty and the social order itself are not natural postulates but something subject to constant changes according to circumstances and needs, civil power in its turn ceases to be a necessary and absolute principle of all social life; it becomes a purely empirical and phenomenal element. Then the duty to render obedience to legitimate authority is no longer a need founded in the social nature of man, but something purely relative. But if civic obedience is relative to individual preference and desire, why invoke it to combat radical and subversive theories? If naturalism is to be consistent with its principles, then it must approve of every form of rebellion, anarchy, and upheaval.

By denying the transcendental origin of civil power and thereby depriving it of its ethicojuridical basis, naturalism renders itself incapable of explaining, on the one hand, the right of exercising authority and, on the other, the duty of rendering obedience. Such a denial makes authority usurpation and obedience nonsense. Right and law would have no other sanction than that of the bayonet and cannon. Man realizing that he owes no duty to obey would transgress all laws; he would gratify his every whim and passion, subordinating the common end to his private interest. The guiding maxim would be and too frequently is: "Do what you like, provided you don't get caught."

If belief in the hereafter is only hypocrisy, if everything ends with death, why then should man renounce the pleasures and enjoyments of this life; why should the poor man respect another's property, and resign himself to a life of suffering and misery; why should the exploited conquer himself, repress hatred or the desire of revenge against his oppressors? Yet naturalism spares no efforts to extol the dignity of accomplished duty, the beauty of sacrifice, the value of heroic deeds and of civic virtues. But it is to be feared that the masses will ignore such lofty exhortations and will follow the principles of the new morality to their logical conclusion by giving full scope to unbridled passion. The French Revolution is a good example of what this kind of morality is capable of, and the Russian revolution is confirming the facts. The morality of naturalism is working itself into American life, and the daily press gives us constant evidence of the consequences. An ever increasing delinquency; audacious and enormous thefts; political graft; numberless murders and rackets; evil moral customs; the breakdown of family life which threatens the very core of society. Again, the unscrupulous squandering of public funds is of frequent occurrence; high offices are sought not for the common well-being but rather for the gratification of egotistic, selfish, and unworthy motives. All this is but a small part of the crimes which are being committed against property, persons, and public morality.

Such are the devastating consequences which logically follow from naturalism. Of course, there are some exceptional characters who while professing in theory a crass materialism, in practice give undoubted proof of justice, probity, and every civic virtue. But these exceptions here as in other cases serve only to prove the rule. The fact remains that relativist theories lead to an utter ruin of the moral order and at the same time undermine the economic and social orders. The rejection by naturalism of the idea of a personal God and of absolute truth leads to a complete bankruptcy of science and philosophy. The empirical system culminates in the denial of all authority, in the substitution of the ephemeral and phenomenal for the necessary and eternal principles of the social order. It fails to give us the true notion of civil power; it cannot explain and justify the exercise of that power; it makes of civil obedience a puzzling enigma and succeeds only in justifying every kind of tyranny.

2. CONTRACTUALIST THEORIES

a) Hobbesian Absolutism

We come now to the theories which would derive civil authority from a social contract. In order to put an end to the unhappy state of anarchy and war of every man against every other man, Hobbes tells us that all men agreed by compact to surrender completely their natural power to one man, the monarch. In return the monarch gave them peace and security, to compensate them for the forfeiture of personal liberty. Hobbes argues that men can obtain complete and enduring security for their self-interest only by seeking peace; that peace can be obtained only by a complete surrender of personal liberty; and that the advantages of peace can be secured only by fidelity to the obligations assumed under the compact. These three conditions summarize the civic duties of the governed. In this theory civil power is identified with the will of the prince which is absolute and unlimited. This will is sovereign, inasmuch as it alone has rights and is free from all duties.

By way of criticism we may point out that the three aforesaid rules are but conditional imperatives; hence they cannot of themselves create a genuine right, nor beget a stable and lasting obligation. If man is forced mechanically into civil society, this society will lack cohesion and finality. Such a society could not impose obligation, for it would have no higher authority than that surrendered to it. If the family and society have no other foundation but self-interest, everything becomes relative, that is, subordinated to utility. Thus, in absence of personal interest or in case of one interest conflicting with another, there would be no ground for any obligation nor for civic duties. As a consequence, disobedience to authority and anarchy would become the incontestable right of every individual.

According to Hobbes society is constituted of individuals destitute of morality or conscience, having only utility and pleasure for their orientation. Now history proves that as soon as egoism prevails over other ideals society suffers. National upheavals and bloody revolutions are, as a rule, cleverly planned and carried out by a few unscrupulous criminals who find in social chaos and anarchy an opportunity for satisfying their selfish motives and baser passions. The French and the Russian revolutions give eloquent proof of this. Hence it is hard to see how a society having no other bond than the free interplay of interests and passions could exist. In such a case the State is doomed to extinction from its very birth.

Hobbes' attempt to discover the true notion of civic right and duty and his explanation of civil power is vain and illusory. The doctrine of social compact is a gratuitous hypothesis. History shows that a social contract among individuals without morality and respect for the rights of others is pure nonsense. As physical coercion may compel but not impose an obligation, so too, self-interest and passion may counsel a thing but never establish an enduring social order wherein the individual may attain his end and satisfy in a rational manner his needs and aspirations. One thing remains unquestionably certain, namely, that political power is something essentially different from the sum total of individual rights. Thus, for instance, civil authority possesses and exercises penal rights, as the right of capital punishment, which do not belong in any way to the individuals themselves. The same may be said of the right to declare war or to make peace.

In reality the Hobbesian theory is not an explanation of the nature, origin, and finality of civil power, but a vindication of every sort of tyranny. The right to govern, according to Hobbes, is directly conferred on the ruler by the members of society; civil authority is but the summation or resultant of individual rights. The consequence of this is the omnipotent State in which the sovereign is vested with every kind and degree of supremacy. Such an unlimited authority, having no duties but only rights, results in the vilest tyranny and despotism. Hobbes, falsifying the very concept of human nature, is incompetent to explain the origin of civil power. He confuses the right to govern with physical coercion and the will of the sovereign. He reduces the duty of obedience to egotism and fear. This materialistic theory destroys all intimate social co-ordinations and makes of the State a juridical person, in the Roman acceptation of the term that the State is the Supreme Master.

b) Democratic Absolutism

Other political theorists begin with the contractualist hypothesis and end in democratic absolutism. They regard civil authority as a merger of all rights and wills in the sovereign and general will, which is the true sovereign. Their fundamental principle is that all power comes from the people in whose name only can it be validly exercised. Whenever the people empower a certain person to exercise their power, they retain the right of exacting from him an account of his actions and of punishing and even depriving him of his office according to the circumstances of the case. To add prestige to this theory an appeal is sometimes erroneously made to such authorities as Bellarmine, Molina, Suarez, etc. Concerning these theologians more shall be said in the sequel.

The basic dogma of the Genevan philosopher, Rousseau, is that men are equal by nature and free from all social obligations. No individual can alienate this natural freedom without an act of betrayal against his own personality. The sole means for preserving this freedom is to obey only one's self. But social order and peace are necessary to every society and cannot be obtained without a ruling power. Social life, therefore, demands an authority capable of directing all of its members toward the common good. The difficulty consists in finding the proper way to conciliate obedience to civil power with the original right of every individual to liberty and independence. This conciliation will be effected when the ruling power becomes to all citizens an indivisible, inalienable good. Authority, then, should be blended with the general will of the people in such a way that each citizen may receive, in place of obedience, an equivalent of authority. Thus it comes to pass that every individual commands and obeys only himself. Sovereignty or social authority is, therefore, an inalienable attribute of the general will; and the sovereign is a collective entity, produced by the sum total of all the components of society. The citizens cannot be represented by others, but only by themselves, since no individual will can be surrendered.

To continue with Rousseau's political theory. The content of social authority consists in legislation. Though every enactment of sovereignty always constitutes a law, this law has no juridical value if it does not emanate from the general will; that is, from the people who promulgate it as a law equally obligatory for all. It is obvious, then, that sovereignty belongs to the entire people and is vested by the general will. Sovereignty is not only inalienable but also indivisible, since there is no other will outside the entire social body. The general will having always in view the common good cannot err. It must not be confused with the will of each one, in so far as the former has for its object the common good and the latter has for its scope private well-being. The content of the general will becomes law, provided always that the common good be not subordinated to the good of an individual or a class. In such a case it would cease to be a real emanation of the general will. Law is a decision of the general will in regard to some object of common interest. But though the general will is always right and tends to the public advantage, its judgments are not always enlightened, and consequently it does not always see where the common good lies; hence the necessity of a legislator. However, the legislator has no authority of himself, he is only a guide. He drafts and proposes laws, but laws can proceed only from the body of citizens who have constituted the State.

In the State it is not sufficient to enact laws, it is also necessary to enforce them. But though the general sovereign or will alone is vested with legislative power, it cannot by itself exercise the executive power. It needs an intermediary to apply the laws under the direction of the general will. This is precisely the role played by the government which is the agent or minister of the sovereign will. The government is merely to carry out the decrees or acts of the will of the sovereign people; magistrates are only representatives or agents delegated to transmit to the people the orders of the sovereignty. The government exists only at the pleasure of the sovereign will and is always revocable by that will. Government, therefore, is not based on a contract between the people and the magistrates, it is simply a law. The officers invested with authority are not masters of the people in virtue of a contract but servants; by fulfilling their functions they simply discharge their duties as citizens. Authority is a creature of the aggregation, in consequence of which the members, whether they are the governing or the governed, remain equal in rights of all kinds, social as well as natural.

This is essentially Rousseau's teaching on the origin and nature of civil authority as embodied in the Social Contract. Immense has been his influence, but alas! great also are his errors. Hobbes' theory culminates in Monarchic Absolutism; Rousseau's system culminates in Democratic Absolutism. As has already been observed, there is no historical confirmation of these theories. If on some rare occasions there have been treaties or accords as to the choice of a sovereign, such events took place only in abnormal times, as during civil wars or during a sudden and violent change of a determined form of government. Such a fact is no proof of Rousseau's contention that civil authority arises necessarily from a compact. A compact may designate a certain person or persons to be vested with authority, but it cannot create authority. As a general rule the designation of a sovereign does not result from the free choice of a people expressed by universal suffrage. In other words, a State cannot be created by formal agreement between individuals, as postulated by the social compact theory, nor brought into being by a compact between sovereign states. By a surrender of private rights, individuals cannot create a public right; by a treaty agreement, there cannot be created a political authority superior to that of the parties establishing it.

An unsuccessful attempt has also been made to portray the State and the social contract as a mere juridical fiction.[7] This fiction always indicates an analogical explanation. In the first place, there is no appropriate analogy between the origin of the State and the stipulation of a contract. For if the State is an exigency of human nature, a necessary and universal fact, while a contract is an effect of the free agency of the contracting parties, it is clear that there is no resemblance between the two concepts. In order to apply *juridical fiction* to them, we would have to identify the concept of something necessary, constant, and universal (which applies to civil society) with the concept of something deliberative, contingent, and accidental (which applies to a stipulation or contract). But this is contrary to all logical reasoning. Like and unlike are not the same and cannot be made so to prove a point.

In the absence of proof the social contract theory remains a gratuitous assumption. Why should men in homage to a gratuitous hypothesis renounce their wills and subject themselves of their own accord to the yoke of civil authority? We are here concerned with the philosophical basis of the obligatory character of juridical norms; in other words, we want to know upon what grounds does civil law impose an obligation upon its subjects? A mere agreement is incapable of explaining this, because the

---

[7] Juridical fiction is an assumption of a possible thing as a fact, irrespective of its truth.

effect would be greater than the cause, since the agreement, being among individuals, would be particular while the force of the obligation is general and universal. Obviously, the social contract is not only void of truth, but also is self-contradictory in itself.

The supposition that the people by obeying the law render obedience only to themselves is another gratuitous hypothesis. If the supposition were to be even slightly true, proof would have to be given that every statal law is approved by a unanimous suffrage of the people, which obviously is not the case. For how can one be so illogical as to obey a law that is against one's will and against one's personal interests and still regard such obedience as an homage or a submission to one's self? In a specific case we should vainly seek for an equivalent between what is given and what is received. One who obeys under the sting of a lash cannot be said to be in favor of a law that impugns both his aspirations and interests. Again, it is foolish to suppose that the citizen obeying a law antagonistic to his own well-being does but obey the general will approved by all, through which he has pledged himself to acknowledge as legitimate every law enacted by the majority. This explanation, however plausible, cannot be accepted unless we admit the axiom that all the citizens have *unanimously* and blindly adhered to the social contract, and have taken upon themselves the obligation to obey everything which the majority is pleased to promulgate. Such a blind and absolute assent to the social contract is inexplicable. History proves that human conscience will sooner or later rebel against immoral and tyrannical laws. Instead of taking it for granted, Rousseau should have established by argument the fact that each and every citizen adhering to the contract has pledged himself to obey all the laws, and that by complying with a tyrannical and unjust law they are but rendering obedience to themselves. An argument of this kind was necessary and would have proved the whole theory. But here, as elsewhere, Rousseau is unconcerned about the proof and quite content to build castles in the air. The lamentable fact is that his daydreams have been used by modern states as basic principles of government. We cannot close our eyes to the sad fact that many citizens unless compelled by force do not comply with the law, while others prefer to face punishment rather than to obey.

"If society is but the voluntary aggregation of individuals and not an ordinance of God, if the governing power has no consecration beyond the free acknowledgement of the governed, then no right exists, and no right is violated when the individual disobeys or withdraws altogether from the pact. No one may complain when all are equal. The 'sacred right of insurrection' or rebellion, just or unjust, whether it be against law or government, or against society at large, is the inalienable privilege of every man. Indeed, there never is rebellion, because above the individual himself there is no authority against which he may rebel. Rousseau's theory of society is political Protestantism — the supremacy of the individual.

"Under the terms of the social contract, no right of obedience exists or can exist. If one man in his own name exacts obedience he is a tyrant, for he assumes over other men a power that does not belong to him. If many men or even the majority of men exact obedience in the name of numbers, they also are tyrants, for mere numbers give no power except such power as robbers and murderers claim (the power of might). Small wonder that authority is called The Enemy."[8]

PART II

CHRISTIAN THEORY

In this section we consider civil authority first as a unitive principle which moves man to live in society, and then as an obligatory principle, namely, a principle capable of imposing an obligation upon its subjects. The latter implies that if civil

---

[8] John Ireland, *The Church and Modern Society* (Chicago and New York: D. H. McBride and Co., 1896), p. 16.

authority has the right to command, the people or the subjects have the duty to obey. Civil power is then considered as a regulative principle necessary for the harmonious co-ordination of all activities toward a common end and for the preservation of peace and order. This is followed by a treatment of the traditional Christian position which claims that all authority comes ultimately from God. Finally we show how authority is exercised through the medium of law.

1. CIVIL AUTHORITY AS A PRINCIPLE OF UNITY

The origin and basis of political power must be sought not in custom or self-interest, nor in tradition, nor in a purely fictitious and arbitrary convention, but in the social nature of man and ultimately in the Creator. In analysing the concept of the State, we find that its outstanding characteristic is the moral or social unity which binds the people. The principle that moves man to social unity is not of a physical or mechanical but essentially of a moral nature. Undoubtedly social unity must be considered not from a subjective but from an objective viewpoint. The subject of this unity or union is neither the intelligence nor the will, neither the soul nor the human body, but man's external activity. This social union is formed because the members of society pursue a common end and orientate their proper activities toward this end. It is not a mere logical union, but a true and real union, as the common end is true and real. If the union that binds the people in the State is of such a nature, it follows that civil power is a unitive principle, one capable of effectively imposing an obligation upon its subjects. Thus with regard to the people civil power is simultaneously a unitive as well as an obligatory principle. It is a unitive principle because it moves men to live in civil society; it is an obligatory principle because it binds the citizens to obey legitimate authority.

If the social end were always well defined, and if each individual knew that end and the means necessary for its attainment, he could in an adequate manner contribute toward its realization. In such a situation social unity would be perfect and there would be no need for civil power. But this is far from being true, as is known from daily experience. While a unanimous agreement as to the end of civil society may obtain in theory, in practice it will encounter all kinds of difficulties. Again, as the means whereby a certain end may be obtained are well-nigh infinite, a choice will have to be made among the most suitable ones. In many circumstances the end may be clearly perceived only in its general aspects but not in its particular details. There is also the difficulty of deciding precisely in what measure the contribution to the *common good* should be made by each individual. Finally, self-interest, personal differences, ambition, jealousy, hatred, and other human passions must be taken into consideration. It is evident, then, that in the absence of a unitive principle the State could not subsist, much less prosper. Hence civil power is necessary to curb human passions, to spur the indolent to the fulfillment of their duty, and to inspire all according to their individual abilities to cooperate for the common well-being and prosperity.

The unitive principle of civil power manifests itself in every form of human society, whether free or necessary, from the ultimate unit which is the family to the more complicated unit which is the State. Even human liberty, however sacred, is subject to its restrictions. We have then, on the one hand, liberty in all its inviolable greatness, and on the other, the civil power which places limits and restrictions on human freedom. These two general principles are not mutually exclusive but mutually perfective, and, incidentally, demonstrate that civil power is a postulate of the social nature of man and not merely a product of chance, egotism, or convention. Precisely because man is social by nature he will, notwithstanding his love for liberty, submit to the yoke of civil laws imposed by the State, since he realizes that in no other way can the common well-being be attained. All this emphasizes how necessary civil power as a unitive principle is to society. The fact of a unitive principle is evidenced analogically in the animal kingdom. We say analogically to indicate that among animals there are no societies in the strict sense.

While instinct is the impelling and guiding force of animal activities, there is some kind of union especially among those
species of animals that follow the guidance of a leader, as bees,
migratory birds, sheep, monkeys, elephants, etc. This unitive
principle was supplied directly by nature, that is, by the Author
of nature, by God Himself.

2. CIVIL AUTHORITY AS A PRINCIPLE OF OBLIGATION

Civil power is not only a unitive principle, it is above all else
an obligatory principle. Because civil power is a unitive principle in society, the same power can validly prescribe whatever
is necessary for the realization of social unity. Every right has
an obligation as its correlative. A right without a duty is meaningless. If civil authority has the right to command, the people
have the duty to obey. Civil power as a unitive principle would
be a mere figment of the brain, if it lacked the right of obligating the people to cooperate according to their ability for the
common good.

The State being a natural and necessary society, its right to
command is not conditioned by a free act or by a convention
but by nature itself. (A pseudo-society, on the contrary, has no
right to impose moral obligations on its members.) Admitting
the principle that man is social by nature, the State has a right
to prescribe whatever is necessary for the realization of social
well-being, and the people have the duty to obey. The direct
source and basis of these rights and duties is the general order
whence all this power is derived. Now it would be repugnant
to reason and to common sense that the State should have a
determined goal without possessing the means necessary to attain that goal. If civil power is the most important means among
many intermediary agencies, it follows that civil power is absolutely necessary. Once more we conclude that civil power derives from nature the right to command, as the subjects are
bound by nature to obey.

The necessity of civil power is evident from reason. In the
universe every being occupies its proper place, and according

to the law of finality every being is endowed with an internal tendency to realize its own end and to strive for its own good and perfection. The inorganic world is ruled by physicomechanical laws, the vegetative by biological laws, the animal kingdom is guided by instinct. Rationality which essentially distinguishes man from the brute assigns to him a very privileged place. The intellective principle in man includes and recapitulates all the forces and perfections of the lower beings. It dominates the biological and sensory activities. Now if order, harmony, and finality prevail everywhere in nature, it must all the more be verified in man, since he is at the pinnacle of visible creation. He cannot be an exception to the general rule.

Reason as well as the aspirations of the human heart are in perfect harmony on this point. Man must attain his proper goal established by nature. He must, therefore, conform his activities to objective laws not depending on his option. These laws or norms imply obligation, and consequently they cannot be of the physical but must be of the moral order. Physical force may constrain us to perform an action or to leave another undone, but it cannot engender in man's conscience a moral obligation. The characteristic note that distinguishes moral laws from all others without destroying or lessening human freedom is their obligatory force. When the civil power enacts a law in view of the common good, the citizen realizes that he has the duty to obey. This persuasion is so profound that man has a natural tendency to observe it. As the State is a necessary and natural institution, so obedience to civil laws is natural and necessary.

It might be said that civil power does not concern itself with the agent's intention, that it is satisfied with the external observance and execution of the law. If this were really the case, if civil power were but a mechanical device for the choice and application of the external means best suited to the maintenance of social unity, every research into the basic reasons of civil obedience would be in vain. The problem of the origin and nature of civil power would be confused with the power possessed by bandit chiefs. Although civil power aims chiefly at establishing and preserving external order, and with this end in view makes use of diverse means, yet essentially it assumes and eminently represents a moral character. The logical inference is that social actions cannot be called human unless the external activity is a manifestation and an externalization of the internal moral activity. Consequently, civil power can neither create nor preserve the moral unity binding its citizens without influencing their will which is the intrinsic source of all human activity. From these considerations it follows that no society, however rudimentary, can exist without an obligatory principle. Here is the alternative: either the citizen is morally bound to conform his activities to the legitimate laws of civil power, in which case we shall have an obligatory principle; or he is not bound, in which case we shall have only compulsion or physical force. Needless to say, the consequences of the second alternative are disastrous; the whole moral basis of civil power is undermined and coercion is made supreme; might alone makes right, and the power of the bully and gangster is vindicated. Following the second alternative, the modern science of the State has done everything in its power to divorce politics from morality and religion. It is due to this ill-omened tendency that the State is gradually losing all vestiges of morality. Once morality is destroyed anarchy steps in.

When no other principle but physical compulsion governs the State, the whole question as to the origin and basis of civil power is reduced to the choosing of the most suitable means to keep the people in subjection; the common well-being of society ceases to be of primary importance. The great object of the State will be the continuance of its tyranny and the extension of its power to other nations. Then human brotherhood will no longer be based on love, but on egotism and passion; justice, no longer a principle of order, will be abused by the stronger imposing his will on the weaker by arrogance and machine guns. Civil power so organized will ignore duty and personify brute force and violence. The employment of the most dishonest methods, of the most suspicious means, of corruption and of treason, in a word everything will be justified in this scheme provided it serves to attain the desired goal, which in this case would not be the public good but the good of one man, a despot, or of a small group of men, an oligarchy.

It is clear that if absolute truth be denied, if moral principles be ignored, it will be impossible to establish the true nature of civil power. But for one who regards the State as a necessary and natural institution, the nature of civil power will be clear since it is impossible to conceive a true social order without an underlying obligatory principle. Therefore for the preservation of the unity or order within political society, some regulative force is necessary. Unless the moral organism of the State is endowed with some principle to guide and direct its members toward their common good, each will go his own way and the whole body will be disrupted. This regulative principle in society is authority, which like society itself has its source proximately in human nature and ultimately in God.

3. TRADITIONAL EXPOSITION

The traditional Christian position on the question of the philosophical origin and basis of civil power has always held that all authority comes from God, as Christ declared to Pilate: "Thou wouldst have no power at all over me, were it not given thee from above."[9] But this principle has also given rise to fantastic interpretations, as for instance, the divine-right-of-kings theory. How, then, is the principle to be interpreted or worked out in accordance with Christian tradition?

For a clearer solution of this important question it will be helpful to recall to mind certain points already stated in reference to the nature of civil power. The divine origin of civil power results, first of all, from the fact that it is a necessary need of all forms of social life. "Nolens volens," a well-ordered society requires authority for the harmonious co-ordination of all activities toward a common goal or end which is the social well-being. As soon as several families unite for the attainment of a common

---

[9] *John,* 19:11.

end, the need of civil authority is felt. In other words, as the birth of a son engenders in the father paternal authority, so the permanent union of several families is but a condition under which nature directly communicates civil authority to a person designated for such a purpose. Another proof is derived from the nature of the rights inherent in civil power. It is apparent that whenever several persons unite for the purpose of establishing a conventional society, such as a baseball league, they are perfectly free to outline the extent and limits of authority to be vested in the leader or in the administrative council. But in regard to the State the situation is entirely different, because the State is a *necessary* institution, having an end assigned to it by nature and ordained for that purpose by God. Now since the State has an end, it must also possess the means necessary to attain that goal. It would certainly be contrary to God's wisdom, if He had deprived the State of the necessary means for reaching the goal set by Him. The rights required by the State for attaining its end emanate from nature; hence they are not subject to any modification by man. The exercise of civil power may be shared by several individuals; the more important task may be allotted to some and the less important ones to others; but authority itself in its specific scope is always limited by the social end; it is immutable and ordained by God. The Creator Himself placed the basis of the State in human nature that order and harmonious cooperation might reign among men. He ordained, therefore, that power should be entrusted to the head of civil society so that under his direction the joint activities of all members might redound to the common good and prosperity.

Law implies command, not any command, but a rational one. No matter what its origin, a law cannot impose an obligation unless it commands in the name of Him to whom obedience is due on the part of free and rational beings. As reason must be a herald of God in order to impose a duty on one, so civil power in order to impose obedience must command in virtue of a superior force, in virtue of Divine Authority. A created will cannot of itself impose obedience either on itself or on others. One cannot impose an obligation upon one's self, because it would be a contradiction in terms that the same *I* and *Me* should at the same time be a ruler and the subject of the ruler. It cannot command others because the nature of man, as such, is equal in all men. When it is said that in a contract a man obligates himself to another, it is meant that the existence of the contract being granted, it is one's duty to comply. The source of obligation or a duty imposed on a free and rational being comes directly or indirectly from God. If the people were not bound to obey, the right of the State to command would be a chimera. Therefore the ultimate source of obligation cannot be other than God.

The State possesses many rights that exceed individual prerogatives, such as the right to declare and wage war, to make peace, or the right of life and death; rights which certainly are not inherent either in the family or in the individual citizen. If the rights of the State exceed the individuals' rights, they cannot come from them; therefore they must emanate from God who has dominion over all things. According to Scholastic philosophy civil authority is of God, not by any revelation or positive institution, but because God is the Author of nature.

4. THE ULTIMATE GROUND OF CIVIL AUTHORITY

Civil power is of divine origin in so far as God made man social by nature. As such it is considered apart from any particular form of government. Naturally, authority demands a subject as well as a specific governmental form for its exercise; it must be inherent in a physical or moral person. Hence a distinction between authority in the abstract and its concrete determinations is necessary. "We must beware of saying," as J. Rickaby wisely observes, "of any particular form of authority, monarchy for example or democracy either, what is true only of authority in the abstract."[10] In the first connotation it denotes an immutable right, an essential content of civil authority, a right to command in view of the common well-being. Here power indicates a need of the rational nature of man, and hence ordained by God as a

---

[10] *Catholic Encyclopedia,* Vol. II, p. 139.

constitutive element of civil society. Only in this acceptation is it found equally and constantly everywhere, in the monarchic, in the aristocratic, and in the democratic State. The content of civil authority is thus once and for all limited by the specific and natural end of the State or by the common well-being. As a need of the rational nature of man, authority is not subject to an increase or decrease; it is equal and constant always and everywhere, regardless of time or place.

The divine origin of power far from leading to absolutism, as some seem to fear, is the most powerful guarantee against the whims, caprices, and tyranny of rulers. Those who are vested with supreme authority to command are bound to use this right within certain limits established by God, namely, within the limits of justice and honesty. Authority is not conferred on rulers in order that they may act according to their whims and caprices, but only in view of the common welfare. Hence it is clear that civil power cannot, without contradicting itself, infringe upon the basic natural rights which man, in virtue of his human dignity, has from God prior to his entrance into political society. If civil power derives all its dignity and value from a divine source, it also finds therein a secure and rational limit for its activities. The rejection of the divine origin leaves us with one sole right and one sole duty — it arms the State with the right to command anything and everything, and imposes on the people the sole duty to respect all legal enactments, no matter how wicked or unjust.

SELECT READINGS

Catholic Encyclopedia, arts. "Civil Authority," "Social Contract."

Encyclopedia of the Social Sciences, arts. "Authority," "Popular Sovereignty."

Haas, F. J., *Man and Society* (New York: Century Co., 1930), Ch. IX.

Hoffman, R. J. S., *The Will to Freedom* (London: Sheed and Ward, 1935).

Ireland, J., *The Church and Modern Society* (Chicago: McBride, 1892), pp. 9–47.

Leo XIII, *Immortale Dei* (Christian Constitution of States); *Libertas Humana* (Human Liberty).

Ryan-Boland, *The Catholic Church and the Citizen* (New York: The Macmillan Co., 1928), Ch. II.

Rickaby, Joseph, S.J., *Moral Philosophy* (New York: Longmans, Green and Co., 1918), Part III, Ch. VIII.

Willoughby, W. W., *The Ethical Basis of Political Authority* (New York: The Macmillan Co., 1930).

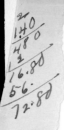

CHAPTER III

THE PROXIMATE ORIGIN OF THE STATE
AND CIVIL AUTHORITY

THE preceding chapters have proved that civil society or the State is not a mechanical and accidental product but a postulate of human nature, finding its full justification in God, and that social life is impossible without a directive force, called civil power or authority. In so doing these chapters proved that the ultimate source of both the State and civil power is God. Yet God does not intervene in any special way to determine what form authority should assume. Any form of government that can fulfill the mission of the State is lawful. Therefore, the proximate origin or immediate source of the State and of civil authority must be considered. Answers must be found for: What in the concrete actualizes civil society and civil authority? Is civil authority transmitted directly by God to the rulers, or indirectly through the people? How can one know that civil power has actually been conferred upon a particular king, president, or parliament?

PART I

THE FORMATION OF THE STATE AND ITS ELEMENTS

Before discussing the proximate origin of the State and of civil power, it will be well to consider briefly the elements and then the formation of civil society. The State consists essentially of a twofold element, one material, the other formal. A multitude of families or individuals permanently united in a fixed territory constitutes the material element, the moral bond uniting these families constitutes the formal. The ultimate explanation of this permanent union cannot be found in community of language, of customs, of traditions, or of blood, but only in the social nature of man. Such a union is prior to the birth of single individuals, or to the founding of single families, and perpetuates itself by means of civil authority.

The formation of civil society is to be sought both in philosophical causes and in historical factors. As an historical fact, civil society begins in diverse ways according to the influence of various factors and circumstances. It may arise by the diffusion of many related families held together by reason of their common ancestry and interests; or by the migration of independent families to a given territory, either to escape persecution or to improve their economic condition. Again, force, physical or moral, of certain individuals or common needs and self-protection may be the determining factor. Irrespective of the way in which the State is formed, it is always a natural and sovereign society comprising a group of families bound together for mutual protection and the common good.

In the formation of the State and the creation of civil power, God is the ultimate and the social nature of man the proximate cause. Man may be regarded, in a sense, as the proximate and immediate cause of civil society and of political power, just as parents through the generative act are the cause of their offspring. They are the dispositive causal factor in that their act is responsible for the human body but God is the determining factor in that He creates the soul and infuses it into the body. Man is the dispositive cause of the State and of civil power in that he predisposes the material element and brings together groups of families. But God alone is the supreme determining cause in that He infuses a social nature into man.

The historical factors responsible for the formation of the State cannot explain the causes which give rise to the bond of legal justice making the united families a moral unit.[1] Nor can they fully explain the origin of the juridical bond or the unity of purpose under the guidance of a common ruler. How does the ethicosocial bond originate? and how do these previously separate families constitute a moral whole? This point is very important, because the ethicosocial bond justifies the right to command and ennobles the duty of obedience to civil law. In other words: "History alone exhibits only the manifold confluent causes which moved man into an organized civil unit. The juridical cause is quite another matter. This is the cause which of its character under the natural law puts the actual moral bond of civil union upon the many in the concrete, imposes the concrete obligation involving all the rights, duties, and powers native to a State, even as the mutual consent of the contracting parties creates the mutual bond of initial domestic society. This determinant has been under dispute among Catholic philosophers."[2] According to Suarez and his followers this determinant is the consent of the people, and civil power is transmitted by successive delegation from God to the people and from the people to the ruler. Others, while admitting that the State can sometimes arise from the free consent of the people, maintain that it can also have its origin *juridically* in the natural and normal expansion of the family into the State without the consent of the constituent members. They hold that civil authority arises when the possessor of that authority is designated. We defend the latter opinion as more probable. Positivistic theories, like those of Rousseau and Hobbes, which exclude the natural character of civil society have no place in this controversy.

---

[1] Legal or social justice demands that the activities of the individual citizen or group members be so conducted as to benefit the community and that, in return, the individual shall be adequately compensated by the community. Legal or social justice includes all actions that bear, directly or indirectly, upon the common good.

[2] *Catholic Encyclopedia*, Vol. XIV, p. 76.

NONACCEPTABLE THEORIES

Certain philosophers would explain the immediate origin of the State and civil power by means of a social contract. The social-contract theory of Pufendorf is in the main quite unacceptable; that of Suarez, Bellarmine, and their followers is acceptable but not preferable to the natural-juridical theory.

1. PUFENDORF

Following in the footsteps of Grotius, Pufendorf holds that man, being free by nature, cannot be compelled to execute the orders enacted by civil authority without first freely subjecting himself to that authority. In consequence he conceives the State as the result of a double compact. By the first compact single individuals pledge their adherence to the State; they promise to form part of civil organization for the attainment of the common good and to comply with civil laws. In so doing they obtain the right to choose a particular form of government by majority vote. By the second compact the person or persons designated to exercise civil power pledge themselves to bring about a realization of the general welfare. At times one compact is sufficient, as, for instance, when groups of families almost spontaneously submit to a leader, prince, or other ruler. While Pufendorf regards the social contract as a necessary condition for the actual organization of the State, he implicitly admits that civil society is a natural institution.

2. SCHOLASTIC CONTRACTUALISM

To explain the proximate origin of the State and of political authority, certain scholastic philosophers and their followers have recourse to a social contract. This social contract is a necessary condition which being present gives rise to the State and consequently to legal justice and to civil rights. They claim that

without this social contract or free consent there can be no obligation on any individual to strive for the common good, no
obligating bond of legal justice. In this theory the obligating
bond of legal justice includes not only free adherents to the
social contract but all others residing within the State. All citizens are in virtue of legal justice bound to respect civil laws and
to cooperate for the general welfare. How each individual
becomes a part of the State is of secondary importance.

Suarez and Bellarmine do not regard this social contract as
the efficient cause of civil power, but only as a necessary condition or moral cause. For a group of families assembled in a fixed
territory to form a State, it is necessary that, first of all, they
constitute a moral whole or a community. The attainment of
this end requires an explicit or implicit consent, whereby single
individuals bind themselves to contribute to the common good.
Through this compact or mutual consent they actually form a
moral or political organization. From the very nature of this
moral union and independently of the will of the contracting
parties civil power follows as a natural consequence. So necessary
is the latter that without it a stable and well-ordered union of
individuals and families for the realization of the general welfare
can be hardly conceived. From the above premises Suarez concludes that the original subject or possessor of civil authority is
the multitude or the people forming the State. All men, he
argues, are free by nature; hence no one has *per se* a right to
command or to exercise jurisdiction over another. While there
is no reason why civil authority should be in the hands of this
or that particular person, the totality of citizens may surrender
civil power or the exercise of the same to a designated person or
group of persons. The ruler or sovereign cannot legitimately
exercise and retain political power, unless he has received it
directly or indirectly from the people.

Suarez expresses his opinion as follows: "No monarch has authority directly from God, but only indirectly, viz., dependently
upon human choice and human ordinance."[3] This same view is

---

[3] Suarez, *Adversus Errores Sectae Anglicanae*, Lib. III, Cap. 2.

expressed by Cardinal Bellarmine: "Political power, as to its subject, resides immediately in the whole state, for this power is by Divine law. But Divine law gives this power to no particular man, therefore Divine law gives this power to the collected body. Furthermore, in the absence of positive law, there is no reason why in a multitude of equals one rather than another should dominate. Therefore, power belongs to the collected body."[4]

According to Suarez, Bellarmine, and their followers, the mutual consent of the members contracting to form society is an indispensable condition for the actual existence of the State; every State must depend on such a social contract. In their view a ruler cannot retain and legitimately exercise sovereign power, unless this power has been first conferred directly or indirectly upon him by the community. Their position may be summarized as follows: By nature man is born to live in society. Since society is not a spontaneous, much less a mechanical, product, the original consent of the people is necessary for its actual and concrete formation. With this end in view the people enter into a compact to follow a directive power or authority for the realization of the general well-being. True, the State or the supreme political collectivity finds its ultimate basis in human nature and in God; but its proximate and immediate source must be sought directly in the consent of the people. This consent may be either explicit or implicit.

It should be carefully noted that the social-contract theory advocated by these Catholic philosophers is poles apart from that of Hobbes and Rousseau, for nothing would be more erroneous than to claim (as some have done) that these Scholastics were precursors of Rousseau and Hobbes. While both agree that civil society depends for its actual existence on the mutual consent of the members contracting to form society, and that civil authority originally belonged to the people, in other respects they

---

[4] St. Robert Bellarmine, *De Laicis* (Trans. by K. E. Murphy) (New York: Fordham University Press, 1928), Ch. VI, p. 25.

differ as the sun from the moon. While Scholastic contractualists regard the social contract as an indispensable condition, in so far as the State is necessary to man, they consider the State as a natural institution and not a mere conventional arrangement. They accept as a self-evident axiom that God created man social by nature and that He engraved on man's heart a set of moral principles necessary both for individual and social life. They unanimously teach that civil authority comes ultimately from God, as the source of rights and moral obligation. They maintain, it is true, that civil power rests originally in the community as an organized whole and that the community has full right to surrender it to a designated person; but they also hold that this authority once handed over to the ruler cannot be recalled arbitrarily. Since stability is a most important element of social order, changes necessarily must not take place save for the gravest reasons.

The theories differ especially on two basic points, the nature of man and the obligation of legal justice. In the view of Rousseau and Hobbes man is not social; he is antisocial or extrasocial, and forms the State only for reasons of expediency. Civil society is a mere collection of elements without cohesion or moral unity, an artificial institution, a human invention. For Rousseau not only is every individual a sovereign, but his sovereignty is inalienable; it belongs to him exclusively. The ruler or the persons charged with the government and administration of the commonwealth are but mere representatives of the sovereign people. The ruler has duties but no rights in regard to the people from whom he receives his mandate; the people are the sole sovereigns. If the prerogative of sovereignty is at times attributed to the ruler or rulers, it is attributed in an improper sense. In the light of this doctrine one cannot seriously speak of seditions or of popular rebellions. Every revolution or popular uprising in Rousseau's theory loses its antisocial and subversive character, and becomes simply a change of public administration, a change fully justified since the people are supreme and not bound to account for their actions.

a) Scholastic Social-Contract Theory Examined

If man cannot be held to obey civil authority without a free submission on his part, then the individual dissenting would not be obliged to cooperate for the common good. One could not seriously blame the nonadhering members for enjoying all the advantages of civil society without making any sacrifices or contributions to the general good. Although the compact has the common good in view, it can never make the obligation intervening between the contracting parties a duty of legal justice. A contract can give rise only to a duty of commutative justice. By their nature contractual duties are duties of commutative and not of legal justice. Having in view the relations and regulations that intervene between subjects and civil authority, legal justice already presupposes the State. Utility or advantage to the community is not sufficient to elevate a duty of commutative justice resulting from a contract to the level of legal justice. The truth of this will become clearer if we consider the end or goal of legal justice. In this connection a few passages from St. Thomas on legal justice will not be out of place.

"It is evident," St. Thomas says, "that all who belong to some community have to the community the relation of parts to a whole. Since it is the nature of the part to belong to the whole, any good of a part must be referable to the good of the whole. Accordingly, the good of every virtue, whether regulating a man in regard to himself or in regard to other persons, is referable to the common good, which is the object of justice. From this standpoint justice is called a general virtue. Since it belongs to law to regulate for the common good, such justice, which we called general, is called legal justice, because by it man conforms to the law which regulates the acts of all virtues unto the common good."[5] Again: "Legal justice is a special virtue according to its specific nature, that is, because it has the common good as its specific object."[6]

---

[5] St. Thomas, *Summa Theologica*, II–II^{ae}, q. 58, a. 5.
[6] *Ibid.*, II–II^{ae}, q. 58, a. 6.

Legal justice cannot be derived from the individual because it imposes upon him the duty of obeying civil power and of working for the common good. Nor can it be derived from the community because legal justice gives civil authority the right to exact whatever is required for the common good. Hence legal justice must proceed from the natural law.

Scholastic contractualism holds that only the democratic form of government rests on divine right, and that the monarchial form rests on human right; but this is obviously contrary to all facts confirmed by experience. If the people had been originally vested with political power, they would in all probability not have surrendered it to others, rather they would have kept it for themselves. The history of the most ancient times from Egypt to Assyria, from Persia to India makes no mention of republics, only of kingdoms.

b) *Arguments Against Scholastic Contractualism*

Modern States though more advanced than the primitive ones have the same goal and the same essential characteristics as the ancient. But if the State really required for its actual existence a free compact, it would be impossible to explain this essential uniformity which persisted and persists amid so many accidental variations.

Even if civil society depended for its actual existence on mutual consent, it would not follow that political power should be considered as the exclusive prerogative of the community. From the fact that paternal authority must look out for the welfare of offspring, it cannot be lawfully inferred that parents are the mere agents or mandatories of their offspring, or that the authority to command belongs equally to all the members of the family. Likewise, from the fact that political power has for its end the common good, it cannot be validly inferred that the ruler is merely a mandatory of the sovereign people. Such an inference has no basis in truth.

Another dangerous assertion of Suarez and Bellarmine is: that each citizen being free and equal by nature, no one can arrogate to himself the right to command others or to bind them in conscience to obey. Such an assertion is a half-truth and highly ambiguous, for it considers man only in the abstract and is true only if we speak of the equality of nature. Men are equal by nature; they have the same organism composed of body and soul; they are subject to the same physical and moral laws; they have the same functions and the same ultimate end — God's glory and their own happiness. But in the concrete men are not equal; there is diversity of sex, of age, of culture, of talent, of health, of economic and social conditions. A babe in the cradle is not equal to the father who supports the family; a lazy lout is not equal to the workman who by his toil helps his fellow men as well as himself; a child is not equal to the soldier who risks life in defense of the State.

Again, if political organization and authority depended exclusively on mutual consent, and if all civil rights and duties were simply nonexistent prior to the social contract, it would follow that an actual adhesion to the contract should be a necessary condition on the part of each citizen, both for the creating of civil rights and duties and for the placing of a moral obligation to keep the contract. Hence the majority could not bind the minority, if the latter did not actually consent to the contract, for duty according to contractualism follows contract. However, the unanimous consent required by the social contract is well-nigh impossible in view of the passions, ignorance, and diversities of opinion which influence man in his judgments. There would always be some who preferring to retain their liberty would refuse their free consent. Now as these could not be forced against their will to participate in the social agreement, the State could not be granted civil power. A contract without the free consent of all the contracting parties cannot be a true contract.

It has even been asserted that the contract once stipulated would bind not only the contracting members but also their posterity. But that a pact which had been wholly voluntary on the part of the original contracting members should be forced upon their descendants is most inconsistent. Even the advantages included in such a contract are incapable of binding posterity, for the latter had no say in the original compact. If this were the case, it would logically follow that all citizens should have been constrained even against their will to adhere to the agreement. This, however, would repudiate the contractualist principle which demands that the social contract be by free and unanimous consent.

Suarez shrewdly remarks that, in the patriarchal scheme, consent could have been verified *paulatim et quasi successive.* In other words, the descendants of the patriarch would have first obeyed him as their father; then as the community through various stages of development reached a more perfect form, they would have extended their consent to political power. But this does not explain at what point the community reached a stage of relative perfection, and how a simple patriarchal family could have been transformed into a State. Moreover, why should the community have submitted itself to political authority as soon as it had reached this stage of perfection? It would seem more logical to say that the community could not have become perfect until obedience due to the patriarch as head of the family had been extended to him also as the political head. The hypothesis that civil society came into actual existence "slowly and as it were successively" while political submission to a person was in the process of formation does not explain the proximate source of the State. It would have been enough for the illustrious theologian to have distinguished between matter and form, namely, between the material and the formal elements of the State in order to see that the content or material element of the State can develop slowly and almost imperceptibly, while the formal element or political authority with its rights and duties must take place instantaneously. When there is question of authority, the *more* or *less* is not sufficient, and the phrase "slowly and successively" does not apply. Power or authority by its very nature either exists whole and entire or not at all. As marital and parental authority does not come into actual existence slowly and gradually, so civil authority as such does not arise slowly and successively.

Gradual submission to civil authority, at most, explains the development or unfolding of the State but not the origin of this power. The origin of the State is something different from its development; one can exist without the other. They are necessarily exclusive; they cannot be subordinated to one another. Thus it would not be correct to say that the proximate source of the State must be accompanied by a certain development or growth. Here is the alternative: either we have to admit that the patriarch could command not only as father but also as judge and legislator, or we have to deny this right. According to the first alternative, the offspring and other members of the family are bound to obey and respect the patriarch both as father and as judge and legislator. Herein we have the essential elements of the State. No essential change can be brought about by posterity, because the relations between subjects and ruler, between the one who commands and the one who obeys, are established once and for all. From the very beginning of the patriarchal regime, all subjects without distinction must "willy nilly" fulfill their duties as subjects and as citizens unless they prefer to withdraw from the patriarchal family and emigrate. According to the second alternative, descendants have no other duty toward the patriarch than that of filial obedience. Now it would be extremely interesting to know how and why the parental authority of the patriarch evolved into the political power of the patriarch and then passed down to his future generations. Briefly, it must be shown how the patriarchal family could have been transformed into a State. To say, as Suarez does, that this political submission to a single person could have taken place "slowly and as it were successively" is quite obviously an inadequate solution.

c) Additional Difficulties

An examination of the logical consequences of the contractualist view will bring to light certain theoretical difficulties. The

theory makes political authority dependent on a presumed transmission of power by the people to the ruler. It contends that
civil authority results from a double agreement, either implicit
or explicit. Having the social contract for its basis, this view presupposes all the relative conditions of a contract in relation both
to its actual existence and to its validity. The first and the most
important of contractual conditions is the following: Whenever
one of the contracting parties betrays his trust, that is, violates
an essential clause of the contract, the other is freed from the
assumed obligations. Thus Bañez holds that whenever the ruler
after repeated admonitions refuses to perform his duties toward
his subjects, the people having no other alternative may banish
him from the State. This is not all; if the government degenerates into tyranny, "it will be in the power of the community
to depose the prince, or even to inflict capital punishment upon
him in defense of the commonwealth." This, however, would
endanger the already weakened stability in social relations, and
the consequences would be all the more disastrous on account
of the anarchical and revolutionary theories which nowadays
advocate a new economic order, based on absolute equality and
on the abolition of classes, of private ownership, and of all
authority.

d) *Specific Suarezian Tenets*

The people, according to Suarez, surrender political power to
the ruler on the condition that he exercise it for the common
good of all. This axiomatic principle is not subject to any exceptions or changes, finding its most ample justification in a
right inherent in the community. On the other hand, the people
cannot deliver up the exercise of supreme authority in such a
way as to deprive themselves of all rights of intervention; they
must reserve at least an implicit or explicit right of legitimate
self-defense. "If a lawful king," says Suarez, "rules tyrannically,
and there is no other way for the kingdom to protect itself except to depose him, it is lawful for the whole community by a
solemn act to do so. This action is sanctioned by the law of

nature which always allows us to repel force by force, as well as by the terms of the original contract under which the first king accepted sovereignty from the people."[7] The people as a moral whole would have reserved to themselves the right to depose the ruler on account of a serious and prolonged tyranny and to confer political power on a more reliable person who would use it for the general good. This doctrine whether taken from a practical or a theoretical point of view involves many difficulties.

Although the contractualist theory of the scholastic differs essentially from that of Rousseau, it may nonetheless lead to certain conclusions never intended by its exponents. If the State depends for its actual existence exclusively on the implicit or explicit consent of the contracting parties, it may happen that certain contracting members may tire of obeying the designated ruler and long for their former liberty. Obviously, withdrawal from the social contract would engender disorder and anarchy. Hence, though the scholastic thesis does not sanction unjust rebellions and revolutions, it lends itself to interpretations that are vague and often harmful for the social order.

It does not seem expedient to invoke the authority of the great theologians of the Church in order to justify and establish so controverted a theory as scholastic contractualism, particularly where unanimity of opinions is wanting. Some theologians claim, for instance, that Adam as father of the human race was already vested with political authority; others contend that he could not have possessed civil authority except in virtue of a contract. Still others believe that the submission to power by many individuals, formerly free and independent, must have come about by cunning contrivances of wealthy and influential persons. In view of such diversity of opinions it would be rash to appeal to the so-called unanimous consent of the School. Not a few have recourse to St. Thomas' teaching as favoring the contractualist theory, but uselessly. True, Aquinas holds that the

---

[7] Suarez, *De Defensio fidei*, I, 3, c. 2, n. 9.

ruler derives laws from the community.[8] This, however, must
not be taken in the sense that the ruler has derived the right to
command from the people through an implicit or explicit social
contract, but in the sense that the rule should be directed to the
common welfare. St. Thomas asks the question: "Can the reason
of any one, whosoever it be, make law? In other words, whose
reason has the duty of ordering things to the common good?"
He answers: "Law properly and principally looks to the common
good. But to ordain things unto the common good is the office
either of the entire multitude or of him who takes care of the
entire multitude. Hence the establishing of law is the function
either of the entire multitude or else of the public person having care of the entire multitude. For also in all other matters
the directing of things to their end is the duty of him to whom
that end belongs" (I–II, 90, 3). There is no indication here of
a compact. It would be in vain to look for it in the works of
St. Thomas. He does not indicate whether such authority is immediately derived from God, or from a contract, or the manner
in which it was possessed by the first patriarchs. One thing is
certain — the contractualists, as Suarez wisely observes, will never
be able to make advantageous use of the aforesaid Thomistic
passage.[9] Therefore it is useless to appeal to the unanimous consensus of the scholastics, because it does not exist except perhaps
in the imagination of their adversaries.

The scholastic contractualist theory, as already stated, is not
concerned with matters of faith. It is merely a philosophical
question allowing the widest field for discussion. It is well to
bear in mind that the problem of the proximate source of the
State and civil power did not acquire such great importance
until the time of Rousseau and other precursors of the Revolution. In the writings of medieval theologians we find only remote allusions to the question. Suarez himself gives but an
abridged exposition. It is certain, however, that if scholasticism

---

[8] St. Thomas, *Summa Theologica*, I, II, q. 97, a. 3.
[9] Suarez, *De Legibus*, I, c. 8, n. 9.

had attacked the problem with the same zeal and earnestness as
it had done in its other undertakings, we would have a better
solution. At any rate, scholastic theologians would have appreciated the necessity of distinguishing between the material and
the formal element of civil society — the material denoting a
plurality of men and families assembled in a fixed territory, the
formal denoting a unity of cohesion under the same common
authority and with the same organization. Admitting this distinction, it is easy to see that while the former element is more
or less voluntary, the second is necessary.

3. C. L. HALLER's THEORY

It will be interesting now to give a critical account of C. L.
Haller's theory. His claim is that man has no direct part in the
conferring of political power. Though depending on God, authority belongs always and necessarily to a citizen who excels
others in pre-eminence and influence. In proof of this he appeals
to the general law according to which some pre-eminently qualified person has a natural tendency to dominate over the less
powerful and influential. From the very fact that the pre-eminent
person is, as it were, assigned by nature to rule over civil society,
the weaker must, in view of the common good, subordinate his
activities to the enactments of civil authority (as represented by
the more capable). The pre-eminence given by nature must not
be confused with physical superiority or might, or with abuse
or oppression. This natural pre-eminence is something entirely
different from violence and despotism. The relationship which
mediates between subject and sovereign is in conformity with
the principle of justice and a source of good for both. The acquisition of civil authority in this theory is conceived and
regulated in the same manner as the right to the acquisition of
property. In both cases the one who succeeds is the more efficient,
the more cautious and prudent; consequently such superiority
or pre-eminence is not in any way opposed to the rights of justice. Considered in its essential character, authority does not
differ from other private rights except in so far as it implies

independence from all others but God. The law of subordination reigns everywhere; in the hierarchy of beings between the organic and inorganic world, in marriage between husband and wife, in the family between the parents and the offspring, in the household between servant and master. All these relations have their natural source and crown in God. The State presupposes such relations with the sole difference that the sovereign authority possesses a higher degree of independence, power, and liberty. For this reason the State cannot be regarded as a mere human institution or an artificial society.

Haller's theory resolves itself in favor of monarchy, since no one in the State but the monarch possesses all the aforesaid qualifications, he alone can be independent of others, though he must render to God an account of his actions. Authority does not differ essentially from other private rights. For Haller the purpose or goal of the State is but the sum total of the individual or private goals or ends. The Hallerian theory is recapitulated in what we may call a *private juridical* conception of the State.

Haller has had many followers. Among the recent ones is A. Fouillie who regards civil power as the sum total of all private juridical relations which in an effective and lasting way bind together groups of families in the same territory. The State consists of numberless families brought together by diverse private-juridical relations, being independent of any superior power. However it does not seem probable that a mere summation of private legal relations in favor of a certain person can satisfactorily account for the origin of the State and of civil authority. It may, indeed, happen that in a group of permanently united families there should be a person enjoying such economic and social superiority as to make him altogether independent and of such influence as to compel others to obey him. It may even happen that such independence and such subordination may effectually lead to a State wherein the civil power falls into the hands of the said person without any popular consent. There would be no absurdity in such a conception; in fact history gives many examples. It seems, however, inadmissible that a person must necessarily be vested with civil power simply because he enjoys complete independence in his private juridical relations. The mere existence of private juridical relations, no matter how well established, is not of itself sufficient to create the State. Of course, there will be a civil society or a State whenever in the aforesaid private juridical relations there is a sovereign authority capable of exercising its proper mandate in the common interest. But all this does not indicate *how* the civil power came into being. If the State resulted merely from the private relations of superiority and dependence, neither the moral union nor the rights of civil society could be explained.

Haller's theory cannot account for the moral bond that characterizes the State and distinguishes it from every other form of society. It cannot explain the State's right of life and death, which by way of contrast is not a prerogative of private individuals. If the bond that unites diverse families into a moral whole be lacking, we should at best have an aggregate of individual interests but never a common authority vested with the right to command. Moreover, a natural right cannot be regarded as a summation of individual rights since both by nature and finality it differs essentially from them. Even though an individual person possessed all possible rights as master or owner, and on that account excelled others in power and wealth, he could not boast of any legal right of command. A number of such rights may increase the quantity but it does not change the quality. The following fact will serve as an illustration. A master has no right to punish his servant for those faults not explicitly specified in the contract, because he has no true jurisdictional power. The defenders of this theory forget that by identifying the political rights with individual right, they destroy all distinction between superior and subject, between master and servant. This, obviously, implies a denial of legal distributive justice which presupposes a community of goods, and of juridical relations regulating public order.

Again, the same theory would grant the ruler the right of

exemption from all social duties and of following his caprice and fancies rather than the general welfare.

On the contrary, the ruler though at the head of civil society must have in view the common good by supplementing and perfecting the individual activities. The citizens must be regarded not as mere servants but as subjects having rights as well as duties. All this goes to show that not only commutative but also legal and distributive justice belong to the State. Hence, the State embraces private juridical relations and relations of public order. The bond which groups citizens and families into a moral whole and binds them in justice to obey the laws and to cooperate in social welfare has nothing in common with the series of private juridical relations. The solution of the problem must, therefore, be sought elsewhere than in a system that confounds private rights with common rights, the relation of servitude with the relation of dependence and subordination.

PART III

THE NATURAL-JURIDICAL THEORY

A theory more consonant with truth is the natural-juridical origin of civil society. According to this theory both the State and civil authority are immediately grounded upon nature; and the subject who originally possesses the right to govern is designated, as in the case of parental authority, immediately by God in a divine yet *natural*, not positive, designation. This view does not in any sense imply that the ruler vested with political power is in *all instances* directly designated by nature. Whenever a plurality of mutually independent families and persons decides to migrate into an uninhabited territory, they can by a social contract form a State and choose the type of government best suited to their needs. In such cases the people are perfectly free to set up either a democratic, or monarchic, or even an aristocratic form of government. There are also instances where civil power reverts to the people, as when a monarch dies without legitimate successors to the throne, or in cases of abdication. But at certain times, especially in the era of ancient patriarchal families, political authority could easily have been vested in one person, in consequence of determined circumstances and juri-dical-natural relations.

In a multitude of families occupying a fixed territory either because of moral and material necessities, or because of affinity and kindred, an individual might arise, say a patriarch, who is superior to all others and who is the only one capable of form-ing a government of even elementary efficiency. In such a case the only reasonable solution is the exercise of political power by this man. From the fact that someone must rule, it follows logically that all the members of the community must recognize him as their ruler and conform to his commands. Even though the community should not consent but should oppose his au-thority by physical force, his moral right to rule seems im-pregnable. Since he is the only one capable of ruling, he is the only one who has the right to rule. Because his rule is necessary for their well-being, the people have no right to refuse their consent. The welfare of the people is the supreme determinant of human rights. The patriarch, therefore, does not require either the explicit or implicit consent of the community.

A multitude of families can, without the compact required by the scholastic contractualists, create the State and confer political power upon a designated person. This reflection will become more apparent by a close study of human nature. As man creates a family in order to satisfy his needs, so families unite into civil society in order to provide more effectively for their self-protec-tion and the general welfare. Such a union must be permanent because the needs of reciprocal protection and cooperation are constant and permanent. But a permanent union of families cannot be conceived without a ruler commissioned to safeguard social order and to care for the general welfare.

The above fact is again verified in the following instance. "Let us consider the case of a savage or semisavage people that possesses some rudimentary show of political organization, but that exhibits conditions little better than those of anarchy. Life, limb, and property are always in jeopardy, and there are no such institutions as schools or churches. Although the territory occupied by this people contains natural resources which would be of great benefit to the human race, the native rulers are unwilling or unable to exploit and utilize these great natural bounties. Suppose now that a civilized power desires to intervene in the affairs of this impotent community in order to set up a stable government, and to render the natural resources available for the satisfaction of human wants. . . . In this situation the outside nation has surely the right to intervene and impose its government upon the helpless community. The latter has no right to oppose or resist, no right to choose some other government, no right of "self-determination." And the sufficient proof that no such right exists is to be found again in the end of all rights, human welfare.[10]

How much the more so has a superior person within a community the right to rule, if there are no other means present for the preservation of unity and the fostering of the common good. Such a person has an impregnable right to rule based upon the natural law and ultimately upon God. The subjects of this person have an indisputable duty to obey him and to cooperate with him for the common good.

According to our theory, the ruler does not possess civil authority as coming directly from God but in virtue of numerous factual relations dependent in large measure on human free will. Hence it is not so much a divine right as a human right. As the right to property in its immediate origin is human or positive; so civil power considered in relation to the ruler is merely a human right. If God directly designated David and

---

[10] J. A. Ryan, *Catholic Doctrine on the Right of Self-Government* (New York: The Paulist Press, 1920), pp. 14, 15.

Saul to govern the chosen people, it was by way of exception. In the natural order of things as well as in the economy of Divine Providence, the right to designate a ruler belongs to human free will. Such designation ordinarily takes place under the influence of numerous circumstances. These circumstances depend on human will only in so far as in their totality they are influential in bringing into permanent union a plurality of families in a fixed territory. If the first patriarchal families constituted a union of families with numerous slaves and progeny; if at the head of this organized society a patriarch was necessary, because in such circumstances nobody else could exercise political authority with such efficiency and because in all probability the patriarch would not tolerate in his place others who might deprive him of his right to judge and legislate for the families subordinated to him by patrimonial bonds and kindred; if all this be admitted, then evidently the patriarch alone could possess the right of supervising public order and of providing protection against internal and external enemies. The patriarch was, as a rule, judge and master in the community dependent on him. Hence the actual existence of civil power can be justified apart from the consent of the community.

Since a moral organism or a permanent union of families would have been impossible without political authority to settle disputes, to right injuries committed against persons, honor, and property, and to direct the members toward their common end, the patriarch had a natural right to rule. In virtue of the same natural law everyone was bound not only to recognize the patriarch as the supreme head of the community, but also to respect his orders relative to social interests. The only alternative was migration. Here obviously civil power is not transferred by the community to the ruler; on the contrary, the community submits to an already constituted power which is independent of the consent of the governed.

It may be asked here: "Where did authority rest before it became attached to the patriarch, council, or king? Nowhere. It is not like a physical entity that must have a local habitation before it can come into a person's possession. It is an attribute which attaches itself to the ruler through the occurrence of certain particular events, just as parental authority attaches itself to the father and mother by the fact that a child is born to them. They then receive the authority from God. In similar fashion the legitimate ruler receives his authority directly from God.

"Why should we assume that God gives authority to a king or a president through the people. Why should He not confer it upon the accredited ruler directly? . . . Is it not enough to assume that the people have the exclusive right to designate the ruling person, and that God invariably bestows the authority directly upon the person thus designated?"[11]

The pretended fear that this theory might obliterate the distinction between family and State is also without foundation. A State is based neither on bonds of kindred and love, nor on a mere community of life and interests. It comes into being from the family only in so far as family development is required for the formation of a tribe in a fixed territory. In this process is precisely verified the fact that while the bonds of blood are gradually disappearing, there arises an intensified "togetherness" of common interests which finds an efficacious safeguard in civil power alone. In other words, it demands a ruler functioning as a leader in case of war, and as a judge in time of peace. Hence, the patriarch in virtue of his position, is called upon to exercise this double task in his quality of political head. In this light civil authority is distinguished from paternal authority. Both conceptions find in God their full justification, with this difference, that while paternal authority by its nature belongs exclusively to the father and cannot be taken away or limited; political authority, on the contrary, may depend to a great extent on human consent.

The natural-juridical theory is not opposed either to a democratic or an aristocratic State. It can be reconciled with any form of government.

---

[11] J. A. Ryan, *op. cit.*

SELECT READINGS

Aquinas, St. Thomas, *The Governance of the Rulers* (Tr. by G. B. Phelan) (New York: Sheed and Ward, 1938).

Bellarmine, St. Robert, *De Laicis* (A Treatise on Civil Government) (Tr. by K. E. Murphy) (New York: Fordham Press, 1928).

Cronin, M., *The Science of Ethics* (New York: Benziger, 1922), Vol. II, pp. 490–530.

Leibel, J. F., *Readings in Ethics* (Chicago: Loyola University Press, 1926), No. 164.

McNamara, "American Democracy and Catholic Doctrine" (Brooklyn: I.C.T.S., 1925), pamphlet.

Ryan, J. A., "Catholic Doctrine on Right of Self-Government" (New York: The Paulist Press, 1920), pamphlet.

Ryan-Boland, *Catholic Principles of Politics*, Ch. VII.

Ryan-Millar, *The State and Church* (New York: The Macmillan Co., 1930), pp. 68–98.

CHAPTER IV

PURPOSE AND FUNCTION OF THE STATE

ANY question of governmental jurisdiction or of the right of the State to use authority must ultimately bring us to an inquiry into the purpose of the State. Starting from the moral purpose of civil society, we must determine the duties of civil authority on the one hand, and the lawful use of its powers on the other.

It has been shown that civil society exists not merely as the result of accident or of extrinsic historical circumstances — which since Hobbes, Rousseau, and Kant has come to be the generally accepted view — but rather because man is formally and intrinsically determined to a social and political life in the very depths of his intellectual and moral nature. Moreover, from the fact that man's countless needs can be properly satisfied only in and through civil society, and that civil society existed *de facto* from the very beginning of the human race, it follows that man is social by nature and that civil society is natural for the purpose of helping him to attain the end for which God created him. Now since civil society is a natural institution, its end or purpose must also be determined by nature. Hence the approach to the problem of the purpose and function of the State must be philosophical rather than historical.

The philosopher's task differs from that of the historian. The latter studies the constitutions of states in their development and political workings with a view of determining how far they have adapted themselves to existing needs and fulfilled their original purposes; whereas the philosopher seeks the basic principles that should regulate governmental activities and legislative functions. The philosophy of the State, then, is not merely an historical exposition comparing and classifying the diverse ideas proposed

85

to regulate the various political organizations, but it is a direct
investigation of the necessary and underlying principles that
should determine the purpose and function of the State.

The philosophy of the State is not concerned with this or that
particular State, say the American or the English or the French
State, but with the State in general, namely, with its essential
and unchanging elements. The object of political philosophy is
to investigate the basic and necessary principles underlying the
social phenomena and to point out the supreme standards according to which political activities *ought* to take place. As the
certainty of all philosophical sciences is derived from the necessity and universality of their principles, so also political philosophy derives its certainty from the absolute character of civil
society and from the purpose and functions of the State.

Indeed, it is nature that specifies the life of every being and
determines its purpose. In other words, as the purpose or end
of an organism is determined by the nature of that organism, so
the purpose of the State must be determined by the nature of
civil society. Hence it is easily seen that erroneous views concerning the end of the State result from false conceptions of
civil society and of man.

PART I

ERRONEOUS THEORIES

The liberalistic and absolutistic conceptions of the purpose
and functions of the State are varied. Certain views deny a
specific purpose to the State. Others consider self-protection and
social peace the ultimate aim of the State. Economic individualism contends that the proper end of the State consists in an unlimited economic competition. Kant, Humboldt, and Spencer
advocate a minimum of State authority and a maximum of individual freedom. Under the absolutistic conception there are the

tenets of ancient and modern Machiavellianism and the Hegelian doctrine of statolatry. Finally, there are the socialistic and the sociological theories which would completely merge the individual into the State.

1. LIBERALISTIC CONCEPTIONS

a) Denial of a Proper Statal End

Certain philosophers, though admitting that the State is a necessary and natural institution, deny to it a proper end or specific purpose. They confuse the specific and common end of the State with the particular ends of other societies, in other words, they confuse the end with the means. Montesquieu, for instance, teaches that while all States have in common their preservation, each State has a peculiar end of its own. "Aggrandizement," he says, "was the chief aim of Rome; war, that of the Lacedemonians; religion, that of the Jews; commerce, that of Marseilles; public tranquillity, that of China, navigation, that of Rhodes."[1] In spite of the authority enjoyed by this author, it is obvious that the natural end of the State is something different from the means suitable or necessary for its attainment. The purpose of the State is as immutable as its nature is immutable; the means are variable and change with the various needs of life. Rome is known for her wars of expansion and conquest, but certainly not for the sole purpose of subduing new peoples and dominating the world. In this polity Rome of the Caesars saw primarily a suitable means for attaining her supreme end, namely, her material development and general welfare. The same may be said of the Jewish people in regard to religion, of the city of Marseilles in regard to commerce, and of Rhodes in regard to navigation. The distinction between private ends and the proper purpose of civil society is of vital importance, and it is surprising that it should have escaped the sagacity of a Montesquieu.

The same opinion is advocated by Haller, who after a brilliant confutation of the revolutionary conception of the State en-

---

[1] Montesquieu, De l'esprit des lois (Genève, 1749), I, XI, c. 5.

deavors to show that civil purposes are all specific to each individual state. According to his theory, instead of a generic purpose native to all civil society, there are as many diverse ends or purposes as there are states, and these ends vary *ad infinitum*. Haller erroneously identifies the specific purpose of the State with the various motives which prompted men to establish a certain governmental organization. A sophism is also added to his error, for Haller asserts that civil society is demanded by nature and yet considers the supreme end of the State as something particular and purely accidental. Haller's theory cannot be admitted, because it would leave society to the guidance of human caprice. Haller's erroneous teaching was very detrimental to political philosophy. It is but a step from the denial of a proper and common end to the State to the affirmation that the State is the supreme source of all law. Right would again be surrendered to the caprice and whims of the ruler, and the Hobbesian formula "what the State commands is good; what it prohibits is bad. Its will is the supreme law" would be vindicated; but this is morally evil.

b) Self-Protectionist View

For some the ultimate aim of the State is self-protection and social peace. The proponents of this theory hold that the specific end of a State is self-protection. But if this is so, small States lacking the means of self-protection would have no specific end and, hence, would not be States. But history and reason prove this false. The armed power of Switzerland contrasted with that of the great nations is insignificant, yet it is a true State. A larger or smaller territorial extension does not change the essential characteristics which remain substantially the same in all political organizations. Moreover, facts show that a small State in the same manner as a large one aims at self-preservation, attends to the internal order, and takes care of the general welfare; that it is equally jealous of its independence and ever ready to defend its territory and its right of sovereignty by force of arms. Many small nations that recently fought so bravely in defense of their liberty and independence are brilliant evidence of this. These considerations prove the shortcoming of the self-protectionist view.

c) Economic Individualism

Now it may be asked whether the purpose of the State is limited to negative functions of maintaining order and protecting rights, or whether it has the function also of promoting the common good in a positive way. The vanishing race of liberalists favors exclusively the first alternative. The theory of economic individualism holds that the best good of all can be obtained through the economics of free exchange; that each individual should look out for himself; that there should be no government interference either in the production, distribution, or consumption of economic goods. This theory profoundly influenced political philosophy, and its tragic consequences brought about a radical reaction.

To this triumph of liberalism such men as F. Bastiat, J. B. Say, Adam Smith, and D. Ricardo generously contributed. In order to obtain the best economic good for all men, Smith claims that it is necessary for each man to strive after his own interests alone. The good of society will then take care of itself. According to him the government should keep its hands strictly out of business and let well-enough alone. Smith's original error was not malice but an exaggerated optimism in human nature, an optimism doomed to failure. Men like Rousseau and Kant favored an absolute and unlimited personal liberty. In the nineteenth century, human life and society came to be viewed under the ascending star of materialism. The law of selfishness was applied to national as well as to individual life. Naturalism taught that, just as there was no other religion than that of brute force, there was no other law than the natural law of struggle for existence and survival of the fittest, which they claimed had dominated all history.

The theory of economics places the supreme good of all in material prosperity and riches which can be realized only under the empire of free economic competition. The sole aim of the State must be to provide for each individual the widest sphere of action. Only one thing is demanded — the juridical protection of the citizens. Everything else would but hinder the provident work of nature and militate against the common good of all. If man, as they claim, is essentially good by nature, then all must respect the free manifestation of his goodness. Accordingly the State on its part is bound to protect the natural inclinations of man, allowing him the widest personal liberty. The common good is felt to be automatically achieved when everyone pursues his own individual interests to the greatest degree. This hypothesis is in harmony with that of Darwin as to free natural selection for the development of a better type of (brute).

In unison with the above view the "physiocrats" revived the *laissez faire* theory — "Keep your hands off"; "Let things alone." Social activities, according to them, are subject to natural laws in the same way that nature is subject to physical laws. National well-being can be secured only by obeying these natural laws. The function of the State should be limited to the protection of life, liberty, and property; and the individual should be permitted to pursue his own interests and make the best of his labor. Evidently this doctrine is rooted in Rousseau's teachings. If man is emancipated from all order superior to himself, then the only purpose of civil society will consist in securing for all its citizens a maximum of personal freedom. The obvious consequence of this is an unlimited economic freedom.

d) Theory of Kant

The Kantian view has several points of contact with liberalism. Kant considers the purpose of the State from a purely negative aspect. He emancipates man from every external authority but advocates an equilibrium for individual liberties. In other words, Kant would subject man's liberties to no other restriction than that demanded for the safeguard of an equal sphere of activity for all. For Kant the primary function of the State consists in securing for all an equal measure of liberty and not in promoting the general welfare. In other words, there should be a minimum of State authority and a maximum of individual freedom. The State in the Kantian scheme is emancipated from every order superior to itself; it becomes an absolute master, free to do what it pleases.

In criticism of this view, it may be noted that liberty considered in itself and abstracted from any definite purpose does not as yet represent a moral good; it can lead to evil as well as to good. Hence individual liberty cannot be the ultimate purpose of the State without emancipating the latter from God. If this were true, the State would cease to have a positive purpose — its exclusive function would rest merely in safeguarding personal liberty. Should the nation be afflicted by some public calamity, as for instance, famine, pestilence, or earthquakes; should the people live in suffering and privations, misery or ignorance; should personal liberty be directed along the path of licentiousness and debauchery rather than along the path of moral goodness and virtue; it would not matter. Provided this individual liberty is secured, nothing can be said against adultery, immorality, or vice. The State in the Kantian theory is expected to check only what would harm or hinder another's liberty. In this scheme the State would then no longer be a moral body but merely a guardian of public order and tranquillity; it would not have to conform to any ethical laws but only to a mechanicomaterialistic principle, which is contrary to logic, to human needs, and to daily experience.

The consequences of this theory are disastrous both in the moral and the social field. If the State has no right to busy itself with the common good of all, except in the measure required to safeguard personal rights and liberty, then the State has no right to suppress an immoral press, obscene pictures, lewd plays, etc. Rather, it has the duty to aid by passivity the affront directed against what is most sacred and dear to the family and society itself. Provided personal freedom be safeguarded, it matters little whether good habits fall into disuse and the incautious youth be driven into moral depravity, whether religion be ridiculed and

Christian virtues contemned. Under the aegis of this theory, vice
and corruption will find a fertile soil for growth and expansion.
While the State immolates whatever is most sacred and esteemed
on the altar of juridical protection, it gradually and imperceptibly paves the way to its utter ruin. Juridical protection culminates in State destruction.

The assertion that the State is an end in itself is the foundation of the Kantian theory. His doctrine of the autonomy of
human reason leads directly to State autonomy. But this proposition is untenable, for neither the individual nor the State is an
end in itself, an autonomous institution. What is created is essentially dependent on God and therefore has no absolute power;
not existing of itself it is subject to Him. So too, the State and
man are limited in their activities by the moral law. This does
not in any way degrade their mission, it rather ennobles them
by safeguarding governmental functions from the whims and
arbitrariness of rulers. The individual is not created for the
State, but the State for the individual. To maintain that the
State is absolutely autonomous and an end in itself, is to make
it the supreme arbiter of public and private rights. It is to enslave the individual to any governmental form, be it ever so
revolutionary or despotic. Thus, in the Kantian theory, the
autonomy of the individual is destroyed by the autonomy of the
State because human rights and dignity are sacrificed to the
statal deity. The very nature of man rebels against such a crude
theory of political society. Why should man be prompted by
nature to create a family and live in society only to be enslaved
by it? This system is contrary to sound logic and experience,
and is repugnant to human dignity and to the highest aspirations of the human heart.

e) Theory of Humboldt

The honor of putting the finishing touches to this picture of
liberalism belongs to the German philosopher, K. W. Humboldt.
The State according to Humboldt may limit the citizen's liberty
only in so far as the protection of the State against internal and

external enemies requires it. Every other method of State activity would be detrimental to the well-being of society and would culminate in a hateful uniformity of action. Moreover, the State out of regard for individual liberties has no right to judge individual actions whether good or bad, just or unjust. In the words of F. La Salle, the State becomes only a night watchman, a mere guardian of law and order.

It matters little that Humboldt extends statal functions to the tutelage of ideal interests, and allows the widest liberties to spiritual values, to culture, science, and religion. Modern industrialism with the steam engine, the division of labor, the rapid means of transportation by land, sea, and air, has brilliantly demonstrated that liberalism far from reflecting a high principle of order and social prosperity tends to favor *rugged individualism*. Had Humboldt closely examined the motives that prompt man to live in society, he would undoubtedly have reached a different conclusion. At any rate he would have been convinced that juridical protection demands also a positive cooperation from the State (only then will the citizens be enabled to attain their spiritual and material well-being). Furthermore, Humboldt would have realized that many other goods beyond the reach of the individual, intended to embellish and develop individual as well as family life, cannot be obtained without effective State cooperation. Finally, he would have learned that all governments, ancient as well as modern, have never limited their function to simple juridical protection, but have positively promoted the common welfare and prosperity. The thesis of liberalism or of juridical protection is, therefore, untenable, as being contrary both to fact and to truth.

f) Theory of Spencer

Under a philosophical aspect Spencer also advocates the theory of juridical protection. Starting from his principle of the struggle for existence and of the survival of the fittest, he comes to the conclusion that the purpose of civil society is "to bind man in the social State, and to check all conduct endangering the exist-

ence of that State."[2] Again, "He who would have the State do
more than protect, is required to say where he means to draw
the line and to give us reasons why it must be just there and
nowhere else."[3] This conclusion is but the logical result of the
axioms assumed by Spencer. The struggle for existence proceed-
ing in an orderly way cannot but lead to a natural selection, to
the triumph of the strong over the weak.

Spencer forgets that in addition to the instinct of self-preservation man is also guided by certain laws corresponding to his
rational nature. Although the instinct impelling man to struggle
for existence is strong, nevertheless, it has certain limitations
which regulate commerce, property, and domestic relations. If
the law of the survival of the fittest finds a constant and practical
application in the animal kingdom, this may hold for the brute,
but certainly not for the rational creature. Spencer includes all
beings, man not excepted, under the general law of struggle for
existence, but he fails to prove that man is a mere evolution of
the brute. Man as a rational being cannot be subject to the
common laws of the brute.

g) Refutation of Individualism and Liberalism

The ideas of liberalism embodied in the aforesaid theories
spread and showed their evil influence in various domains of
human life. According to this doctrine the state should confine
itself to the task of protecting the legality of contracts and the
freedom of individuals, but beyond such police and judicial
power it should not go. The full development of liberalism has
shown itself, above all, in what may be called economic individualism and in the influence of this upon various phases of
human activity. It holds that there is no moral law higher than
man; that all laws are man made and can, therefore, be unmade
by man. The entire domain of the economic life, namely the
domain that has to do with man's relations to the goods of this

---

[2] Herbert Spencer, *Social Statics* (New York: D. Appleton and Co., 1903),
p. 127.
[3] *Ibid.*, p. 131.

earth, is considered free from any higher moral law. This is the notorious separation of economics from ethics and from the natural law.

Most certainly the State has a duty to protect the life and goods of its citizens and to punish any misdeed against property or person. The very advocates of juridical protection urge severe punishment for those who are guilty of arson. Not satisfied with this, they even insist on legal prevention of whatever may cause a conflagration. But why should governmental functions be limited to this? Why should they not be extended also to those things which, although not included in juridical protection, are nevertheless of the greatest benefit for all? Is not the State bound to look after public health and to prevent, to the best of its ability, the spreading of contagious and infectious diseases? Why should the State, through fear of invading individual liberty, be deprived of the right to build hospitals, orphanages, insane asylums, etc.?

"The strongest objection against unrestricted individualism is that it leads to the opposite extreme, state absolutism. . . . In a monarchy, the weaker and oppressed section of the people will clamor for relief, and, if conditions become intolerable, they will demand a new government to protect their interests. . . . This was substantially the condition that preceded the French Revolution. Under a democracy, injustices can be remedied in a more orderly way. . . . For in a democracy, if the wrongs of the many are ignored by the "do nothing" government, there will be a demand for legislators who will protect the interests of their constituents. These legislators will respond to the demands of the people who elected them and will pass laws, perhaps indiscriminately, to compensate for what the state had failed to do. Probably much of the new legislation will be unwise. But, whatever the character of the laws passed, whether good or bad, their number will be multiplied. Thus *laissez-faire* paves the way for excessive state action. The pendulum of rigid individualism always swings to its opposite extreme, paternalism.

"It develops into what its advocates are most horrified at —

state absolutism. . . . Under an individualistic government the liberty which is maintained is, in reality, a very specious kind of liberty. True, it is liberty, but only for some. It is not the liberty of opportunity for all, as it confers new advantages on those already strongly intrenched in power. Consequently, only a small minority in the nation enjoy absolute freedom, and the great mass of the people are subjected to rigid necessity."[4]

The State must safeguard personal liberty, protect commerce, foster industry and private ownership, but this is not all. There are many other functions from which it cannot exempt itself without failing in its duties. As a matter of fact, modern States have extended their activities to numerous problems in the economic, social, scientific, philosophic, and cultural fields. All these facts militate against the theory that regards the State as a policeman or a night watchman. On the contrary, from the very fact that civil society is a natural institution and necessary to man for the realization of his material and spiritual development, it follows that its chief function consists in integrating individual and family activities. By this it is not implied that the State should intervene in all particular cases of individual and family need when private initiative is self-sufficient. But there are certain calamities that reduce thousands of families to beggary and throw entire regions into destitution; a prompt and effective intervention by the State is here absolutely necessary. It would be idiocy to maintain that public authorities in such cases do not have a sacred and positive duty immediately to provide food and shelter for the citizens who would, otherwise, be exposed to famine, misery, and death.

But apart from exceptional cases and public calamities, a State, conscious of its civil duties, cannot permit everything in the industrial and economic fields to be left to the caprice and free play of competition. Without positive State cooperation the best initiative, either for want of power or means, would end in failure to the detriment of the common good. The State cannot

---

[4] Francis J. Haas, *Man and Society* (New York: Century Co., 1930), pp. 205, 206.

remain idle when by timely intervention it can successfully crown
so many deserving enterprises, alleviate numerous physical and
moral miseries, and thus deserve well of a grateful people. Hence
the liberalistic theory of juridical protection is illogical as well
as cruel. If man is by nature a social being, it is because through
civil society he can improve his condition and better satisfy his
needs. To maintain the contrary would be equivalent to saying
that man has a natural end to attain without having the means
for its realization.

But if such are the motives prompting men to lead a social
life, the State should endeavor to place general welfare and
happiness, in a measure at least, within the reach of all. As a
father's duties are not limited merely to domestic peace and
order, but also include the welfare of the family, so the State
cannot limit its functions to a mere guardianship of public order
and personal liberty, but must promote the general welfare in
a positive way. Otherwise, it would betray its mission and violate
its most sacred duties to the community. Hence from the fact
that man is social by nature, it follows that the State is bound
not merely to safeguard individual liberty and public order, but
also to promote the common good of all. St. Thomas wisely remarks that "law properly and principally looks to the common
good."[5]

The evil consequences of individualism in general and of
economic liberalism in particular, as experienced by us today,
are graphically summarized by Pius XI: "From this source as
from a polluted spring have come all the errors of the individualistic school of economics. This school destroying the social
and moral nature of economics either through forgetfulness or
through ignorance, held that economics should be considered
and treated as free and independent of public authority because
it had in free exchange or competition a self-directive principle
by which it would be regulated much more perfectly than by
any intervention of human intellect. Free competition, however,
though it is equitable and useful when confined within certain

---

[5] St. Thomas, *Summa Theologica*, I, c. 11, q. 90. 3.

limits, can evidently not direct economic life. This has been proved more than sufficiently by events, ever since the tenets of the depraved individualistic spirit were put into execution." And again: "Unbridled ambition for domination has succeeded the desire for gain; the whole economic life has become hard, cruel, and relentless in a ghastly measure. Furthermore, the intermingling and scandalous confusing of the duties and offices of civil authority and of economics has produced crying evils and have gone so far as to degrade the majesty of the state. The State which should be the supreme arbiter, ruling in kingly fashion far above all party contention, *intent only upon justice and the common good,* has become instead a slave, bound over to the service of human passion and greed. As regards the relations of people among themselves, a double stream has issued forth from this one fountainhead, on the one hand, economic nationalism or even economic imperialism; on the other, a no less noxious and detestable internationalism or international imperialism in financial affairs, which holds that where a man's fortune is, there is his country."[6]

2. ABSOLUTISTIC CONCEPTIONS

a) *Ancient and Modern Machiavellianism*

From individualism and liberalism we pass to a consideration of the other extreme, State absolutism. The former placed emphasis exclusively on individual rights and liberties, the latter is concerned only with social rights and prerogatives. The State here absorbs all individual and family rights; the individual has no rights, not even that of existence, except in so far as he can be utilized by the community. The State is no longer regarded as a means to an end, but becomes an end in itself.

State absolutism was advocated by practically all ancient philosophers. According to Plato the individual must be absorbed by the State, otherwise a genuine social unity could not be obtained. Everything is to be held in common. Private property

---

[6] Pius XI, *Quadragesimo Anno* (The Reconstruction of the Civil Order).

must be handed over to the State. Matrimony is abolished. The education of children belongs to the State. The State alone can determine one's vocation. The State decides the measure and extent in which everyone has to contribute to arts, science, literature. The State is everything, the source of all rights; the individual is nothing, without any rights. Aristotle also wholly subordinates the individual to the State. As a member exists for the sake of the whole body of which it is an integral part, so the citizen exists only for the sake of the community. Without violating any private right or interest, the State can freely dispose of individuals for its own interests. But, on the other hand, Aristotle clearly perceived what the general purpose of the State should be. The purpose of civil society is not merely that all should obtain the material necessities of life, but that they should also attain the higher things of life, mental and moral development, higher social intercourse, etc. It is then the duty and the right of the State to organize and regulate conditions in such a way that all men may attain the purposes of civil society. Aristotle also taught that some individual rights are inalienable despite an all-absorbing State. The phrase *some rights* serves to show that even Aristotle adhered in part to the opinions in vogue in his day as does the fact that he defends the institution of slavery.

An absolutistic view of the State is implied in the Roman motto: *Salus populi suprema lex esto* — "Let the welfare of the people (the State) be the supreme law." Throughout the ancient world the State generally occupied the place of pre-eminence, the individual remained in the background. Political ends prevailed over individual ends, the latter, if not completely absorbed, were subordinated to the first. And yet, even among the ancient Greeks and Romans the individual enjoyed a certain amount of independence or autonomy. Athenian citizens, for instance, enjoyed an extensive freedom of action recognized by all and guaranteed against any State interference. It would be an error to confuse the Greek State in general with the militaristic State of the Lacedemonians. Although among the Greeks and Romans the notion of human personality was rather vague, and the philosophers of that time entertained no clear ideas of individual rights, we would not be justified in concluding that in those days a system of private rights was nonexistent. However, the fact remains that in the Greco-Roman world and elsewhere the good of the State prevailed over that of the individual and private ends were wholly subordinated to the political purpose.

In the course of time the ancient conception was gradually supplanted and excelled by the Christian teaching, which definitely established the true end of man and the relations binding him with his Creator. Hence it became possible to conceive an exact notion of human dignity and of the various rights inherent in the human person. Christianity raised its voice before despots and tyrants and ceaselessly proclaimed the sacredness of personal rights; it defended the humble and the down-trodden classes; and it reminded the poor and the rich alike of their respective rights and duties. The providential mission of the Church produced a double salutary effect, that of bringing the people back to the path of truth and that of gradually emancipating them from the State absolutism which pervaded the entire ancient culture to the detriment of personal rights and liberty.

Under the auspices of the Renaissance the pagan concept of the State revived. Machiavelli was the chief apostle of this revival. The ideas embodied in his *Il Principe* aim at emancipating politics from every superior order. "Utility" is regarded as the supreme purpose of all State activity. Hence the motto "The end justifies the means." Everything is lawful and good provided it helps to attain a good end. Even religion deserves consideration and respect, but only in so far as it is subservient to political ends. We have already referred to Hobbes who advocated State absolutism in all its crudity. The sovereign according to him is the supreme arbiter of morality; he alone can distinguish between good and evil. Whatever he commands is good, what he forbids is evil.

b) *Pantheism and Statolatry*

More recently, Hegel conceived an absolutistic system of politics which culminates in a nauseating statolatry. Here individual right as well as human dignity is completely sacrificed to the omnipotent State. Individual wills contribute to the constitution of the State through the exercise of political duties. From the diversity of individual wills or reasons results the political unity or "general reason," which becomes the standard for all human activities. This "general reason" embodied in the State reigns supreme. In consequence, the State is conceived as the reality of the ethical idea, the reality of the *absolute will,* an end *by* and *of itself.* Therefore, if the State has an absolute right over the individual, the latter has a duty to be a member of the State in order to represent something truly objective and moral. The State is the indwelling spirit in the world, the divine will in the process of self-development in the real and organic form of the world (Pantheism). Hence the State must be worshiped as a deity. All this may seem mysterious; but for our consolation we are reminded that if it is difficult to understand nature, it is even more difficult to understand the nature of the State. The dignity of the State as that of the omnipresent deity requires that the individual should have no rights but only duties. The absolutism of Hegel is complete. It would be almost impossible for the human mind to conceive a more brutal form of absolutism than the Hegelian one which subordinates and absorbs the individual, the family, the moral and religious order, science and art into the State.

In this theory everything is subjected to the optional will of the State, namely, to the caprice and passions of the ruler. Every civil law is necessarily just because the State is the personification of absolute reason and is the ultimate source of right and justice. Freedom and human dignity will be recognized only in so far as the State pleases to grant it. Now, since no norm emanating from outside is valid, the State through "sovereign reason" becomes the absolute standard for all functions and activities. The disastrous consequences of this doctrine should be obvious to all.

From the Hegelian point of view, it is useless to investigate the purpose and functions of the State. The State will no longer be a means to an end but the end itself. Good and evil, right and wrong, virtue and vice will have no other measure than State caprice. Here we have a veritable *Deus ex machina*. This modern statolatry complicates instead of solving the problem of State functions. The Hegelian doctrine degrades and denaturalizes the State and makes of it a tyrannical entity. In sound philosophy the individual does not belong to the State, as leaves to a tree, as members to the human body, as a part to the whole. He is not created to serve the State as a slave serves his master. He has intrinsic rights which are prior to and independent of State rights. Whoever contends that since the leaves are for the tree, the members for the body, and the parts for the whole, the individual, too, is for the State, forgets that while leaves and parts have no intrinsic value save in relation to the tree or to the whole and have no personality of their own, even though they participate in the unity of the body, the individual is a personality of intrinsic worth. Christianity elevated human personality and assigned to the individual, to the family, and to the State a proper place in the natural hierarchy of things, but rationalism and positivism, reviving pagan ideas, attempts to degrade and enslave man.

Although these two currents of thought start from opposite premises — materialism from an infinite quantity of atoms forming the cosmos, pantheism from a unique all-inclusive substance, they lead eventually to the same conclusion, namely, the repudiation of the ethical and moral order. In such a situation it is useless to speak of objective justice or injustice, of duties or vices, of reward or punishment. Wherever citizens are regarded as the exclusive property of the State, individual rights become meaningless. The consequences of the absolutistic principles were glaringly exhibited in the French Revolution, which in the name of liberty and the so-called human rights plunged into every excess and disorder. Whether it be a Roman emperor who sets up his own caprice as a supreme law for all citizens; or a Protestant prince who does not tolerate in his subjects any other religion but his own (*cuius regio, eius religio*); or a legitimate monarch who identifies his own will with the State (*L' état c'est moi*); or a Robespierre who proclaims liberty to be a despotism of reason, a despotism by which an autocrat can impose his will with the guillotine; or a Casimir Perier who identifies liberty with the caprice of the majority of the Chamber; the same practical result follows: the omnipotence of the State is destructive of personal liberty and of human rights.

The individual and the family are prior to the State by nature. The latter was created not to absorb but to supplement the formers' insufficiencies. The State has the duty to supply whatever the individual and the family cannot accomplish by their own efforts. But if such is the function of the State, the latter cannot be regarded as an end but only as a means toward the specified end, which is the happiness and prosperity of the community. To deny this is to abandon the individual to State arbitrariness, to deprive him of his personal dignity and rights.

c) Socialistic Theory of the Statal End

Another erroneous theory is embodied in the famous "Communist Manifesto," of which Karl Marx is the principal author. The practical proposals of the Manifesto include the abolition of property in land and of all right of inheritance, the nationalization of banks, transportation, and means of production. By the application of these measures, class distinctions will be swept away; but in order to apply them the proletariat must wrest political power from the bourgeoisie and make of itself the ruling class. This ruling class becomes the source of all rights. The individual, the family, as well as other societies, are deprived of all rights and liberty and are subjected to this absolute State or collective whole. In this connection it will be enough to quote the words of Pius XI: "Communism strips man of liberty, robs human personality of all its dignity, and removes all moral restraints that check the eruption of blind impulses.

There is no recognition of any right of the individual in his relations to collectivity; no natural right is accorded to human personality which is a mere cog-wheel in the Communist system. . . . Communism recognizes in the collectivity the right, or rather the unlimited discretion to draft individuals for the labor of the collectivity with no regard for their personal welfare; so that even violence could be legitimately exercised to dragoon the recalcitrant against their wills."[7] An ample proof of this prophetic statement is to be found in Soviet Russia.

d) Sociological Theory

The sociological theory sacrifices the personal dignity of the human individual to the transcending majesty of society. One of its foremost proponents was Émile Durkheim. He begins by postulating that the normal typical man is primarily a sociological fact, not an individual animal. Whatever characterizes man and confers upon him a moral dignity is the result of collective life and is explained by the social structure of the group. Man is composed of two entities or circles of intrinsic life: the individual entity, definable by a morphological consideration of man's organism, which is of animal nature; and the social entity, definable by a morphological consideration of the group constituting man properly so called. In this latter capacity man receives from the collectivity the logical and moral imperatives, his religious well-being, his reason, his spiritual element, his personality, and the sacredness of human dignity. Man is truly a man only in virtue of the society in which he lives; in other words, it is society that constitutes man. Society itself is a being superior to and distinct from the individuals, and therefore has moral authority to command obedience. Hence social solidarity is also the greatest possible social good. "We postulate a society specifically distinct from individuals, else morality has no object, and duty hovers in the air with no basic support." "Morality commands us to will society." "The individual is not

---

[7] Pius XI, *Divini Redemptoris* (Atheistic Communism).

morally free or permitted to repudiate society. The latter is the supreme end of all moral activity."[8]

The theories that consider society the ultimate goal of the individual usually argue their point by stating or trying to show that the individual actually does find his greatest good in the society of his fellow men, and not apart from them or by himself. Yet it does not follow from this that the end of human conduct must be the social well-being of all, certainly not in the sense that the whole purpose of the individual is to subserve the growth and integrity of the social entity. Nor does it follow that the social entity is something over and above the individuals comprising it.

Granted that we are in a large measure debtors to society, yet whence does society draw the precious possessions which it distributes so lavishly among individuals? It is more in harmony with facts to say that society owes everything to individuals than the individuals to society. The moral ideas and the scientific truths that constitute human progress have their first source in individual consciousness and intelligence. Society may be compared to the surface soil, surrounding atmosphere, or the sum total of conditions in virtue of which an individual plant grows and flourishes; but the vital principle, the prolific germ, is in the plant itself which in the hierarchy of beings is far superior to the azoic mass. Society is not so much the end of man as it is a means to the higher development and perfection of all individuals alike. This interpretation of the relation of the individual to society is far from minimizing the importance of society for the individual. If society is necessary for the higher perfection of man, then social relations are of the highest importance for the individual. And the social effects of his conduct are of the highest consequence and influence on his moral status. The social factor is a very important element in human conduct, but the attainment of the individual's ultimate end is still more important.

---

[8] Quotations from various writings of Durkheim, as to be found in *Annales de l'institut superieur de philosophie*, III, pp. 347, 354, 369, *et passim*.

CHRISTIAN TEACHING

The principal points of this section are as follows: The end of the State is not a mere safeguard of public order, but the promotion of the common good in a positive way. The State is obliged to protect the natural and acquired rights of the citizens. The State has the duty of securing economic justice and equality. The State has no right to interfere in private and family affairs except in so far as the common good demands. Those possessed of civil authority have a moral duty to do everything possible to enable the individual citizens to attain their moral and material well-being. The State must recognize the moral and juridical order founded in the natural law.

1. PURPOSE OF THE STATE

In dealing with the true end and function of civil society, it will not be out of place to state once more that the State must guard against two dangers: first, the danger of leaving too much to private initiative; second, the danger of leaving too little. The one extreme, liberalism, would restrict the State to a mere police supervision for the enforcement of agreements made by private citizens. The other extreme, paternalism and socialism, would have the State do everything. Incidentally, there is at present a strong tendency in people's minds to expect everything from the State and to see in it a sort of substitute for Divine Providence. The true purpose of the State stands between these two extremes as between two natural poles, and it is impossible to displace the true purpose without upsetting entirely the social order. Naturally, here on earth, private well-being will never reach perfection. It can be possessed only partially; and even this partial attainment is not a constant quantity; it varies with age, sex, and the moral and physical needs of each individual. Such

needs, lying outside of State control, cannot constitute the proximate purpose of the State. Otherwise the end of the State would
consist in the sum total of private ends, and the State would
have no specific purpose of its own, because the private end of
the individual and of the family would be identified with that
of civil society.

While the State, in seeking the general welfare, must have at
heart private well-being, such is not its direct end. If the purpose
of the State were identified with the private purposes of individuals, then the State would also have the right to interfere
with the life and private affairs of its citizens, which is obviously
contrary to the most elementary principles of personal freedom.
The solution of the problem must, therefore, be sought in the
general welfare. But here a difficulty immediately presents itself.
It could be said that if the individual well-being were subordinated to the common good, the statal end would take absolute
precedence over the private end and would be superior to it.
But *subordination*, it must be remembered, is something entirely
different from *sacrifice*. In the case of *subordination* the private
good can coexist with the common good; in the case of *sacrifice*
the private good must give place to the general welfare. Hence,
whenever private welfare is antagonistic to the general welfare,
the former should be sacrificed to the latter. The State, therefore,
is merely a means for the attainment of the common good of all.
The subordination of the private to the common good is not
incompatible with human dignity; rather, in this subordination
the individual finds a rational satisfaction for his needs in harmony with the order established by nature.

For the sake of clarity it will be well to define the different
characteristics or specific notes of the common good. As already
remarked, the end of any being is derived from the nature of
that being; likewise the State. It is necessary, therefore, to outline
the various needs which prompt men to live in society. Leo XIII
supplies the argument: "Man's natural instinct moves him to
live in society, for he cannot, if dwelling apart, provide himself
with the necessary requirements of life, nor procure the means

of developing his mental and moral faculties. Hence it is divinely ordained that he should have his life — be it family, social, or civil — with his fellow men, amongst whom alone his several wants can be adequately supplied."[9] If this were not the case, the very craving for greater freedom and independence, instead of prompting man to live in society, would impel him to wage war against the State, regarding it as a dangerous and parasitic institution. But just the contrary is the case, which emphasizes the fact that man needs the State as fish need water and birds air. The manifold variety of spiritual and material needs which only the State can supply, prove it to be an institution demanded by nature. Hence the whole purpose of the State is to foster the common good, the good of all and the good of each. St. Thomas Aquinas and, in fact, the entire Christian tradition down to our own times have considered the State a basic natural society; that is, the State is demanded and justified by the natural moral law. St. Thomas appropriately says: "The end of civil society and the very reason for its existence is the common welfare of its members; that they might not only live but live contentedly."[10] "For a good life two things are essential; virtue and a sufficiency of material goods. Of these, virtue is the more important, for the happiness and welfare of man on earth consists primarily in living virtuously. Virtue implies both knowledge and moral goodness; hence, for a virtuous life mental development is necessary as well as moral development."[11] "A sufficiency of material goods is likewise required for the proper development of man, but these goods are secondary and instrumental, the means to an end, which consists in virtuous living. For the realization of these two ends it is necessary that happiness and prosperity be enjoyed, not only by the community as a whole, but also by the individual members who are parts of the whole."[12]

"Because of its ability to provide all things necessary for the temporal happiness and well-being of man, the State is desig-

---

[9] Leo XIII, *Immortale Dei* (Christian Constitution of States).
[10] St. Thomas, *In Pol.*, Lib. III, lect. 7.
[11] St. Thomas, *Summa Theologica*, I, II, q. 58, a. 3.
[12] St. Thomas, *In Pol.*, Lib. III, lect. 5.

nated as a perfect community. Among all natural societies it holds the highest rank as being the most perfect, subordinate to none other in its own sphere."[13] Hence it is the duty and the right of the State to organize and regulate conditions in such a way that all men may attain the purpose of civil society. If the established conditions are such that men with the best of will are by force of circumstances excluded from attaining the purpose of civil society, then the State most certainly has the duty and the right to interfere and to use its full power toward setting up and regulating conditions in such a way as to enable all to attain the good life.

The State, however, has no right in normal circumstances to interfere with private affairs or to intrude into the sacred family precincts. Says Leo XIII: "The contention, then, that the civil government should at its option intrude into and exercise intimate control over the family and the household, is a great and pernicious error. True, if a family finds itself in exceeding distress without any prospect of extricating itself, it is right that extreme necessity be met by public aid, since each family is part of the commonwealth. In like manner, if within the precincts of the household there occur grave disturbances of mutual rights, public authority should intervene to force each party to yield to the other its proper due; for this is not to deprive citizens of their rights, but justly and properly to safeguard and strengthen them. But the rulers of the State must not go further; there nature bids them stop."[14] This is a most important point to remember in our day of growing State intervention, of increasing bureaucracy and of totalitarianism. We shall return to it later on. In conclusion the State is neither a mere guardian of public order and individual liberty, nor a deity to be blindly obeyed by its subjects. If these facts and teachings are kept in mind, solving the problems will be easy and natural.

Since the end of civil society consists in the common good of all, the common good must be accessible to all men of good will.

---

[13] *Ibid.*, *Summa Theologica*, I, II, q. 90, a. 2.
[14] Leo XIII, *Rerum Novarum* (The Condition of the Workingman).

The State must so regulate the ordinary conditions of life that every man is really able to take the initiative and to acquire for himself the means necessary for a good life. It is not the duty of the State to provide the citizens directly with the means of temporal prosperity, but to provide the opportunities favorable to the free play of personal initiative. If the individual fails to make the proper use of these opportunities, the blame cannot be imputed to the State. The notion of the common good is very elastic; hence, it cannot be determined *a priori*. It varies greatly according to places, times, and the development of the active faculties of the people; it varies with the unfolding needs of society, with the disappearance of the old and with the rise of new needs. The principle, however, remains always the same. Accordingly, the State must never act in a partisan spirit which would endanger peace and the general welfare. It must esteem and protect public morality and good customs which play so important a part in the common welfare. Temporal well-being and morality are closely allied. Immorality leads to temporal as well as to spiritual disaster. While ancient and modern paganism regards the individual as a humble instrument in the hands of the State, sound philosophy assigns to him his proper place, maintaining that the State exists for the individual and not the individual for the State. It follows from this that the State has no end apart or distinct from the end of the individuals comprising it.

2. FUNCTION OF THE STATE

State authority must possess adequate power to fulfill its purpose in the government of political society. In other words, civil authority must exercise the following three functions: (*a*) *legislative,* namely, the power of making or enacting laws; (*b*) *judiciary,* namely, the power of applying laws to particular cases and of punishing all infractions of the laws; (*c*) *executive,* namely, the power of enforcing these laws and judgments. In the United States these three functions are entrusted to three distinct departments.

a) Legislative Function

Political authority is exercised through the medium of law, which, according to St. Thomas, is an ordinance of reason enacted for the common good and promulgated by those who govern the State. Reason, he states, is the prime principle of human conduct. It is the business of reason, so to say, to direct all things to their proper end or goal. Naturally, there is no law without the action of the will, but the will to have the force of law must be guided by reason. Law is, therefore, one of the essential elements of civil society.

All civil or positive law must be derived from the natural law. This derivation takes place in two ways: (a) by deduction: as when from the principle, "Do not to others what you do not want them do to you," we deduce the laws: "Do not steal"; "Do not defraud," etc.; (b) by specific determination or application of a principle to a particular case. A law punishing commercial fraud with imprisonment is a further determination or application to a particular case, of the principle: "All injustice deserves punishment." Thus natural reason determines the punishment due to a particular transgression, by taking into account the circumstances of time and place, customs and general interests. In making such choice or determination, positive law must, even in its concrete circumstances, have its basis in the natural law. Whenever civil law disagrees with the natural law, it is no longer a law but a corruption of law.

Being an ordinance of reason, a law has force only when it fulfills its office. Since it is made for the good of the majority, a law when it becomes injurious need not be obeyed. Although the natural law is immutable, its application to variable conditions can necessitate change in the positive law. The civil law, then, is not rigid but flexible. Men learn by experience and should, therefore, improve their laws in the light of better experience. However, the norm of such changes must always be the greater public good.

The primary function of the State is to render justice.

The latter as aiming at the general good and directing actions toward general interests is called legal justice. Legal justice is commutative or distributive. Positive law is nothing but an instrument or means of attaining legal justice. Civil law regulates relations of citizens among themselves and to the State; hence it relates only to acts of social justice. From the above considerations, it follows that the State has the right of making laws or setting norms for social justice.

Since the State has the duty of directing its members to a common end, it follows that at least those laws oblige in conscience whose violation would be positively injurious to the common good. The specific duty of the citizens is obedience to laws; this obedience is based on right reason and not on any one's mere will as such. Legislative power resides only in the public person possessing supreme jurisdiction; in others only in so far as it is communicated to them by the supreme power.

b) *Judiciary Function*

By judging here is meant defining right in a particular set of circumstances. Judiciary power is necessary for the settlement of civil disputes, and for the punishment of transgressors of the law. It is obvious that public order could not be maintained and individual rights would not be protected in the absence of judiciary power.

Penal action is a necessary complement of the judiciary function. Transgressions are punished to repair the social disorders. Punishment should be a reprimand to the guilty; but it should also procure their amendment, act as a deterrent, secure peace, and preserve justice. Punishment must also be related not only to the nature of the crime, but also to the social harm done and to the scandalous example given. All this makes it clear that the State has the right to punish crime.

c) *Executive Function*

The purpose of this function is to carry the laws into effect. A State requires for its government executive offices, an armed force, and a treasury for the remuneration of public officials. Without these executive essentials the legislative power could not attain its end. Moreover, there is need of a power to settle individual cases for which, perhaps, no special law exists. It is the special task of this function to represent civil society internally and externally. The State must not only organize internal peace and prosperity, it must also safeguard against external aggression.

Since the State, unlike the individual, has no future life, its primary end is the temporal welfare, moral and material, of all its citizens. The basic State functions are thus summed up by Leo XIII: "The first duty, therefore, of the rulers of the State should be to make sure that the laws and institutions, the general character and administration of the commonwealth shall be such as to produce of themselves public well-being and private prosperity. This is the proper office of wise statesmanship and the work of the heads of the State. Now a State chiefly prospers and flourishes by morality, well-regulated family life, by respect for religion and justice, by the moderation and equal distribution of public burdens, by the progress of the arts and of trade, by the abundant yield of the land, by everything which makes the citizens better and happier. . . . Among the interests of the public, as of private individuals, are these: that peace and good order should be maintained; that family life should be carried on in accordance with God's laws and those of nature; that Religion should be reverenced and obeyed; that a high standard of morality should prevail in public and private life; that the sanctity of justice should be respected, and that no one should injure another with impunity.

"To the State the interests of all, whether high or low, are equal. The poor are members of the national community equally with the rich; they are real component parts, living parts, which make up, through the family, the living body; and it need hardly be said that they are by far the majority. It would be irrational to neglect one portion of the citizens and to favor another; and therefore the public administration must duly and

solicitously provide for the welfare and the comfort of the working people, or else that law of justice will be violated which
ordains that each shall have his due. To cite the wise words of
St. Thomas of Aquin: 'As the part and the whole are in a certain sense identical, the part may in some sense claim what belongs to the whole.' Among the many and grave duties of rulers
who would do their best for their people, the first and the chief
is to act with strict justice — with that justice which is called in
the Schools *distributive* — toward each and every class."[15]

Thus the State has the right to supervise commerce and trade,
and to take an active hand in the regulation of economic life.
For the attainment of the purposes of the State, that is, the
promotion of a good and virtuous life among its citizens, a certain share of economic goods is not only generally necessary but
entirely indispensable. The true good of the citizens is not something that can be attained by a momentary sufficiency of the
necessaries of life, it is something more than that, and the duty
of the ruler is to provide the security essential to permit each
citizen to work out his own destiny. Moreover, since men must
provide for their temporal future, the State must see to it that
the economic institutions enable men to provide themselves
against sickness, old age, unemployment, and the like. In so doing
the State must safeguard justice and equality of rights among
citizens. "Free competition and, still more, economic domination
must be kept within just and definite limits, and must be brought
under the effective control of the public authority, in matters
appertaining to this latter's competence. The public institutions
of the nations must be such as to make the whole of human
society conform to the common good: i.e., to the standard of
social justice."[16]

Differing in natural endowments and subject to many vicissitudes of life, men must provide for the future. The institutions of economic life must, likewise, look ahead to more than
momentary relief of needs; they must be so organized as to

[15] Leo XIII, *Rerum Novarum* (The Condition of the Workingman).
[16] Pius XI, *Quadragesimo Anno* (The Reconstruction of the Social Order).

enable men to provide themselves against sickness, old age, unemployment, and the like.

Thus the common good of all is the sum total of conditions necessary for all citizens to attain freely and of their own initiative their temporal well-being. So conceived, this end characterizes and distinguishes the State from all other societies. In the State which actually fulfills its purpose of securing the temporal good, there will be found the unity and peace which constitute the true perfection of society. For real peace is nothing else than the harmony which results from the proper order in human relations.

SELECT READINGS

Cahill, E., S.J., *The Framework of a Christian State* (Dublin: Gill and Son, 1932), Chs. IX–X.

Encyclopedia of the Social Sciences, art. "Government Regulation of Business."

Haas, F. J., *Man and Society* (New York: Century Co., 1930), Ch. X.

Leo XIII, *Immortale Dei* (Christian Constitution of States); *Rerum Novarum* (The Condition of Labor).

Michel, V., O.S.B., "St. Thomas and Today," "The Nature of Capitalism" (St. Paul: Wanderer Press, 1936), pamphlets.

——— *Christian Social Reconstruction* (Milwaukee: The Bruce Publishing Co., 1937).

Pius XI, *Quadragesimo Anno* (The Reconstruction of the Social Order).

Ryan-Boland, *Catholic Principles of Politics* (New York: The Macmillan Co., 1940), Chs. VIII–XII.

CHAPTER V

THE TOTALITARIAN STATE

THE philosophies of the eighteenth century sought to free man from the tyrannical oppression of absolute monarchism. But they lost the golden mean and proclaimed man an autonomous entity, the supreme arbiter and master of private and social life. In place of monarchical despotism they substituted a democratic despotism and raised it to the level of sovereignty. The multitudes eagerly assumed and exercised this role of sovereignty. But social upheavals, wavering of governments, and a prolonged paralysis of the vital organs of society followed. Finally, in due course of time a reaction took place, a reaction which was but a spontaneous reawakening of the forces latent in the social organism, so long torn by internecine wars.

Philosophy undertook the task of formulating certain ideal principles that might protect and defend the State collectivism against the invading hordes of political atomism. With a quick gesture the new philosophy canceled all individual rights, rejected all justice of a higher order, and struck at the heart of man by denying him a true personality. Reverting to old pagan ideas, it regarded man only as an instrument of power and expansion. Above the ephemeral individuals the new philosophy placed an eternal nation, namely, a unitary organism possessing a proper personality, a life of its own governed by the vital laws of development and evolution. To complete its work it placed the State, the organizer and unifier of national society, above the nation. This is totalitarianism.

In less than a quarter of a century, the totalitarian State has changed the whole perspective of men's lives and is attempting to plunge large parts of the world into a new slavery. Obviously, this subject merits serious consideration. As it would take volumes to treat totalitarianism adequately and in detail, we will confine ourselves to a general presentation of totalitarian ideologies, showing chiefly how on two fundamental points the totalitarian conception of the State is diametrically opposed to sound Christian ideals.

PART I

EXPOSITION

1. FROM LIBERALISM TO TOTALITARIANISM

The liberalist outlook of the nineteenth century has received a rude shock by several radical departures from concepts of State that seemed to have become sacrosanct. "There is on the one hand the unavoidable necessity of governmental regulation — whether in the interests of owners, workers, or consumers — of commercial, financial, and industrial relationships; and, on the other, the evident ineptness of legislatures, as now constituted, for dealing effectively with the problems thus presented. The question appears to be whether adequate agencies for such regulation can be created while a general function of co-ordinating and supervising is left to elective legislatures, or whether a still further centralization of authority is required, involving the disappearance or drastic-curtailment of representative government as now understood. The second alternative, given effect in the fascist governments of Italy and Germany and in Communist Russia, has again thrown into strong relief the totalitarian conception of the State, the doctrine that the State is not only sovereign in a legal sense but has also the function of regulating every department of social life — education, religion and art, as well as capital and labor and the whole national economy. Both systems (Fascism and Communism) involve the abolition

of opposition parties and a substantial elimination of parliamen-
tary institutions."[1]

The most recent totalitarian ideologies have initiated and actively carry on a bitter attack against individualism and liberalism, attributing to them the social chaos into which the life of
States has gradually sunk. Unquestionably, the criticism and
scorn heaped on liberalism and individualism are fully justified
by the sad story of the recent past. The liberal system was positively and purposely agnostic. It divorced morality, natural
rights, and the State from the only foundation that could give
a secure support to individual and social life, and tried to erect
the superstructure by eliminating God, His laws, and His Church.
No wonder then that these weak constructions, resting upon
such unstable grounds, should have been shaken to their foundations and fallen into utter ruin. The totalitarian philosophy of
the State naturally spurns the doctrinal idols of liberalism, in-
sisting on a vigorous and strong State, free from the vacillations
and uncertainties of past governments. So far so good, but it
should have renounced certain idealities inherent in the liberal
system.

In spite of the bitter lessons of the past, the totalitarian philosophy retains as the outstanding achievement of modern
thought the autonomy of morality, the autonomy of natural
rights, and the autonomy of the State, practically denying or
purposely ignoring God. Thus, notwithstanding the changed
consequences, the basic principles in the old and the new systems are the same. While individualism ignored God and attempted to supplant Him by the individual will, regarding that
will as the sole and independent source of morality, of natural
rights, and of the State itself, the societal trends of today are
trying to supplant God by the State, investing that State explicitly or implicitly with the attributes of divinity.

It is well to remember that this idea of the State is peculiar to
modern times. During the Middle Ages every group had a life

---

[1] *Encyclopedia of the Social Sciences*, Vol. XIV, p. 330.

of its own, its own liberties, privileges, and immunities. Machiavelli was the first to identify the State with the prince, claiming that the ends of the ruler demand the subordination of the ends of the subjects. For the wily Florentine means are indifferent, they may be honorable or dishonorable. Religion is good in so far as it is necessary to keep people quiet; morality is useful inasmuch as it promotes the common good; but politics dominate both religion and morality. Whereas Machiavelli only subordinated the ends of religion to the ends of the State, Luther placed religion entirely under the control of princes. Luther separated morals from faith, and left both morality and religion in the hands of the State.

2. PHILOSOPHICAL SOURCES OF TOTALITARIANISM

In passing, we may advert to the fact that the philosophy of the totalitarian State is implied in the political systems of Spinoza, Bodin, Hobbes, and Rousseau. Some of the most recent totalitarian conceptions originate in the spiritualistic pantheism of Hegel; others are embodied in the dark pathways of the idealistic systems of today, which firmly adhere to the monistic pantheism of the spirit, and arrive at the same conclusions. The State is absolutely autonomous, being the supreme actualization of divinity immanent in the world. It is the supreme omnipotent will, the sole and absolute source of all rights. Before this superwill the individual is practically annihilated and divested of all rights and privileges.

Other totalitarian conceptions emanating from agnosticism conceive the State as a superindividual entity; that is, a reality superior to and distinct from other individuals, an organism governed by its own laws. In France A. Aspinas, A. Fouille, and E. Durkheim militantly advocate such a conception of the State. In Germany A. Schaeffle described minutely the various organs of social organism — the skin, the bones, the nervous system, the blood. Bluntschli succeeded even in discovering the sex — the State is male and the Church female.

In these points of view, the individual does not constitute

society, rather, he is constituted by society — by being born into the State and receiving from it all he has and possesses. Moreover, the end of his life cannot be other than that of service to the State. As an organic cell of the whole, the individual does not possess any right independently of the State, since every right is derived from the statal will wherein it finds its reason and its coactive force. There are no natural rights prior to or above the State; a right is either positive or not at all.

3. Totalitarian State Defined

Totalitarian States claim the right to regulate everything, regardless of its character or relation to man, and acknowledge no right inherent in individuals as apart from the State, no rights that are not created by the State itself for its own pleasure. The classical definition of the totalitarian State is: "Nothing outside or above the State, nothing against the State, everything within the State, everything for the State." Theoretically then, the word totalitarian applies to the deification of the State at the expense of every other conceivable social organism. The State is made an *absolute* entity in accordance with either Marxian materialism, Hegelian nationalism, or Machiavellian empiricism. "All that goes on in the life of society, all economic and cultural activity, all intellectual expression, all associational enterprise, is brought under the rule of the State; not, of course, to be undertaken or managed and directed by the State, but made subject to whatever regulation the State may choose to impose. No right exists save as grants of permission; no sanctions of freedom rooted in a natural law anterior to and beyond the reach of State authority have any recognition whatever."[2]

---

[2] Ross J. S. Hoffman, *The Will to Freedom* (London: Sheed and Ward, 1935), p. 60.

PART II

REFUTATION

We will now give a critical analysis of the basic tenets of the totalitarian State as summarized in the following propositions:

1. The State is absolutely autonomous.
2. The State is the sole fountain and source of rights.
3. The State is the only guarantor of individual and family rights.

1. THE STATE NOT ABSOLUTELY AUTONOMOUS

The first fundamental proposition of totalitarianism is the absolute autonomy of the State. It is necessary to distinguish between the relative and absolute autonomy of the State. The relative autonomy is that intrinsic and essential independence which every sovereign civil society possesses in regard to other civil societies. Since these are equal in the natural order, they can exercise their sovereign power for the general welfare independently of the individual will of each member of the social organism. It is sufficiently clear that such relative autonomy can be granted to the State. The States which form part of international society represent such a perfect moral entity, each having an end particular to itself, possessing sufficient means for attaining that end, and not being subordinate to other moral entities. Independent both as to the end and the means, such States are also independent or autonomous as to their internal social action. In an analogous manner States are distinct one from the other as the individuals, families, and entities that dwell within the State are distinct one from the other. Just as the individuals, the families, and the minor groups are autonomous and free to act within the limit of their sphere, so also are the States free and autonomous within international society. But as between individuals and families arise mutual rights and mutual duties, so also between the states arise, as a necessary result of international intercourse, certain reciprocal rights and duties, which form the complexus of international law. On the contrary, absolute autonomy, besides attributing to the State absolute independence, also divorces the State from every external bond, from every law that is outside or above it, from all external and immutable laws, and consequently from God Himself, the supreme Legislator.

Anyone that retains a just and rational concept of God will perceive the absurdity of absolute State autonomy. All created beings depend ontologically on their Author, and this dependence is essential. To say that creature is absolutely independent is a contradiction in terms. The very origin of the creature through the creative act implies an essential relation which entirely encompasses the created being and refers it to the creative act. Now God, who created man and endowed his nature with exigencies and necessities that irresistibly impel him to seek social life and to be compacted into the State, determined the existence of civil society in the same way as He determined the existence of the family. The State, therefore, being an object of the creative will of God, must, like all other contingent beings, depend ontologically on Him. When we say that the State is natural to man, that man is naturally social, we refer only to the proximate and immediate origin of society, and do not and cannot deny the first transcendent Cause.

Again, this ontological dependence implies another, the teleological. When God creates He must, as a personal Being create with an end in view. In its external operations, divine intelligence always fixes upon an end worthy of its infinite perfections and does not launch any creature into the great sea of being without assigning to it a particular scope and end. Every created being, then, must by natural exigency tend to this end either knowingly, if rational, or unknowingly, if irrational. The particular ends like the notes of an immense harmony combine into that order which makes the universe similar to God, reflecting the order and harmony existing in the divine mind.

But the State is an organism demanded by nature itself, since man cannot be born, live, nourish, cover, and defend himself, speak and love, without the concurrence of other men; man's physical, intellectual, and moral life is maintained, modified, and enriched by society. Hence, the State as a natural institution must have an end assigned to it by the will of the supreme Ruler. Moreover, this must be an eternal, absolute, and immutable end, such as is the act of the divine will, such as are the essences of things intuited by the divine intellect and actuated by the creative will.

If the State did not have a universal and stable end corresponding to its natural constitution, it would be impossible to construct either a philosophy of the State or of right and duty. A systematic study of contingent facts, of intermediary and temporal ends, and of the means employed to meet the exigencies of the historic moment does not furnish us with a true philosophy, one concerned with the investigation of universal principles and immutable laws. If the State be deprived of a stable and external end imposed upon it by the Creator, an end which determines the point of convergence of all social actions, which binds under the yoke of duty both subjects and rulers, whence shall we derive the moral obligation of working for social welfare — an obligation binding both the individuals in and the rulers of civil society? Duty is an absolute bond, a categorical imperative, compelling free agents. Now such a bond cannot originate in the State, if the latter is prescinded from the essential end imposed upon it by God of furthering the common welfare. Without an eternal law and a higher order, the most a State can do is to employ violence and external coercion. It cannot pierce the interior part of man and impose duties on free beings.

The difficulty increases when from the subjects we pass to the man or men at the summit of power. In their regard even recourse to coercion is of no value, because might is in their hands and the instruments of coercive power blindly obey their commands. Who will impose obligations upon them? Where shall we find the source of duty? Shall we have recourse to the social welfare which the State has the mission to protect and promote? But from where does this mission come? Is it from an objective order independent of the will of him who governs? In such a case does not absolute autonomy disappear? It becomes necessary, then, to relate the State to God, to His divine will, to an absolute and transcendent law by means of an immutable end imposed by God Himself on civil society. Without such a foundation every superstructure will inevitably crumble.

This end indicates the limits within which the action of the State must be contained, and determines independently of the ruler's will what is licit or illicit, just or unjust. In moral actions, the end is the beacon which enlightens and directs; it is the criterion by which we judge of the goodness or malice of such actions. It follows, therefore, that the State depends upon God not only ontologically and theoretically but also in the exercise of its power. This dependence is obviously an external limitation which proceeds from a will distinct from that of the State. Thus the State finds the field of its activity well-defined, outside of which it cannot operate without violating the laws of justice. There is, then, an order of justice above and outside the State, which is founded on the eternal law.

2. The State Not the Absolute Fountain of Right

The second proposition of totalitarianism is that the State is the absolute and exclusive source of right. Let us examine this statement in the light of natural reason and of Christian philosophy. The totalitarian theory leaves international law, regarded by all jurists as a true and peculiar right, without a logical explanation and devoid of moral obligation. It is without a logical explanation because if an order of universal and transcendent justice be excluded, we cannot assign to international law a source of origin. Maintaining that the State is the source of origin might appear true in the ambit of the internal life of nations, but this semblance of truth will disappear like fog before the wind when we consider the State in its external relations.

In such relations States appear as fully autonomous entities, endowed with a moral personality, possessors of rights; only higher exigencies can induce them to curb their national egoisms and to respect certain laws and certain universal principles of equity. But in order that such laws may be imposed on international society, they must be endowed with the characteristics of universality and necessity, and they must gravitate with their weight equally on all States. On the other hand, the laws and rights which emanate from the State are particular and contingent and cannot be raised to that universal and necessary sphere which embraces the whole international society.

International law, therefore, cannot emanate from the State; for in such a supposition international relations would remain unstable. We know from history that governments fall, that ancient constitutions decay, that the various forms of State are subject to change. But we also know that the higher exigencies and laws which form the cornerstone of international law do not change. All the various social formations, all the new governments must be governed, guided, and directed by these immutable rules.

The totalitarian theory, moreover, deprives international law of moral obligation and coactive force. If there is no order superior to the State, then there can be no order superior to the states as a group. Unless one admits the existence of a transcendent order, he must consider international law void of any binding force. Either international law obliges of itself, but this is a contradiction in terms, or it obliges because of a superior order, but this denies the basic tenet of totalitarianism, absolute autonomy.

But is an international law, possessed of moral obligation and coactive force because of a superior order, necessary in political society? States are bound to respect the rights of other states. They must abide by their contracts and treaties, and must keep their promises. Whence does this obligation proceed? Is it from the State that freely binds itself? But in this supposition the bond would lose that absoluteness which is peculiar to moral obligation. For as the State freely binds itself, it will also be able to break contracts and to reject freely any inconvenient or onerous measure. Moreover, if we exclude a sphere of higher justice, where shall we find a criterion for judging the justice or injustice of actions in the international field? Do we not, for example, speak of the unjust burdens imposed on the defeated nations by the treaties of Versailles, and of many other similar events? No answer can be given to these legitimate questions, if we do not admit the existence of universal and immutable laws emanating from a source distinct from the States.

The absurdity of the totalitarian system becomes even more apparent, when one considers the inner life of society. As we have already remarked, according to totalitarianism, single individuals become mere units in a rigid collectivity, to such an extent that individuality is lost in the collectivity and the collectivity is absorbed by the State. Here we have a very deification of the State. The State is everything; the individual nothing; the State is an omnipotent and absolute master; the individual a servant and a slave.

Such a system is repugnant juridically and in the light of personal dignity. In the order of Providence, God has ordained everything for man's welfare, to whom He has assigned an end transcending the limits of time. If there be an end to which all contingent beings must be subordinated, this cannot be other than man's ultimate end. Consequently, the individual directed to that transcendent end by a higher power, must make use of creatures as a ladder and means. In the words of Pius XI: "the State is not the end of man, but man the end of the State." And again: "Man is truly the end and the centre for which everything is ordained; it might be said that this is true even of the invisible universe, because in it the angels themselves are employed for the protection of human creatures."[3]

The State, therefore, cannot be regarded as the ultimate end assigned to man; it is rather a means to help him attain that end. "The fundamental tragedy of the totalitarian State," says

---

[3] Pius XI, *Non Abbiamo Bisogno.*

Maritain, "seems to us to consist in this, that while they require for themselves the complete devotion of the person, although they have themselves neither the understanding nor respect for the person and his interior reserves, they must fatally drift towards the myth of external grandeur and must seek a principle of human exaltation in the never completed striving towards external power and prestige. This way, necessarily lies war with the self-destruction of civilization."[4]

Christianity has given the world the basic doctrines, the assertion of the dignity and value of human personality, and the theory of natural rights. Outside of the Christian scheme there is no real security for the individual. The true freedom and dignity of man rests "on the basic fact that man as a person possesses God-given rights, which must be preserved from all attacks aimed at denying, suppressing, or disregarding them. To pay no heed to this truth is to overlook the fact that the true public good is finally determined and recognized by the nature of man with its harmonious co-ordination of personal rights and social obligations."[5]

If there are no rights outside the positive rights emanating from the statal will, the binding force of law would presuppose another which gives the State that binding right; this right in its turn would presuppose another, and thus *ad infinitum*. But this process *ad infinitum* is repugnant; we are compelled to halt and arrive at a right that does not presuppose any other law, to a right, namely, that is not a positive right.

It may be said that the State, being an absolute will or a superindividual, possesses such a right. This, however, would be either a filthy pantheism, which militates against reason, or an abstract construction, which has no correspondence in reality. Again, it may be said that such a right belongs to the State in virtue of its mission of promoting the social good. Here again we ask: Is this mission something which the State finds determined by the intrinsic constitution of its nature? In this

---

[4] Maritain, *Irish Ecclesiastical Record*, May, 1938.
[5] Pius XI, *Mit Brennender Sorge*.

case we find ourselves in the field of natural rights. Or is it a self-imposed mission? But if this be so, we cannot explain whence arises the governmental duty to work for the social welfare. Here again we are reminded of the necessity of assigning to the State a stable end that must be imposed upon it by the divine will, without which one cannot explain duty or obligation. Otherwise, duty has no logical explanation either in regard to the directive organs of the State or in regard to the individual.

Society is not a mechanical entity but a spontaneous and natural union of intelligent beings seeking mutual aid for the attainment of the high ideals of human life, and willing to co-operate in promoting the public good for motives very different from coercion. They are prompted by the noble sentiment of justice, suggested, dictated, and imposed on them by human nature itself. To explain this peaceful and prolific social union, one must admit the motive of moral obligation emanating from a higher law independent of the will of the State, from an absolute and universal order which imposes an absolute obligation and a true internal bond both on the State and on the individual.

In the absence of this higher law, nothing can be explained; not even the State, as Petrone many years ago wisely remarked, "The naturalist who conceives of right as a pure and simple product of the State, forgets that the State, divorced from the right, is no longer a State, but an amorphous multitude, and that he derives the right from the State after having by a mental anticipation derived the State from the right."[6]

3. Totalitarianism Destructive of Individual and Family Rights

The third proposition is that the State is the sole guarantee of family and individual rights. Man is a being *sui juris*, standing in his own right, endowed with rational and volitional faculties, a being destined to a supernatural end, a being capable of developing his internal and external activities. The primary scope

---

[6] Petrone, *La fase recentissima della filosofia del diritto in Germania* (Pisa, 1895), p. 138.

of social philosophy is to proclaim, defend, and safeguard the natural and acquired rights of the individual, of the family, and other minor groups within the ambit of the State.

But what guarantees do we find in the totalitarian theories of State? Most certainly not a safeguard of the natural and acquired rights which man may possess, because he cannot claim any rights over against the State. There can be no appeal to a higher and transcendent justice, since justice itself is coextensive with the all-inclusive State. Again, no limitations *ab extra* can be imposed on the social activities of the State for the simple reason that the State being supreme cannot recognize or tolerate any limitation from the outside. Some totalitarian theorists claim that the best safeguard of individual, of group or family rights, is the very nature which constitutes the real basis of the State, or the interests that the State is called upon to protect and interpret. The mission of the State, they say, is the promotion of the well-being of the nation, a well-being which cannot depend on individual whims or the ideological fanaticism of governors. Such a well-being is manifested by history and it is easily recognized not only by the cultured classes but even at times by popular intuition.

The guarantees of the individual and minor groups, according to this view, would arise from the spiritual and material incorporation of the individual into the nation of which he is a part and member. The individual is vivified by the current of life circulating within this vast organism. As the State, they say, has for its primary aim the realization of the immediate historic exigencies, and as these are easily perceived by the cultured, it logically follows that the rights of every man, family, and group will be safeguarded from all whim and oppression because of the necessary coincidence and harmony of private with national interests. The foundation of this system rests on a partial truth capable of deceiving certain minds not accustomed to severe analysis of concepts. It is based on an organic conception of the State, a true conception if restricted to the proper limits of analogy.

The ultimate end for which man is destined does not consist entirely in helping to further the common welfare. The purpose of man's existence, being eternal and absolute, transcends the limits of the temporal and the contingent. The purpose of the State, on the other hand, belongs within the ambit of time and contingency. The bond, therefore, which unites and cements man in a social body, subjecting him to the constituted authority, is not the result of a fatalistic and necessary law. Rather, it is only a moral bond, influencing man's will but not depriving him of the physical liberty with which nature endowed man.

Therefore, contrary to totalitarian teaching, the well-being of the social organism is not produced necessarily, as in a living body, by physico-organic forces but depends on the free cooperation of individual wills. Moreover, the welfare, prosperity, and security of the individual do not arise spontaneously from statal society; rather they are subordinated to the rule and dependent on the will of the ruler. Mere inclusion of the individual in the social organism, and mere citizenship in a nation or national State, do not constitute a sufficient guarantee of his freedom, nor a safeguard of his individual rights. This will become more evident from the following consideration.

Even in the bosom of society, man preserves his intelligence and free will and remains an active principle. Very often his activities will give rise to conflicts and differences of opinion between him and State authorities. In virtue of what laws can harmony be restored in such conflicts? Obviously not in virtue of a necessary physical law. Such a law when applied to the free actions of man would be an absurdity. Nor in virtue of a moral law or of a superior order, for such is denied by totalitarian theories. It follows, therefore, that the only factor capable of intervention is that of might. Then right will always be on the side of might; and the almighty State may without reference to justice or legality compel by brute force the helpless individual to bow his head, if indeed it doesn't deprive him of it. In this manner the dominion of violence will be established, the moral order will be suppressed by brute force, and the gates will be opened to tyranny and oppression. But it may be said that in a legally constituted society there is always a code of laws which serve to regulate the relation between citizen and civil authority, and to safeguard the individual from possible oppression and the whims of the rulers. However, once we accept the false principle that man receives everything from the State, personality, life, rights, and that the State cannot have any external limitation in social activities, all positive laws and regulations will become a very insignificant guarantee and in particular cases will cease to function.

The State, in fact, would be able to abrogate laws, modify regulations, create new bases of public rights while the individual would be unable to raise a single protest. And, in truth, on what ground and in what name could he protest? If every right is given him by the State, obviously the State cannot commit any injustice by withdrawing any rights provisionally accorded. An absolutely autonomous will is not bound to respect a superior order of justice; it is free to do what it wills. It can say with Juvenal, *Hoc volo, sic jubeo, stat pro ratione voluntas* — "This I wish, thus I command, be my will sufficient reason." Once social life is reduced to such a level, then rights and duties will be reduced to pure legalism, and every excess will be legalized with impunity.

a) No Distributive Justice in Totalitarianism

Moreover, a mere inclusion of the individual in the social organism, cannot safeguard a just distribution of the goods to which the individual is justly entitled according to his cooperation in the national prosperity. In the living organism this just distribution is brought about automatically on the principle that the well-being of one member redounds to the benefit of the whole body. In society free will often disturbs the right order of things and prevents the common well-being from flowing equitably unto all the single parts of the social organism. The only principle for remedying an unbalanced social situation is distributive justice, the moral law which imposes the duty of just distribution. But if this moral law be denied, then the will of the ruler or of powerful individuals will *ipso facto* become the absolute and supreme criterion of distribution. It is easy to see how in such a scheme equity and justice will become myths, and how a kingdom of preferences and of privileged classes accompanied by ostracism of other opposing social groups will be established.

The State might, of course, be idealized into a being transcending the individuals and absorbing in itself the life of all. It might be regarded as a divine something, a full expression of the becoming of the Spirit, a synthesis of the individual and social life, a source of faith, passion, and action. This, however, does not agree with reality. The State is not an abstract entity inhabiting the clouds of the ideal, but a reality made up of men who have reached the summit of power, but who have not, on that account, become more perfect, more just, or more disinterested. Like the rest of mortals, they have a nature agitated by noble as well as base passions. If from these passions we take away the restraint of a superior law, the guarantees of the people and of the individual will remain under the supreme sway of a deified human will.

Subjected to analysis the above system of guarantees may seem poetical, but it is in no way based on the reality of facts and the teaching of history. In dealing with social problems we must not be guided by enthusiasm or transported by luminous fancies. Rather, we must focus our eyes on the real factors which dominate the relations of rational creatures; we must keep our feet on solid ground.

b) God, the Cornerstone of Society

As the higher law, or the order emanating from God, is the only means capable of checking and moderating the passions of individuals, so the same is the only breastwork capable of keeping the power of the State within its proper limits and of controlling the arbitrariness of rulers. The true guarantee and safeguard of individual and family rights is the eternal order estab-

lished by God. Without this superior order there could be no
security either for the individual or for the State, because the
relations between the individual and the State, instead of resting
upon moral obligation would be based on violence. Now violence
does not engender peace but war, not harmony but disorder. It
stirs up passion, foments suspicion, jealousy, and hatred, and
gives rise to those social upheavals which not infrequently destroy thrones, kingdoms, and democracies. Apart from God there
is no peace, no order.

c) The Totalitarian State and Christianity

From these considerations of the nature of the totalitarian
State, we can indicate, by way of summary, the several aspects
which make it incompatible with Christianity. Totalitarianism
holds that the individual exists for the State; Christianity that
the State exists for the individual. Christianity holds that each
individual has certain natural rights which every government
must respect and protect. Among these rights are the right to
life, to a reasonable amount of liberty of movement, of self-
assertion, of association. Totalitarianism seeks to control the
total activity of a people — their religion and philosophy, their
social and economic life. It interferes with the freedom of religious worship, with religious education, with the family and
private enterprises. Pius XI has declared that the ideology of
Fascism "is no less in contrast with the natural rights of the
family than it is in contradiction with the supernatural rights
of the Church." The hierarchies of England, France, Belgium,
and Holland have condemned both Fascism and National Socialism (Nazism). They have made it clear that what they condemn is not dictatorship but totalitarianism. Undoubtedly the
State has a perfect right to maintain law and order, but it has
no right to dominate over religious liberty or to interfere with
parental rights, unless parents forfeit them by criminal or negli-
gent conduct. In the field of international relations, totalitarianism promotes an exaggerated nationalism which is incompatible
with the teaching and practice of Christian brotherhood. And

finally it believes in war as a normal means of promoting national welfare and aggrandizement. The immorality of all this is obvious. In the words of Pius XI, "Whoever exalts race, or the people, or the State, or a particular form of State, or the depositories of power, or any other fundamental value of the human community — however necessary and honorable be their function in worldly things — whoever raises these notions above their standard value and divinizes them to an idolatrous level, distorts and perverts an order of the world planned and created by God: he is far from the true faith in God and from the concept of life which that faith upholds."[7]

In similar vein Pius XII wrote: "Whoever considers the State to be the end toward which all is directed, to which all must bow, is of necessity an enemy and an obstacle to all true and lasting progress among the nations. That is true, whether this unlimited competence has been entrusted to the ruling power in the State by a decree of the nation or of some class within the nation, or whether that power has simply usurped the right to rule, regarding itself as the all-competent master of the situation, responsible to nobody."[8]

d) A Word of Warning

State totalitarianism or anything approaching it cannot be sufficiently condemned. If, however, one should think that dictatorships or absolute monarchies have a monopoly on totalitarianism and that democracies are so many delightful utopias, let him ponder these words of Douglas Jerrold: "If a government claims that its powers are absolute, it is making a claim contrary to Christianity, and it make not two pennyworth of difference whether that claim is put forward by a legal dictator, a rebel general, or a legally constituted democratic Government. Christians, if they are sincere, are bound to challenge the claim of any Government to interfere with the practice and teaching of religion, to secularize education or to place religious education

---

[7] Pius XI, *Quadragesimo Anno* (The Reconstruction of the Social Order).
[8] Pius XII, *Darkness Over the Earth.*

THE TOTALITARIAN STATE 135

at a disadvantage, or to lend prestige and authority to a secular and pagan morality by legalizing immorality or attacking the independence of the family institution."[9]

---

[9] Douglas Jerrold, *The Future of Freedom* (Oxford: Sheed and Ward, 1938), p. 114.

SELECT READINGS

Belloc, H., *The Crisis of Civilization* (New York: Fordham Press, 1937).

Berdyaev, N., *The Fate of Man in the Modern World* (New York: Sheed and Ward, 1935).

Dawson, Christopher, *Religion and the Modern State* (New York: Sheed and Ward, 1936).

Encyclopedia of the Social Sciences, arts. on "Fascism"; "Communism"; "State"; "Liberalism"; "Liberty"; "Absolutism"; "Dictatorship"; "Autocracy."

Gurian, W., *The Philosophy of the Totalitarian State,* in the "Proceedings of the American Catholic Philosophical Association, 1939," Vol. XV.

Kohn, H., *World Order in Historical Perspective* (Cambridge: Harvard Press, 1942).

Neumann, F. L., *Anatomy of Nazism* (New York: Oxford Press, 1942).

Pius XI, *Mit Brennender Sorge* (On the Present Position of the Catholic Church in Germany).

Pius XII, *The Christmas Eve Allocution,* 1941.

Rauschning, H., *Totalitarianism or the Revolution of Nihilism* (New York: Alliance Book Co., 1940).

CHAPTER VI

STATE AND RIGHT

IN THE past century a strong reaction set in against all the so-called rationalistic philosophies. This reaction was inaugurated in the name of positivism, the philosophy that would apply to all fields of thought and life the experimental attitude of the natural sciences. Positivism denies the value of fixed abstract principles in general, and would substitute for them the concrete data of experience. For positivism nothing exists except that capable of demonstration through the senses or that capable of scientific truth. Hence there is no personal God, no absolute standards; abstractions like truth, liberty, justice, right are mere words. Positivism turned political philosophy into an empirical science, a science strictly limited to the investigation of actual political and social occurrences, past or present. In this view political philosophy can have meaning and value only by discarding all metaphysical luggage and by confining its investigations exclusively to historical facts, in which alone the ultimate source of rights can be found. Positivism contends that juridical, politico-philosophical, and religious postulates must be established on the historical, economic, and social structure of the State. It claims that language, religion, and rights are not absolute but relative truths, and that the modern ways of thinking are essentially relativistic or historico-genetic.

The positivistic conception of life necessarily leads to a naturalistic view of the State and of right, and to a denial of all permanent values. It results in the following: (1) Rights are nothing but the outcome of human customs or of the approval of men. (2) Rights, being dependent upon human legislation, have only legal sanction. (3) The might of the State is the creator of all right. Obviously, such a view strips life of any higher meaning, and in so doing denies all natural rights. These and like statements may surprise the unsophisticated; but they logically follow from the postulates of positivism.

Necessarily so, positivism identifies right with might. The characteristic determining the value of an action is no longer its intrinsic goodness but its mere occurrence and utility. The directive standard of all human activities is egoism in individual life and Machiavellianism in public and international relations. And the so-called juridical problems discussed by diverse classes and persons are reduced to a mere question of force. As a result, the great social and political problems are left entirely either to the caprice of the strongest, or to a small group of supercapitalists, or to the majority of the "have nots." From the viewpoint of positivism, it is a waste of time and energy to inquire into the nature of right and into the ultimate sources of juridical authority.

Positivism discarded and derided the highest truths of traditional philosophy, but not with impunity. Just as excesses in the physical and physiological order are sooner or later avenged, so also are excesses in the social and political order. Positivism is now reaping a vast harvest of devastating consequences, as the present-day naturalistic culture clearly shows. It elevated brute force to a place once reserved to justice and natural right, and now the war god, militarism, scourges and bleeds the entire human race, plunging nation after nation into the maelstrom of war, hindering international progress and good will, and undermining the bonds of brotherhood that Christian civilization had established throughout the world. It is necessary, on the one hand, to expose the fallacies and aberrations of the positivistic theories, and on the other, to bring to light the forgotten teachings of Christian tradition as to the State and natural right.

PART I

ERRONEOUS DOCTRINES

This section is devoted to a general criticism of positivism in itself and in reference to the traditional teaching on the origin and objective value of the first principles of knowledge and of moral judgments. It is pointed out that the State cannot be the ultimate source of right, because the enactment of any positive law necessarily presupposes the right to command, which right cannot be justified on such positivistic grounds as custom, self-interest, or general utility. This is followed by a critical analysis of right and coercion, of coercion and commutative justice; by an examination of the origin of right according to Rousseau and Kant; and by a discussion of right and social sanction.

1. POSITIVISM

a) General Criticism

Since positivism as a philosophy of state is a reflection of its own philosophy of knowledge, we can best begin by discussing the latter and contrasting it with truth. Experience, that is, observation and classification of moral and social phenomena, is the supreme criterion of juridical realism, and a criticism of the latter is reduced to a critique of positivism or empiricism.

While experience manifests that which exists, it does not reveal whether things exist necessarily or not. Experience registers what takes place in this or that circumstance; but it can never affirm categorically what *must always be* in the past, present, or future. By experience we know that man lives in society. Past as well as present history shows that man is everywhere moved to create a family and a political organization, but experience cannot assure us that sooner or later things might not undergo a complete transformation for either better or worse. In other words, experience is acquainted only with the past or the present, with what has occurred or is occurring in this or that place, at this or that time, but not with what must be, now and always. Thus experience alone is unable to discover either the universal and necessary characteristic of right, or the necessary causal nexus of juridical phenomena, or the causal nexus of any other order of phenomena. Experience furnishes us with the coexistence and succession of phenomena; it can even give the empirical laws of phenomena, but it can never furnish us with the law of necessity. From experience we may gather repetitions of coexistences and of successions of certain events, but not the law of such repetitions. It can tell us that an event is repeated one hundred, or one thousand times, but not the why or the cause of that repetition. The last term of the progressive series of experiences tells us neither more nor less than the first. The increment of material experience is merely quantitative progress. No matter how accurate and extensive, experience alone cannot establish a general and necessary principle, nor furnish us with the true notion of right, nor explain social order.

As it was noted, positivism categorically denies the validity of general principles in the field of knowledge, and of universal and absolute norms in the domain of ethics; it contends that their value is purely subjective, differing with time and person. In this light, truth, justice, and right become a matter of individual opinion, and people rationalize that what is advantageous to them is ethically correct. But if all objective certitude is impossible, as positivists maintain, philosophical knowledge becomes nonsense, because philosophy in its true acceptation is a certain and evident knowledge of things in and through their causes. Yet, if before Kepler and Newton, solar eclipse could have been predicted with certainty (as *de facto* it was), it must have been known that this phenomenon was founded in the nature of things, and the principle that similar causes always produce similar effects could have been applied to this occurrence. But from a purely empirical viewpoint all this would have been impossible. As long as empirical data are subject to change, there is a possibility of hypothetical conjecture but not of real and certain scientific knowledge. Experience builds only for the present and in a provisional manner; philosophy and true scientific knowledge build for the future and without fear of self-contradiction.

Experience, resting solely on sensory perceptions and excluding the rational element of human knowledge, must ignore such general and directive principles as: "every effect presupposes an adequate cause"; "an effect cannot contain any perfection which does not in some way pre-exist in the cause"; "the same thing cannot both be and not be at the same time and under the same formal relations"; or "a statement cannot simultaneously be true and false." And yet the principle of causality, which is the foundation of all philosophical and strictly scientific knowledge, is used by all natural sciences. A denial of it leads to the complete bankruptcy of science itself. Again, without the principle of contradiction there can be no certainty in human knowledge, for it is the necessary presupposition of all scientific or certain knowledge.

In these principles the relation between the terms is known from a mere analysis of the two concepts expressing them, and is seen to have its basis in the intrinsic nature of the contents examined. Hence the principles are universal and necessary, valid in the realm of thought as well as in the realm of being, and metaphysically certain. Their denial means mental annihilation and the utter negation of any and all knowledge. Being self-evident, they cannot be demonstrated. They go to the foundation of knowledge, telling us what must be under all circumstances and cannot be otherwise. Their justification is found in the very analysis of themselves, or not at all.

Reflection shows that the certitude with which we assent to these truths is the greatest possible — by far surpassing the firmness with which we assert that the majority of experienced facts *had to be* as they were. The assent, however, is not a spontaneous act of the intellect in the sense of not being objectively motivated by the concepts and arising out of them; but it is due entirely to the objective nature of the relation itself; the nexus is as objective as the contents. The necessity of these principles is not a mere psychical disposition of the mind, but belongs to the conceptual contents themselves, to the matter or objects of knowledge.

Positivism denies the validity of these universal and necessary principles. But in so doing it is guilty of a contradiction, for to deny that any principle is certain is to affirm that at least one principle, that of the denial, is certain. Moreover positivism, paradoxically so, appeals to the very principles which it rejects, if doing so serves its purpose.

By his intelligence man can penetrate into the very essences and nature of things. From sensory knowledge the intellect forms abstract and general concepts. For instance, we know not only this or that tree but the nature of tree in general, namely, what is common to all trees and distinguishes them from everything else. Likewise, we form the notion of being and nonbeing, of cause and effect, of motion, of quantity, of animal, of man, of order, of right, and of social relations. These concepts are not innate but are derived from experience through the process of intellectual abstraction. By comparing these concepts, the mind deduces general and absolute principles, as for instance, "if two things agree with one and the same thing, they must agree with each other"; "the same thing cannot at the same time and from the same point of view be and not be"; "the existence of a non-necessary being demands a cause." By means of such principles embodying both experience and a rational factor, man expands his field of knowledge more and more.

By intellectual abstraction we attain not only the notions of being and nonbeing, of good and evil, but also those of justice and injustice, of order, of right, and of civil society. In order to develop and perfect ourselves, we use our faculties to investigate whatever corresponds to our rational nature. From earliest childhood we are naturally prompted by intellectual curiosity not only to form the notion of right and wrong, of justice and injustice, but also to formulate judgments that "good ought to be done and evil avoided"; "everyone ought to render to each his own"; "no one ought to harm another." The fact, for instance, that the child resents and protests against undeserved punishment evidences this. Every normal man easily acquires knowledge of his duties and rights, for instance, that he must not steal, or kill or injure anyone, that he must keep his promises, and render to everyone his due. By means of these principles, and guided by experience and education, he acquires an adequate knowledge of his moral and social duties. These basic moral principles find their reason of being proximately in the rational nature of man and ultimately in God. The moral-juridical order has, therefore, a value independent of individual caprices and other accidental features. Consequently, the principles: "you ought to render to another his own; you ought not to injure anyone; promises ought to be kept; civil authorities ought to be obeyed"; are not a product of pure experience. The *ought* is not derived from experience. These principles are absolute and immutable; they are true everywhere and always. Although what each individual must render to another will vary according to circumstances of time and place, the general principle, "you must render to another his own," remains immutable.

Science proclaims that there has been no basic change in the rational nature of man, despite the vast extrinsic changes in his conduct and conditions of life. Moral principles are grounded in human nature; and as human nature is immutable, immutable too are the laws governing it. The principles that man is a being composed of body and soul and that he is a social being by nature are unalterable. Therefore, man must behave in such a way as to enable society to subsist and to attain its proper end. To achieve this, every individual is bound to forego whatever action is detrimental to society and to do whatever is required of him to promote its welfare. Hence follows the citizen's obligation to obey civil authority, without which social order and the attainment of the common good of all is impossible. In the absence of stable and absolute principles and standards there can be no duties or rights. Absoluteness is the distinguishing characteristic of moral-juridical principles. While other rules of human conduct are limited to counsels, these principles are imperatives. To deny the absoluteness of moral principles in their general formulation is equivalent to denying the moral law altogether. Their reality and value must be recognized by all under penalty of betraying human dignity and the rational nature of man. On the other hand, if everything is relative, as positivism claims, then right, duty, and obligation will *ipso facto* lose their essential characteristics of obligatoriness, absoluteness, and universality.

In this lies the basic error of positivism. If moral principles are relative, mutable, and particular, then the State has no right to command and the citizen no duty to obey, or, equally true, the State has the right to be tyrannical and absolute and the citizen the duty to submit. Positivism would seek the source of right and duty in coercion, self-interest, public custom and utility, and in the State. But reason and fact prove the inability to do so.

Coercion can compel one to perform or to omit an action, but it cannot engender right, duty, or obligation. Self-interest might prompt a man to respect the law, but it will not oblige him to do so. Moreover self-interest might be, and often is, quite at odds with public welfare. Then how can one speak of the obligation to further the common welfare? A country often asks of its citizens sacrifices which it cannot adequately compensate. Thus, it cannot adequately compensate the soldier who died in its defense. Yet that soldier has the sacred duty to defend his country with his life if need be. In this and like cases positivism cannot advance a valid reason why the individual should subordinate his own well-being to the social well-being. The majority may by superior strength compel the individual to obey; but it cannot bind him to sacrifice himself for the community. If right is but a result of force; if everything is only relative in social relations, the ethico-juridical laws will be but a wild fancy; they will have no value because they are devoid of a moral basis.

The consequences of the positivistic conception of right cannot be evaded by a recourse to the legality of laws. Rights, according to positivism, are made and unmade by the will or decrees of the State; and men have as many and such rights as the State has granted them, no more and no less. Every law, on the mere condition of being vested with legality, would constitute a true right. The ill-omened laws of the Revolution, the cruel and bloody laws of tyrants would thus assume the sacred name of right. Hence positivism in speaking of just and unjust laws, of individual and family rights, contradicts the basic postulates of its own system. Whoever denies any moral principle above and beyond the will of the State, ought not to speak or complain of unjust laws. Every positive law, in this theory, represents a right and as such it must be respected. The only, and the absolute master is the State; before it as before a supreme deity citizens must bow and obey. The State is omnipotent and an end in itself; the individual is merely a means to an end or even less, having only one right — the right to obey and to sacrifice everything for the State or for the whims of the majority. Hence such a system, under the mantle of legality, can justify the cruelest crimes and injustices. It is an illusion to seek in the State the ultimate source of all rights and duties. Moreover, if the State were really the supreme source of right, it would cease to be a juridical concern and become a coercive affair based on force and violence. Hence the dilemma: either there are rights prior to the State, and then the State is not the sole source of the juridical order; or there are no rights other than State rights, and then every right has its justification in the State. "The positivist" remarks Petrone "who conceives right as a mere, simple product of the will of the State, forgets that the State, abstracted from right is no longer a State but an amorphous multitude, and that it (the State) derives the right from the State, after having by a mental anticipation derived the State from the right."[1] Or as M. Cronin puts it: "The State cannot be the source of all rights, for it cannot be the source of its own right to existence."[2] Hence, the State divested of its ethical basis will no longer be a juridical but merely a mechanical or coercive institution.

---

[1] Petrone, *La fase recentissima della filosofia del diritto in Germania* (Pisa, 1895), p. 138.
[2] Cronin, *The Science of Ethics* (New York: Benziger, 1922), Vol. II, p. 676.

The specific characteristic of every right consists in engendering a moral obligation, since right cannot be thought of without its correlative, duty. Our rights would have no meaning as moral claims unless there is in others a corresponding moral obligation to respect them. A juridical norm could not be considered valid, unless from the very beginning it did engender a moral obligation on the part of the subjects. Now, this moral obligation pre-supposes that political power has from the first instant the right to command, that is, to impose obedience on the subjects. In order to enact a valid and legitimate law, civil power must have the right to command. If this right should not precede but follow the enactment of the law, the latter would be destitute of all obligatory force. It would be a coercive precept sanctioned by physical force, but not a rule imposing a moral obligation. If the function of all law is to engender certain obligations, then civil power implies a right to command and the subjects have a moral obligation to obey. Such rights and duties cannot originate in tradition or custom, since their existence must precede the enactment of the law. The first civil law already presupposes a first right and a first duty, on the part of civil authority the right to command, on the part of the subjects the duty of obedience. In any other hypothesis the categories of right and duty remain a riddle.

Neither can social utility be regarded as an ultimate source of right. "It is clear," writes A. Rosmini, "that if we repudiate the true source of justice and of rights emanating from it, a source recognized by all ages and by all nations down to our own day, and if we admit no other source of what is right and just than public utility, we thereby place in the hands of the government a limitless authority; we destroy the Magna Charta of human rights, and completely subordinate the individual to the arbitrariness of public authority. Social utility is by itself a vague idea and altogether incapable of establishing the principle of governmental authority and of what is just."[3]

Even granting that public utility were the motivating factor

---

[3] A. Rosmini, *Filosofia del Diritto* (Milano, 1841), p. 194.

of obedience, the utilitarian norm would be relative, namely, left to the arbitrariness and caprice of everyone. Obedience in this hypothesis ceases to be a natural consequence of a right inherent in authority; it becomes a purely optional affair, subject to endless change according to personal interests, profits, and advantages. Moreover, even the advantages resulting from obedience to authority and from respect for social order could not engender moral obligation, which is the basic character of positive law. Therefore, realizing the shortcomings of the utilitarian theory, some positivists have recourse to custom.

But custom cannot explain the ultimate basis of right and duty nor offer a sufficient basis for obligation. True, custom may at times engender a sense of obligation to the accustomed action. If the obligation of obedience were but a result of custom, it would not be a serious matter for one to trample underfoot the most sacred duties, especially when their observance was onerous or required the sacrifice of one's life. Even a cursory study of history reveals that innumerable old and well-established customs have been abolished without serious difficulty. Again, nothing could prevent citizens from rebelling against civil authority, if the latter were but a result of custom. On the contrary, certain actions, as the worship of the deity, filial love, justice, temperance, fortitude, etc., have been held to be laudable in themselves by all men and at all times and in all places; whereas blasphemy, impurity, injustice, adultery, etc., have been regarded as vicious always and everywhere. Why? Because of the profound conviction that such good and bad actions are essentially good or essentially bad, and consequently either conducive to or destructive of social welfare. This essential distinction and not custom makes morals to be morals and rights to be rights. If morals and rights were a result of custom, then what is essentially good today might be evil tomorrow; justice in one might be injustice in another; adultery today a vice might later become a virtue. This would obviously undermine the moral and social order; and moral skepticism would reign supreme.

From the dawn of reason everyone realizes that man is social

by nature; that he must order his life in such a way as to enable
society to exist and prosper; that everyone must keep his
promises, obey legitimate authority, and render to each one his
due. Everyone knows that whatever is detrimental to social life
and order must be avoided; that theft, murder, and perjury are
intrinsically bad. These self-evident principles, absolute and universal, constitute the ultimate standard for the proper ordering
of society. Hence they cannot be the result of either custom, or
utility, or the legislative will of the State; they are a necessary
presupposition for all moral and social life. Jellineck errs in
maintaining that obedience to civil and religious authorities was
at first rendered through fear or some other personal motive,
becoming only gradually an absolute moral norm. All the attempts made by the positivists to explain the ultimate source of
right and moral obligation are obviously unsatisfactory; right
and moral obligation cannot be explained in terms of force,
utility, or custom; they cannot be the product of merely accidental circumstances or conditions of life.

b) *Additional Criticism*

Because of its prominence both in theory and practice, the
positivistic teaching on right and coercion requires further and
more detailed study. Some positivists contend that the State must
be the ultimate source of right, because it alone possesses the
efficacious means for the enforcement of laws. Accordingly, coercive power would constitute the essential element of right. Rights
then exist only in so far as the power to enforce them exists;
where there is no coercive power, there are no rights. But on the
contrary, rights do not lose their obligatoriness, when civil authority lacks the means necessary for their enforcement as happens in times of rebellion or revolution. Right, it must be remembered, has an intrinsic value and persists notwithstanding
the fact that someone may violate it with impunity. Both in the
national and international domain there are certain rights which,
though lacking in proper sanctions, still retain their character
of obligation.

Again, according to the positivists, an evil or a violent act by the very fact that it can be enforced acquires the value of a juridical and obligatory law. But the enforcement or coercive measures used to secure the observance of the law cannot affect either the validity of the right or its nature. The mere enforcement of certain evil and immoral laws does not and cannot change their intrinsic malice. Needless to say, this position is virtually a nullification of all true moral right and of all morality. No wonder that the principle "might makes right" has always meant the subversion of personal moral ideals and values.

To confound right with enforceability would imply that civil power has the right to impose a moral obligation on its subjects only by inflicting punishment on the transgressors of civil laws. However, punishment is not an essential element of right but a remedial and penal measure to secure respect for law, in view of human weakness, malice, and selfishness. Evidently coercion, far from being an essential element, necessarily presupposes right and has a subsidiary role. Coercion has no other purpose than to secure the observance of the law and comes into play only after the law has been violated. The observance of the law does not depend so much on coercive force as on the simple duty binding the citizens to observe it. Subjects should respect the laws and obey legitimate authorities in virtue of moral obligation and not because of coercion.

An analysis of the notions of right and coercion as related to each other shows that coercion, though a derivative character of right, is not its essential basis or nature. Legitimate coercion comes into play only after the violation of rights or when the act of violation is in progress or is immediately imminent. Therefore, coercion presupposes the existence or rights, or else coercion of any kind would *ipso facto* be morally legitimate, and universal moral values would cease to exist. Rights have a value and a meaning in life that lies much deeper than, and is not exhausted by, the ability to exercise physical force. "He who possesses a right has also by law a moral power to uphold that right with all his internal and external force against every ob-

stacle. Hence the inviolability (of rights) and the moral possibil·
ity of employing all human forces against whatever and whoever
opposes them. But it must be noted that coercion comes as an
effect, not as a cause of right. The former causes the latter to
prevail, but does not give existence to it. Hence every right im·
plies the idea of coercion potentially, not actually. . . . In judg·
ing about right, one must look not to physical might but to the
moral order. A right exists even if he who possesses it lacks the
physical force necessary to exercise or uphold it."[4]

Coercive power aims primarily at the preservation of social
order required by the common welfare. While the majority of
subjects will obey the law because urged by a sense of duty,
others will not unless compelled by coercive power. Coercion is
a logical and necessary consequence of the purpose intended by
law. Laws must be observed not only by the majority, but by
all; otherwise social order and welfare would be seriously im·
paired. Coercion cannot be dispensed with; it is necessary for
punishing evildoers, for stimulating the weak, and for instilling
a salutary fear into those who might be tempted to disturb the
social order and the peace of the community.

Undoubtedly civil law cannot do without police, judges, and
tribunals, yet it is not a mere coercive power. Moral persuasion
and duty contribute more to respect for law than coercion or
fear. Force may constrain but it does not impose a moral obliga·
tion. Coercion is something external and of a material nature,
whereas the sense of duty penetrates the human conscience and
is by its very nature spiritual. With physical force it is possible
to overpower and even "liquidate" a man, but never to oblige
him in conscience to perform or to omit a human act. The
robber with a gun can compel a person to hand over his money,
but he will not create a moral obligation in the conscience of
his victim.

Finally, coercion intended to secure respect for law cannot
be left to its own caprice; it must be applied in a moderate and
orderly manner. Otherwise social order would be constantly

---

[4] Tolomei, "Diritto Naturale," quoted in Volpi, *Philosophia Moralis*, p. 180.

exposed to serious dangers because the magistrates charged with the enforcement of the law would be guided not by justice but rather by partisan spirit and passion. Hence to eliminate abuses, civil power sets up certain laws regulating the exercise of coercion. These regulative norms are common to all States. Unless one prefers an infinite regress, such norms cannot presuppose force as an essential and constitutive element. We are compelled to recognize a juridical norm which regulates the use of force without itself including coercion as an essential element. Otherwise civil power would be an instrument of brutal despotism whereby the State would enslave all the members.

Moreover the element of coercion is not essential to subjective right. The term subjective right denotes a faculty or moral power to possess and to claim the use of a thing as one's own to the exclusion of all others. The precept to give each one his due presupposes in each individual a right or moral power to demand that others respect whatever belongs to him. To legal, commutative, and distributive justice corresponds a subjective right or juridical power. To legal justice corresponds the right or power of the State to demand from its members what is necessary for the general good. To commutative justice corresponds the right and power in the individual citizen to demand that each member renders to his fellow members what is equitably theirs. To distributive justice corresponds the right and the power of the subjects to exact that the State distribute public burdens, such as taxation and military service, according to the powers and capabilities of the members; and that it distribute public goods, such as offices and honors, according to the worthiness and service of the citizens. This explanation of subjective right will enable us to see that coercion is not an essential element of right. That to the right corresponding to legal justice belongs the use, as needs require, of coercive power there can be no doubt, since the task of legal justice is to secure respect for law. If civil authority were deprived of this right, nature would have prescribed an end without supplying the means necessary for its attainment. This cannot be. It is not sufficient for civil society to be a necessary exigency of social order, or to have the right to command, it must also have the right to enforce its laws.

Coercion in so far as it applies to right is a moral, not a physical power. It does not denote the right of the stronger, or that might makes right. The highwayman may kill a traveler and rob him of his belongings, but in so doing he obviously does not exercise a moral power. All agree that such an action is morally bad, repugnant to nature, and deserving of severe punishment. Where do the materialists, positivists, relativists, etc., find the ultimate morality or immorality of the said act? By way of contrast the victim's right to life, to personal integrity, and to a peaceful possession of his goods becomes more evident than ever. The right of coercion is a moral power flowing from a divine or human law. Public authority commands in virtue of a moral power which must be carefully distinguished from that exercised by a master over his slave, which though sanctioned by human law at times, never had the sanction of the natural or divine law. Social order being a need of human nature cannot exist without a directive principle or civil authority which, abstracted from the concept of coercion or physical force, has the right to demand from its members whatever is necessary for the attainment of the common good, and consequently the right to compel the recalcitrant to respect the law. But this power of compulsion or coercion must be regarded as an effect or consequence of law and not as an intrinsic element of the same. Granting that law is an obligatory norm for social welfare, it will be readily appreciated why the vast majority are spontaneously, as it were, inclined to observe it, and why public authority has the right to use coercion for its enforcement. On the other hand, private individuals cannot lay claim to this right with regard to distributive justice. The State, as we have seen, has the right and duty of distributing public burdens and public honors according to capabilities and degree of worthiness and service. The private individual, however, cannot employ coercion against public authorities for the enforcement of his violated rights. For if each individual could lawfully take a stand against public authority whenever the rights of distributive justice were violated, we would soon have disorder, anarchy, and chaos. In view of the public welfare it is expedient that coercive power, when there is question of distributive justice, should belong only to the State. Juridical or legal right is coercive only in the measure required by the common good. But the common good does not demand that to distributive justice should correspond a coercive right, rather it condemns every violent act employed in the enforcement of such rights.

All this, however, does not mean that public authority may distribute public goods and burdens arbitrarily. Rulers have sacred duties toward their subjects. To the duties of the rulers corresponds a right of the members. This rule is so clear and evident that even many empiricists have accepted it as an established fact. In the distribution of public goods and burdens the State must make a distinction between persons. Human society is made up of many different members and supported and sustained only by the variant services contributed by the members. There is no absolute equality of men in this regard, since actually there are differences in both abilities and importance of functions and contributions. Here true justice and equality can only be observed, if the proportionate relation of all contributions to the whole social undertaking is kept in mind. True distributive justice must rest upon a proper distinction of persons.

While the individual has no right to coercion with regard to distributive justice, he has that right with regard to commutative justice.

The social order by its very nature aims at safeguarding the liberty and independence of every citizen. Now in order that he might defend his rights efficaciously as for example the right to life and to personal integrity, it is necessary that each one, in the case of an unjust aggression should have the right to employ coercive power. Obviously, if everyone has a right or moral power to the possession and exclusive use of what is his own, he must also have a right to repel force by force in case of an unjust attack upon that right. If Peter owes Paul one hundred dollars, the latter has a right to exact that sum, and the former the obligation to pay it. Therefore Paul, if Peter refuses to pay, may compel him to do so. However, this moral power or right that one has to coerce another, is not an essential attribute of right, but rather an indispensable condition for the enforcement of that right.

As to a legitimate exercise of coercive power, we distinguish between cases of urgent necessity and cases of disputed rights. In the first instance, an individual may directly use force in self-defense by repelling an unjust aggressor; in the second, he must have recourse to legitimate authority. The justification for such a procedure consists in the fact that in the first circumstance the individual has neither the time nor the means for an appeal to public authority; but in the second he has. If everyone could legitimately and directly, irrespective of the circumstances, defend his violated rights by coercive methods, the result would be anarchy. Instead of promoting individual and social well-being and tranquillity, such use of coercive power would open the door to countless abuses. Public order and security demand that whenever possible disputed rights should be settled not by private whim and caprice but by public authority.

2. THEORIES OF ROUSSEAU AND KANT

Rousseau's contention that rights are an expression of the "general will" is equally as fallacious as positivism. Since we have already shown the untenability of Rousseau's statal doctrines, a few general remarks will suffice. Society is not, as Rousseau maintains, the ultimate source of duties and rights for the family and the individual. The State is the protector and helper of families and individuals in the fulfillment of their duties and obligations; its existence is commanded and its authority is limited by this very end.

Kant attempted to solve the problem by regarding right as an aggregate of conditions according to which the freedom of one can coexist with the freedom of other persons whose one perfection is their liberty. The following imperative judgment, according to Kant, summarizes all our juridical obligations: "Act externally in such a manner that the free exercise of thy will may be able to coexist with the freedom of all others, according to a universal law." This conception leads to a most crass type of individualism. Kant separated right and duty from all concrete relation to life. Thus he succeeded in suspending his theory of right in the air without contact with the conditions of life, and at the same time destroying all confidence in reason as applied to life. To assure liberty for all which alone would constitute the purpose of life was his only aim. Being deeply religious Kant could not imagine any human being willing to put forth as a universal law what would contradict the best natural aspirations of mankind and what would be destructive to the nobility of human nature. He was not acquainted with the supermen of today who are willing to do and to allow almost anything. Only in subsequent decades do we meet with the glorification in ethics of the evolutionary principle of struggle for existence and survival of the fittest, or the struggle of all with all, with no holds barred and where the top dog is the kingpin of all the wreckage he can survey. To the person who says: "My categorical imperative commands me to act thus, and so regardless of how this action will affect others or even myself, I will let my action be a universal law for all, and I am perfectly willing to let others do the same," Kant has no answer, and can have none. His principle provides moral justification for every type of agitator, revolutionary or criminal.

Inconsistently with the above principle of universal liberty, Kant elsewhere teaches that all rights originate with the State and are dependent on the will of the ruler. This view has already been examined. Furthermore, Kant maintains that rights have not only a different object but also a different origin than morality. Rights, according to him, originate in the law of the State, and morality originates in the moral law. Such an absolute line of separation between right and morality, as we shall see, is impossible, because rights apart from morality have no meaning.

It will be shown in the sequel that rights originate in the natural moral law, which "regarded as a rule of human action . . . is the moral law."[5] Therefore right must depend on the moral law. If man has a right to life, then other men have a duty to respect that right. Since duty also depends on the moral law, right could have no meaning apart from it.

Many advocates of the historic school have tried to reduce right to social approval or sanction. Rights as ordinarily conceived are by their very nature social if they exist at all. The majority of human acts, in the very nature of things, affect the well-being of others favorably or unfavorably. "All men are constantly affected by the acts of their fellow men. Now, if men possess any right to their well-being, they must have the right to defend themselves against the unfavorable influence of the actions of their neighbors. The most harmonious relation would possibly be attained when all men would perform only such actions as have received the previous approval of their neighbors or are sure to meet with their approval. But this is still far from saying that men have a right to do only what is socially approved, and still further from the view that social approval is the only constitutive factor of human rights. Yet even the latter claim is heard not infrequently in our day."[6] We are told that rights are mere conventions and that if we cooperate in doing the wrong thing, the wrong thing becomes right by natural agreement. Companionate marriage should be legalized because it is being done. So then, should murder, robbery.

Social approval may be a partial index to go by in the determination of human rights; but even as such it need not necessarily be of further use than just an index, since the fickleness of social approval or condemnation is proverbial.

[5] M. Cronin, *op. cit.*, Vol. II, p. 674.

[6] V. Michel, O.S.B., *Philosophy of Human Conduct* (Minneapolis: Burgess Publishing Co., 1936), p. 105.

PART II

THE CHRISTIAN PHILOSOPHY OF RIGHT

According to Christian teaching, right must be grounded in the natural moral law and ultimately in God. Without the reality of natural right, true human authority would be impossible, as there would be no rights in heaven or on earth. The traditional concept of natural right is contrasted here with pseudo-concepts of that right. This is followed by the Christian solution of the problem, and by a discussion of the relation of natural to positive right, showing that the former exists independently of human will and that it is the source of all positive right. The last two sections deal with the relation of right to morality and with the limitation of obedience in regard to unjust and immoral laws.

1. THE ULTIMATE BASIS OF RIGHT

A true explanation of right and moral obligation can be found only in the theistic conception of the universe. This view categorically affirms the existence of a God possessed with intelligence and free will, that is, of an infinite spirit in the state of personality. The traditional proofs for God's existence, in spite of constant attacks, have never been refuted. Moreover, it is a commonplace fact that objections against theism rest almost invariably on a misunderstanding and misrepresentation of the Christian doctrine. Having discarded the true God, the modern man has constructed a god after his own image and likeness. This denial of a personal God is the cause of the chief difficulties in modern ethics and political philosophy.

It will not be out of place to note that without the idea of a personal God, the world would be an incomprehensible enigma. Order cannot be thought of without an intelligent Governor, just as a series of secondary causes cannot be thought of without an uncreated first cause. The law of consistency compels the rational mind to admit that every effect presupposes the existence of an adequate cause; that an effect cannot be superior to its cause. These principles are objective and universally valid. Therefore the application of these principles cannot be arbitrarily ignored or rejected when there is question of God's existence. It is false then to assert, as positivism does, that our concept of God transcends the sphere of human knowability.

Everywhere in the universe, of which man is part and parcel, there is order. We are able to express this order in terms of laws of action, whose general validity can be doubted only by the confirmed skeptic. Since there is order in the universe, man ought to reflect in himself that order and harmony. Just as cosmic laws govern all things according to their nature, so the natural moral order should govern and direct human actions to their proper end. Here we must distinguish between the physical and natural moral laws. The former apply exclusively to the properties of matter; they are indicative of what takes place necessarily and uniformly. Moral laws, on the other hand, apply only to men as intelligent and free agents; they are imperative and indicative of what should or ought to take place.

By moral law is meant a body of moral principles, which reason itself discovers and which are binding on all men. In other words, this law is a participation in the eternal law mirrored in created intellects. It is ultimately a part of the general law of the universe, of all creation, of the law of God as expressed in the nature of things. St. Thomas explains this point as follows: "Since all things subject to divine providence are ruled and measured by the eternal law, it is evident that all things partake somewhat of the eternal law, in so far as they, being imprinted with the eternal law, derive therefrom their respective inclinations to their proper acts and ends. Now among all others, the rational creature is subject to divine providence . . . therefore it shares in the Eternal Reason, whereby it has a natural inclination to its proper act and end. This participation of the eternal law in the rational creature is called the natural law."[7] The following quotation from an eminent modern jurist also shows the value and importance universally attached to the natural law. "There are the eternal, immutable laws of good and evil, to which the Creator Himself in all His dispensations, conforms; and which He has enabled human nature to discover, so far as they are necessary for the conduct of human actions."[8]

By right is meant the privilege of being unhindered in whatever conduct conforms to the moral law. If there is to be any ethical significance to rights at all, their basis must be sought in the moral law. Unless there were a moral law, anybody could do as he pleased and could trespass on the rights of others without being guilty of evil. If human rights are not supported by the moral law, then it is not morally wrong for one to kill his neighbor. The only question for him would be: Am I strong enough to do it, or cunning enough to get away with it? Rights must have their basis in the very nature of the moral law itself, hence they follow as a necessary corollary from the latter. Moral right is based as intimately in human nature as the moral law itself. Like morality in general, rights are rooted in the free rational nature of man and attach immediately to human personality. They are based in the ultimate obligation resting on all men to strive toward their natural end. Therefore, an affirmation of natural rights implies the existence of morality; just as a denial of a natural basis of human rights always implies a denial of morality in general. Human rights stand or fall with the moral law.

Since the moral law obliges all men to strive for moral perfection, then it also obliges them to use the necessary means for attaining that end. Moreover, all men are by nature united through the bond of mutual rights and duties relative to societal life. This engenders in each individual an obligation to contribute to the social welfare on which all depend for the attain-

---

[7] St. Thomas, *Summa Theologica*, I, 2, q. 91, a. 2.
[8] Blackstone, *Commentaries on the Laws of England* (London: J. B. Lippincott, 1897), *Introd.*, Sec. 2, No. 40.

ment of their natural end; only thus can all individuals receive the co-operation to which they have a right and in turn
properly exercise their duty of such co-operation.

The moral good consists essentially in the conformity of an
action with human nature, considered both in itself and in its
relations with other men. In other words, a thing is morally
good if it agrees with the true end of man; morally bad if it
does not. There is an objective distinction between moral good
and moral evil. Whether we like it or not, morality is what it is.
It does not depend upon the caprice of man, and not even God
Himself can change it. Whether we wish it or not, a good deed
must draw us toward our ultimate end, and a bad deed must
separate us from it. Moral law commands doing good and avoiding evil. Under penalty of intellectual suicide man is bound to
recognize this law as rational and in conformity with human
nature. It is on the natural moral law, itself grounded on God,
that Christian tradition bases all true human rights. This law
is binding on all men, both as individuals and as members of
society.

In the light of these principles we can explain man's duties
toward God, toward himself, and toward his fellow men. In
theism moral law and right possess a meaning and an intrinsic
value. No other system of thought offers a moral ideal more in
conformity with human nature. This system rests on a complete
analysis of human nature. The real trouble with practically all
the modern systems of ethics in general, and of political ethics
in particular, is their failure to furnish a complete analysis of
human nature. Their point of view is too narrow, since they
consider only one aspect of man's nature, as for instance mere
reason, or will, or feelings. "Emphasizing the claims of the feelings, utilitarians neglect those of reason. They fail to see the
intrinsic value of actions, and look only at the value of their
results. Kant, on the contrary, considers only reason and will,
and has no regard whatever for the result of actions. Our view
recognizes the claims of both. It is more complete, and more in
accordance with human nature as a whole. It alone accounts

for the distinction between that which is obligatory and that which is good without being imposed, because certain things are strictly required by human nature, while others are in accord-ance with it but not necessary. Right and wrong are known by comparing actions with the exigencies of man's rational nature. This is the true norm or standard according to which morality of actions should be judged."[9]

It is also absurd to regard man as a result of blind evolution. It is revolting to think that man, whose mind spans the past, present, and future, and whose soul craves for complete happi-ness and immortality, should, like any brute animal, be con-demned to a short and unhappy life ending only in death and annihilation. All this is clearly repugnant to the noblest aspira-tions of the human heart, to the dignity and pre-eminence of man over other creatures. True philosophy convinces us that man's highest goal consists in the development of his abilities and in the realization of his moral ideals; that he is captain of his own soul; that upon the proper use of his freedom depends his ultimate happiness.

In the sphere of private, individual conduct, that is, apart from social relations, man is responsible only to God and his conscience. The latter is but the natural law applied to each and every individual in every specific case. This sphere does not come within the scope of civil authority. But when there is ques-tion of social duties and obligations the situation is entirely different. It is natural for man to live in society with his fellow men, otherwise he could not fully develop his abilities, personal-ity, or happiness. In society, therefore, everyone is bound to re-spect another's rights, for a violation of these rights would ob-viously be destructive of the social order. Now since God willed the existence of civil society, He must also will the means neces-sary for its maintenance and for the attainment of its ends. Civil society has the right to make laws, to punish violators, and to bring the recalcitrant back to the observance of his social obliga-

---

[9] C. A. Dubray, *Introductory Philosophy* (New York: Longmans Green, 1928), p. 354.

tions. The members have a duty corresponding to this right.
Each citizen is obliged to live in peace with his fellow men, to
respect their rights, to cooperate for the realization of social
good which otherwise could not be procured. This implies a
reciprocal limitation of freedom. There is, then, an obligation
incumbent on every individual to contribute in a positive way
to the general welfare, as there is also a corresponding right of
demanding such cooperation from others.

All men are not only entitled to the means necessary for the
fulfillment of the moral law, but also to any further development
of which they are capable and which is not destructive of the
fundamental rights of others. Unlike the Kantian teaching,
Christian philosophy wisely restricts individual freedom in such
a way as not to hinder others in the exercise of their rights. The
very existence of the social order demands the omission of whatever conflicts with another's rights, and the execution of whatever is necessary for the preservation of that order. Right, then,
is a directive norm of individual freedom within the orbit demanded by the general good. It is not concerned with internal
motives but only with external actions or their omission; it is
not concerned with private individual life, but only with social
conduct.

Christian tradition has always upheld the existence of natural
rights founded upon the basic requirements of human nature
itself. These rights are rooted in the natural law, which itself is
grounded in the innermost nature of man or of society, independent of convention, legislation, or other institutional devices. Natural rights are always clearly distinguished from positive rights and from social sanctions. They are the cornerstone
of all positive right, and the source of the latter's obligatory
character. But the so-called philosophers, who set the stage for
the French Revolution, substituted positive for natural right.
To accomplish this they subjected both civil institutions and
positive right to a general revision. The directive principles of
the new juridical code were called *the state of nature, social
contract, the inalienable sovereignty of the people,* etc. These

theorists used all the brilliance of their wit, satire, and irony in overthrowing the natural law, the very cornerstone of all culture and progress. In their pride and arrogance they substituted for it a goddess of reason worthy of them, a woman of the streets, a harlot. After the French Revolution, the traditional doctrine of natural law and right was ignored and scorned by the advocates of juridical positivism. These jurists regard the term natural law merely as denoting a generalization of experience or experiment, namely, a customary way of action. All law, for them, is but a statement of customary or general ways in which men and material things happen to act. Rights based on natural law turn into rights based merely on human custom, legislation, utility, and social sanctions.

Even though we have already treated the various positivistic theories, the following remarks will not be amiss. Moral right because of its obligatory character cannot rest exclusively on human legislation; it must be grounded in the moral order. The State cannot elevate to the dignity of right what in reality is an obvious negation of right. The scope of human legislation is not absolute; it is circumscribed by the moral law. To possess an intrinsic value, positive right must be in harmony with the basic principles of natural law, which is the source of obligatoriness. As a negation of natural law necessarily leads to a negation of positive law, so the existence of positive right implies the existence of natural law.

Moreover, positive law cannot derive its obligatory character from physical force. If law were but a result of force, the weaker would have to obey the stronger even against his will. The specific character that distinguishes law from violence is the moral obligation which it imposes. This obligation is not merely a result of the enactment of a law, but must coexist with it from the very beginning. Even the first positive law presupposes in civil power the right to command and in the subjects the duty of obedience. The Christian teaching on this point cannot be better expressed than in the words of Leo XIII: "All prescriptions of human reason can have force of law only inasmuch as they are the voice and the interpreter of some higher power on which our reason and liberty necessarily depend. For, since the force of law consists in the imposing of obligations and the granting of rights, authority is the one and only foundation of all law — the power, that is, of fixing duties and defining right, as also of assigning the necessary sanctions of reward and punishment to each and all of its commands. But all this, clearly, cannot be found in man, if, as his own supreme legislator, he is to be the ruler of his own actions. It follows, therefore, that the law of nature is the same thing as the eternal law implanted in rational creatures, and inclining them to their right action and end, and can be nothing else but the eternal reason of God, the Creator and Ruler of all the world."[10]

The solution of the problem of right and moral obligation becomes intelligible only when treated in relation to human nature and ultimately to God Himself. In order to provide in a worthy manner for his moral and material wants, man needs civil society. But for a society to exist and tend to its end, a power is required to direct it to that end, and with it the right to ordain whatever is demanded by the common good. In other words, authority must have the right to command and the subjects the duty to obey. This right and this duty do not depend on human will but are demands of the natural law, the basis of all positive right. We have the ultimate explanation in God. Hence the alternative: either admit that God, the Author of man and of nature, has the right to command and to enact laws as a necessary presupposition of all social order; or take refuge in relativism and statal arbitrariness. The first alternative has the support of the vast majority of men of all races, nations, and times; the second has the support only of recent innovators who are trying out their experiments, reckless of the cost to morality, unity, and human liberty. Support of the latter has led to the thousands and thousands of unjust laws which, unless quickly remedied, will cause social chaos and disruption and eventually the degradation of mankind.

---

[10] Leo XIII, *Libertas Humana* (Human Liberty).

2. NATURAL RIGHT AND POSITIVE RIGHT

It is important here to point out the close connection between law and right. Right is the result or effect of a law which gives to one the right over something and imposes on others the obligation to respect that right. A particular right must necessarily partake of the law from which it originates. The natural law, then, will give rise to natural rights, and the positive law to positive rights.

Some consider natural right as something elastic, to which every despot and tyrant can have recourse. But natural right is not to be confounded with arbitrariness, since it arises from obligatory laws having the reason of their being in human nature and ultimately in God, the Author of nature. A positive law then will be legitimate only in so far as it conforms with the principles grounded in the rational nature of man. Although positive rights vary according to circumstances of time, place, and person, they must nevertheless conform to the absolute principles of the natural law. There can be no contradiction between the absolute principles of the natural law and true positive rights.

There are two kinds of positive law: laws which are, as it were, a continuation or expansion of the natural law, such as those prohibiting murder, adultery, theft, etc.; and secondly, laws which determine and apply the more general laws of nature to various circumstances of social life, such as those prescribing and determining the equitable cooperation of all citizens in view of the common good. Obviously the first group of laws, far from being opposed to, and separated from, the natural right, reflect the sublime character of the latter, confirm its existence, and render its exercise more expeditious. If there be any doubt concerning the second group, this doubt is easily removed once we remember that such laws find the supreme reason of their being in human nature itself.

All positive laws must proceed from such primary and self-evident principles of natural right as: Man must live in society;

living in society, man needs the cooperation of his fellow men; every individual citizen must equitably work for the general good. For instance, civil laws for the levying of public taxes can be justified on the following grounds: Whoever shares in the advantages of civil society is necessarily bound to contribute to that society in proportion to his ability. Society has an obligation of prescribing such laws, and individual citizens have a corresponding obligation of obeying them. Hence when public authority imposes just taxes, it makes explicit that which nature itself prescribes, by clarifying and determining the vague and general dictates of nature.

Furthermore, just as the form of every moral judgment invariably results from a twofold element, one of general right or justice, and one of fact, so in every enactment of law, public authority must keep in mind both the universal and abstract principle of natural right, and its application in the concrete. Without the former, positive law would be wanting in justice; without the latter, it could not form part of the practical order. Hence positive right is at once fixed and variable; in so far as the legislator applies the general and fixed norms of justice to changeable conditions of social life. These conditions are not dependent, either directly or indirectly on human nature; hence they do not fall within the scope of natural right as such; nor are they dependent on the will of the legislator. Rather, they depend on the force of circumstances, and are relative to the intellectual, moral, and economic status of a given people. Positive law, then, is subordinated to natural right not only because it proceeds from the general principle of right, but also because that principle is applied to concrete cases. Therefore positive right cannot be an arbitrary affair; it is an authoritative expression of what already pre-exists in nature.

This is exemplified by the penal code. It is a principle of natural right that malefactors should be punished; for an unpunished crime would obviously be a contradiction. It is also a principle of natural right that the measure and kind of punishment should vary in proportion to each criminal deed. But just how crime must be punished postulates the entire body of criminal laws. These positive laws determine whether the punishment is to be by fine, imprisonment, etc. In inflicting adequate punishment the political lawgiver presupposes the following two principles: the intrinsic malice of the crime, and the actual conditions of a given civilization. He supposes the first, because in it consists the measure of punishment; he supposes the second, because the severity of punishment must be modified according to custom and the moral and intellectual status of a given people. The first of these elements is a principle of natural right; the second is the specific condition which occasions the enactment of the law.

True, the progress of modern technology, invention, industry and commerce is gradually creating new relations, and consequently new rights and duties. This, however, does not in any way impair the stable relations, ends and means which cannot find a justification except in the natural moral order. These fundamental relations founded in human nature and the basic norms regulating civil society remain unchanged. Thus for instance, the moral law which not merely forbids us to injure ourselves, but also commands us to perfect our nature by developing our spiritual and bodily abilities, is absolute. Fulfilling these duties we act in conformity with the immutable ends which characterize human nature. Again, the right to life, to personal integrity, and to freedom, are so many natural rights resulting from human nature itself, and the essential order of things. Such rights are universally recognized because they are immediately evident in themselves. It is because human nature and experience are so fundamentally alike that we find a universal agreement in regard to them. One may be ignorant of many positive laws, but not of the principle that one man should not injure another in life and property, or of the principle of love of parents and children, of fundamental respect for human personality. Likewise, the family remains to be what it is, a natural institution, even though the State might not recognize or sanction its existence. So, too, the reciprocal rights and duties of the married persons, must be regarded as fundamental and demanded by the immutable ends embodied in the moral order. To contend that these rights and duties spring from the State is like contending that the family does not antedate, but follows, the State in time, which contention is contradictory.

The State does not create natural rights but finds them already established when it begins to exist. The function of the State is to see to it that these rights are respected. These rights are absolute and universal, hence the State cannot abolish or modify them; they are necessary for social and individual life; they impose themselves by their own evidence since they are grounded in human nature itself.

Precisely because natural right was considered as something divine, independent of human will, the ancients entertained such an esteem for the administrators of justice that they regarded this function as a kind of priesthood. This conviction was prevalent among the Persians, Hindoos, and the ancient Babylonians. The Roman jurists considered the administration of justice as a true worship. That the ancients never doubted the existence of the natural right is attested by Cicero: "There is a law, judges, not written, but born within us, which we have not learned or received by tradition, or read, but which we sucked and imbibed from nature itself, which we were not trained in, but which is ingrained in us."[11] Again, "Right reason is indeed a true law, in accord with nature, diffused among all men, unchangeable, eternal. By its commands it calls men to their duty, by its prohibitions it deters them from vice. . . . There shall no longer be one law at Rome and another at Athens, nor shall it prescribe one thing today and another tomorrow, but one and the same law, eternal and immutable, shall be prescribed for all nations and all times, and the God who shall prescribe, introduce and promulgate this law shall be the one common Lord and supreme Ruler of all, and whosoever will refuse obedience to Him shall be filled with confusions, as this very act will be a virtual denial

---

[11] Cicero, *Pro Milone*.

of his human nature; and should he escape a present punishment, he shall endure heavy chastisement hereafter."[12]

Since the advent of Christianity this belief in the existence of the natural law has been part and parcel of human thought and life. It took the de-Christianized, neopagan man of today to deny the existence of such natural law. Fortunately, however, prejudices and errors cannot change the nature of things. In spite of the corruption of the human heart, natural law has always been and will continue to be the only possible source of legitimate positive law. In its true acceptation, natural law is just the very opposite of caprice or violence, for its scope is strictly limited to the self-evident obligatory norms of social life, concerning the applicability of which there can be no doubt. Such norms have the character of universality and are not referred to anything except to what is immutable in human and social life. Thus, natural law demands authority or the right to command on the part of the State, and obedience to its authority on the part of the subjects; for this obedience is a necessary condition of its existence. Nature does not intervene in any special way to determine what form authority shall assume. It does not designate who the legislators or judges shall be, nor does it determine the nature and kind of punishment to be imposed on malefactors. Such determinations belong to positive law. Likewise, natural law demands that promises should be kept; but positive law determines the conditions under which contracts are binding. In all such cases the general provisions and precepts of the natural law stand in need of specific determination by the positive law. The latter therefore is a necessary supplement to the natural law. Positive law, then, has for its special object those duties pertaining to the common good which are not expressly dictated by nature as are the universal principles of the natural law. Positive law adapts to concrete circumstances the immediate prescriptions of the natural law. The relation between the two is described by St. Thomas: "Every human law has just so much of the nature of law, as it is derived from the law of nature. But

---

[12] Cicero, *De Republica*, Bk. III, Ch. 23.

if in any point it deflects from the law of nature, it is no longer
a law but a perversion of law.

"But it must be noted that something may be derived from
the natural law in two ways: first, as a conclusion from premises;
secondly, by way of determination of certain generalities. The
first way is like to that by which, in sciences, demonstrated conclusions are drawn from the principles; while the second mode
is likened to that whereby, in the arts, general forms are par-
ticularized as to details; thus the craftsman needs to determine
the general form of a house to some particular shape. Some
things are therefore derived from the general principles of the
natural law, by way of conclusions; e.g., that *one must not kill*
may be derived as a conclusion from the principle that *one
should do harm to no man;* while some are derived therefrom
by way of determination; e.g., the law of nature has it that the
evildoer should be punished; but that he be punished in this or
that way, is a determination of the law of nature. Accordingly,
both modes of derivation are found in the human law. But
those things which are derived in the first way, are contained in
human law not as emanating therefrom exclusively, but have
some force from the natural law also. But those things which
are derived in the second way, have no other force than that of
human law."[13]

Positive right therefore presupposes the natural law as its
basis. But, while the essential principles of the natural law are
absolute as long as human nature remains what it is, its further
determinations, its particular applications arising out of particular sets of circumstances, may and must change. It is the function
of positive right to work out these determinations and applications and to unfold itself in harmony with the needs of various
times and places. The natural right is, as it were, a skeleton of
the juridical order, the flesh and nerves and sinews to be filled
in by positive laws. Hence the sphere of positive law is much
wider than the sphere of natural law. This is amply illustrated
by the Napoleonic and the Justinian codes of civil law. New

---

[13] St. Thomas, *Summa Theologica*, I, II, q. 95, a. 2.

social and economic conditions, new discoveries and inventions give rise to new rights and duties which must be based on the general principles of justice. All this shows that positive right, though resting on absolute principles of moral law, is nevertheless subject to change and alterations.

That natural right is the source of positive right is also shown from the obligatory character of every true right. A mere coercive precept as such does not constitute a right. On the contrary, a legitimate positive right, though lacking the necessary means of enforcement, does not thereby cease to be obligatory. A right retains its obligatory character whether it can be enforced or not. The mere fact of enactment of a law is not sufficient to make the law binding. Therefore positive law cannot be an adequate and exclusive source of moral obligation. We have already noted that the right to command as well the duty of obeying are grounded in the social nature of man and find their full justification in God. If God created man social by nature, He must have supplied that society with all the necessary means to subsist and prosper. But this cannot be attained without a common authority having a right to command whatever is necessary for the realization of the aforesaid end. Therefore the right to command and the obligation of obedience is founded not in the juridical positive order, but in the natural moral law. Since the preservation of the social order demands coercive laws, civil authority specifies the content of the natural norms, and traces the path to be followed by the subjects. Civil authority is, therefore, a basic postulate of the social order.

Such being the case, it is hard to understand the alarming attitude of certain philosophers, when today, more than ever, the need of reaffirming and restoring the doctrine of natural right is so vividly felt. And yet, the high esteem for, and the interpretation of the natural right were the glory and pride of the Latin genius. The following passage reminds us again of the importance and value of the traditional teaching.

"Before the existence of civil society, before constitutions were framed and human laws were enacted, there must have been some rules of conduct, already possessing a binding force. . . . If so, there must have been a standard of right based on nature itself, and anterior to all human legislation. Again, when legislators devise a system of rules to prevent the clashing of rights and the conflicts of interests, they must have before their minds an ideal of justice anterior to human rules and binding on the human will: this ideal cannot be derived from the laws which they are just then engaged in framing, for the effect cannot exist before the cause, and imitation presupposes a model. Lastly, when unjust laws or pernicious laws have been enacted, and the people wish them to be repealed and replaced by just and beneficial laws, whence do the citizens derive their ideal of what a law ought to be? Certainly not from the existing legislation, since the modification or reversal of this legislation is demanded; then the people must appeal to a higher standard, which existed before the passing of the obnoxious laws, and which has remained unchanged despite the sins of legislators."[14]

3. RIGHT AND MORALITY

That an essential relation must exist between right and morality is undeniable. This is only too evident from the very meaning men have for ages attached to right. The precise relation of right to morality is apparent from a proper evaluation of the former. Morality refers to the conformity of all human actions, of all practical life, with the standard of the moral good, with the rational nature of man. It is grounded in the very nature of man, individual as well as social. Right, on the other hand, refers to the relation of one man to another, especially in regard to his freedom from hindrance in the performance of his actions. It comes into play only where contact or refusal of contact between persons impairs the proper direction of human conduct.

While morality is concerned with all human actions, right is restricted to a certain type of action. Offenses against morality are not necessarily offenses against any particular person, they

---

[14] R. I. Holaind, S.J., *Natural Law and Legal Practice* (New York: Benziger, 1899), p. 37.

may be against God or oneself, while offenses against the strict right of others are always considered offenses against the person and the dignity of a fellow man. Again, there are cases with which morality is directly interested without involving positive rights except indirectly. Blasphemy, drunkenness, lewdness, and many other vices are expressly condemned by the moral law, without being necessarily condemned by positive law; or if they are condemned, they are condemned only in so far as they are detrimental to social life and not as destructive to eternal life.

Right in general rests on the moral order under the following aspects: First, many rights are but the application to social conduct of the principles of the natural moral order. Secondly, a well-ordered society could not exist unless citizens were morally bound to obey civil power. A legitimate positive law is at the same time a moral law, and as such, is vested with obligatory force. Without this character of obligatoriness a law ceases to be a law. All human laws must, directly or indirectly, draw their obligatory force from the natural moral law.

The moral order is a necessary postulate of society's existence. Without such laws of morality as "Render to each his due"; "Keep one's promise"; "Do not kill," etc., society could not continue to exist. These laws engender rights as well as duties. Whoever violates the former and neglects the latter, attacks the moral order. Hence right cannot be separated from morality. A denial of this principle implies that right is one with might, and that positive law is the same as coercive power. Unless man is morally bound to fulfill his duties toward God, his neighbor, and himself, society would be subject to every individual whim and passion.

But if right is an integral part of the moral order and finds therein its obligatory force, it follows that positive laws which are completely severed from the moral order cannot engender obligation. Civil laws are binding on the subjects because they are part of the positive right operating in a State. In regard to unjust and immoral actions, all rights cease, because the said actions are detrimental to social welfare. The fact that ordinarily

jurists are satisfied with mere legality does not impair our principle. Positive civil law is not concerned with intentions or internal motives determining an action, but only with external
social relations. Although the citizen is answerable only to God
for his internal motives which are beyond the scope of human
justice, yet in his external behavior he is bound in conscience to
respect the positive law; nor can he violate it without disregarding the moral order. The fact that a positive law is founded in
the moral order does not mean that it must also be concerned
with private, internal motives. As long as the individual does
not invade another's sphere of action, he is responsible only to
God and to his conscience. But whenever he violates the rights
of others, the State has the right and duty to intervene, not because the individual is ruining his health or wasting his heritage,
but because by such actions he injures his fellow men. Drunkenness, for instance, is a breach of the natural moral law because
it destroys health and life; yet the penal code is not concerned
with it so long as it is not annoying to others. Moreover, in
practice legislators generally agree in regarding right as a moral
factor. Thus in penal cases, as a rule, an attempt is made to
proportion the penalty to the guilt. With this end in view,
magistrates and legislators take into account the moral character,
the good faith, ignorance, want of discretion of the persons in-
volved. Right, therefore, cannot be separated from morality.

With his usual clarity of expression Leo XIII summarizes the
traditional doctrine in these words: "Of the laws enacted by
men, some are concerned with what is good or bad by its very
nature. They command men to follow after what is right and to
shun what is wrong, adding at the same time a suitable sanction.
But such laws by no means derive their origin from civil society;
because, just as civil society did not create human nature, so
neither can it be said to be the author of the good which befits
human nature, or of the evil which is contrary to it. Laws came
before men lived together in society, and have their origin in the
natural, and consequently in the eternal law. The precepts, therefore, of the natural law, embodied in the laws of men have not

merely the force of human law, but they possess that higher and more august sanction which belongs to the law of nature and the eternal law. And within the sphere of this kind of laws, the duty of the civil legislator is, mainly, to keep the community in obedience. . . . Now there are other enactments of the civil authority, which do not follow directly, but somewhat remotely, from the natural law, and decide many points which the law of nature treats only in a general and indefinite way. For instance, though nature commands all to contribute to the public peace and prosperity, still whatever belongs to the manner, and circumstances, and conditions under which such service is to be rendered must be determined by the wisdom of men and not by nature herself. It is in the constitution of these particular rules of life, suggested by reason and prudence, and put forth by competent authority, that human law, properly so called, consists. This law bids all citizens to work together for the attainment of the common end proposed to the community, and forbids them to depart from this end; and the same law, in so far as it is in conformity with the dictates of nature, leads to what is good, and deters from evil."[15]

A final question is that relative to unjust or immoral laws. If we keep in mind that both the right of commanding and the duty of obeying are limited by the moral law, we come to realize that the difficulties of this problem are more apparent than real. Whenever a law degenerates into whim and caprice, either by violating the principles of the moral law, or by exceeding the limits of its preceptive power, obedience to such a law is no longer a duty. However, in the changing conditions of a complex social life, we must distinguish between a law that is intrinsically bad, and a law that is simply unjust. In the first instance, subjects are obviously not bound to obey, because the principle, evil must be avoided, is all-inclusive and holds for all cases. The State's right to command is not absolute; hence the obligation of obedience to positive civil laws admits of limitations.

---

[15] Leo XIII, *Libertas Humana* (Human Liberty).

In the second instance the solution is more complex and involves many factors. Hence it is necessary first to ascertain in what measure the law violates the principle of justice. If the law is indubitably unjust, it does not bind. Sometimes, however, observance of such a law is not illicit; as when a law is not openly opposed to the ethical and moral order, or if there are extenuating circumstances or when its transgression might lead to grave consequences. Thus, for example, it is better to submit to a law imposing unjust taxes than to suffer heavy financial losses by refusing. At times observance of an unjust law may be obligatory, as in cases when its violation would cause great disturbance to social order and public tranquillity. Here, too, the principle that of two evils one must choose the lesser, would operate. Aquinas clarifies this point as follows:

"Laws framed by man are either just or unjust. If they are just, they have the power of binding in conscience, from the eternal law whence they are derived. Now laws are said to be just, both from their end, if they are ordained to the common good, from their author, if the law that is made does not exceed the power of the lawgiver, and from their form, if burdens are laid on the subjects, according to an equality of proportion and with a view to the common good. Since a man is a part of the community, each man, in all that he is and has, belongs to the community; just as a part, in all that it is, belongs to the whole. Just as nature inflicts a loss on the part, in order to save the whole, so for the same reason, such laws as these, which impose proportionate burdens, are just and binding in conscience, and are legal laws.

"On the other hand, laws may be unjust in two ways. First, laws may be unjust by being contrary to human good, through being opposed to the things mentioned above. Such are the acts of violence rather than laws, because as Augustine says 'a law that is not just, seems to be no law at all.' Such laws do not bind in conscience, save perhaps in order to avoid scandal or disturbance, in which case a man should even yield his right. Secondly, laws may be unjust through being opposed to the

Divine good. Such are the laws of tyrants inducing to idolatry, or to anything else contrary to the Divine law. Laws of this kind must not be observed, because, as stated in Acts 5:29 'we ought to obey God rather than men.' "[16]

Positive right presupposes natural right. From it civil power draws the right to command, and the subjects derive the duty to obey. Without natural right a true human authority is not possible, as there would be no rights in heaven or on earth. Under penalty of declaring bankrupt the whole juridical order we must admit the existence of natural right. But natural right cannot be conceived without a legislator, who has engraved in the human heart the general principles of the moral order. Therefore, without a God, the Author of nature and of the laws governing it, there could be neither order nor harmony in nature nor in man. Today, more than ever before, the philosophical and juridical sciences experience the great need of drawing from this source of justice and order a new light and orientation. Only thus can the empire of right under a new era of peace and prosperity, be restored and flourish. The devastating consequences of rights not resting on natural laws are appalling: the whole world is reaping the whirlwind of the four-century-old revolt.

------

[16] St. Thomas, *Summa Theologica*, I, 2, q. 96, a. 4.

SELECT READINGS

Aquinas, St. Thomas, *Summa Theologica*, 1–2, quaestiones, 90–98.
Catholic Encyclopedia, arts. on "Justice"; "Right"; "Duty."
Cronin, M., *The Science of Ethics* (New York: Benziger, 1922), Vol. II, Ch. III.
Encyclopedia of the Social Sciences, art. "Natural Rights."
Haas, F. J., *Man and Society* (New York: Century Co., 1930), Ch. III.
Holaind, R. I., *Natural Law and Legal Practice* (New York: Benziger, 1899).
Leo XIII, *Rerum Novarum* (Christian Constitution of States); *Libertas Humana* (Human Liberty).
Maritain, Jacques, *The Natural Law and Human Rights* (Ontario: Christian Culture Press, 1942).

Michel, V., O.S.B., *Philosophy of Human Conduct* (Minneapolis: Burgess, 1936), Chs. XVII–XVIII.

Rickaby, Joseph, S.J., *Moral Philosophy* (London: Longmans, Green and Co., 1918), Part II, Ch. III; Part III, Ch. V.

Ryan-Boland, *Catholic Principles of Politics* (New York: The Macmillan Co., 1940), Chs. I–II.

CHAPTER VII

MAN'S PLACE IN THE UNIVERSE

IN VIEW of the intellectual, moral, and political chaos reigning in our day and age, it is not only appropriate but necessary to bring into fuller relief certain basic concepts whose validity has been so far assumed. In this chapter, then, we shall consider the problems of human personality, of man's ultimate end, and of God's existence. These concepts are essentially connected with the true doctrine of human rights, for unless man's personal dignity and proper end and God's existence are recognized, there can be no basis for the ethical and juridical order.

It is imperative to reaffirm man's personal dignity because in virtue of human personality alone does man possess rights and duties. Right, as already noted, is a moral power or faculty to perform an action and has its source in the natural moral law. A being devoid of knowledge of law cannot be a subject or possessor of right. Hence "brute beasts, not having understanding and therefore not being persons, cannot have any right. The conclusion is clear. They are not autocentric. They are of the number of things, which are another's; they are chattels or cattle."[1] True, under the impulse of self-preservation brutes defend life and bodily integrity, but they lack knowledge of what right is. Assigning to man the proper place which belongs to him in virtue of his personality is equivalent to a repudiation of materialistic, pantheistic, and positivistic political philosophies.

Furthermore, the determining factor of a thing is its end, hence man's ultimate goal is the determining factor of all social life. Therefore, in order to assign to man his rightful place in

---

[1] Joseph Rickaby, S.J., *Moral Philosophy* (London: Longmans, Green and Co., 1918), p. 248.

society, it is necessary to consider his end or goal in relation to universal finality. Aquinas begins his ethics with the problem of the *end* or *aim* of man. A proper evaluation of this end furnishes us with the only possible norm of merit and demerit in human actions; it is the *Magna Charta* of individual and social liberties. Small wonder then that the darts of positivism and pantheism are directed so violently against the true end of man.

The true end of man cannot be repudiated without proclaiming the triumph of might over right, and without immolating the individual on the altar of the State. In the light of their true end, all men are brethren and sons of the same heavenly Father; the slave becomes conscious of his dignity as a person and realizes that like his master he, too, is possessor of sacred and inviolable rights; the State ceases to be a despot and becomes a helper and defender of individual, family, and social rights.

PART I

THE NATURE OF MAN

1. PANTHEISM

Pantheism has vainly sought to prove that man, as well as everything else, emanates from a unique, absolute, and all-inclusive substance. Since in this system particular objects are only modes or phenomena of the absolute substance, it logically follows that consciousness of self and belief in one's personality and liberty are illusory. Whatever is, is one; there is neither right nor wrong; all is fate and nature. The absolute and all-inclusive substance, in which all qualifications are reduced to unity, acts not in pursuance of a purpose but according to the necessity of its nature. In other words, this absolute substance is an impersonal and indeterminate something.

Pantheism annuls the very concept of right with its fundamental principles and elements which constitute the complexus of the ethical-juridical order. Right, as already noted, requires not only a personality but a plurality of persons; it expresses a correlation of person to person. This plurality of persons is necessarily implied in the distinction between the superior who imposes the law and the inferior who must obey it. The pantheistic denial of personality and of all real distinction between persons necessarily negates the ethical-juridical order, as well as all distinction between right and wrong, between justice and injustice.

Moreover, pantheism militates against experience. In all consciousness of self we know ourselves as persons, namely, as self-subsisting beings endowed with reason and free will. In all knowledge of other objects we know them as different and apart from ourselves, and ourselves as different and apart from them. Every man is convinced of this; no man can be made to think otherwise. In his Allocution of June 9, 1862, Pius IX thus condemns pantheism: "With a perversity only equalled by their folly, they [the pantheists] dare to assert that the Supreme All-wise, All-provident Deity has no existence apart from the visible universe; that God and nature are the same, and similarly subject to change; that God is modified in man and the world; and that everything is God and possesses the very essence of the Divinity. If God and the world then are one and the same thing, there is no difference between spirit and matter, necessity and liberty, truth and falsehood, good and evil, right and wrong. In truth nothing can be imagined more insane, impious, and irrational than this teaching [pantheism]." The Pope shows how absolutism in the State follows logically from pantheism. "They [the pantheists] attack and endeavor to destroy the rights of all lawful property, and with perverse mind and purpose imagine and coin for themselves an unlimited, uncircumscribed right, which the State is to enjoy, the State being, in their rash judgment, the organ and source of all right."[2]

---

[2] Hettinger-Bowden, *Natural Religion* (New York: Benziger, 1900), p. 175.

2. MATERIALISM

Though differing from pantheism in many other respects, materialism likewise denies to man his personal dignity. Huxley, one of its ablest exponents, defines materialism as that correlation of all the phenomena of the universe with matter and motion which lies at the heart of modern physical science. In short, matter and motion constitute the origin and the source of everything that exists. Materialism denies that God or the human soul exist; asserts that all mental activities are functions of the organism; and claims that sensible experience is the limit of human knowledge. Necessarily, all this implies a denial of self, of personality, and consequently of rights.

Materialism substitutes a blind impulse for the sense of duty. the instinct of self-preservation for the laws of morality. It will, at best, give us rights only based on self-interest, custom, social sanction, brute force; it will never give us true rights founded on a stable and permanent basis. Therefore might predominates over right, egotism over public welfare, vice over virtue. Moreover, in denying the objectivity of absolute truths, materialism undermines the rational basis for all research, and reduces man to the level of the brute. Deny thought or intelligence, and man is a lowly brute animal, whose domain is a den or an acre or more of forest or wilderness. In the words of Lacordaire: "Materialism is the result of that exterminating war of evil against good; it is but the supreme effort to stifle remorse. And this is why I call it an abject and an unnatural doctrine. If this should seem rash, I offer no apology. You attack my very essence, you degrade me to mere animality, you treat me as the equal of a dog! What do I say? — you dare to write that 'Man is a digestive tube pierced at both ends.' "[3]

3. CHRISTIAN PHILOSOPHY

The traditional and Christian definition of man as a free and rational animal needs further elucidation. Man is an animal in

---

[3] Lacordaire, *Conferences on God* (New York: O'Shea, 1871), p. 117.

that his nature exhibits all the characteristics proper to animals in general and to sentient life as well. Man is a biological creature, a sentient being, but primarily a rational being. Biologically, man's organism undergoes the various processes common to plant life as well as the subconscious physiological processes common to animal life. The biological activities of his organism are the most active, their function being so constant as to be unnoticeable. We become aware of their essential importance to our well-being only when their proper functioning is impaired. As a sentient being man has a highly developed mechanism of sense perception and the whole gamut of impulses and emotional complexes of animals. To some extent these are more varied and more complex in man than in any other animal.

But above all, man is a rational being, namely, possessed of intellect and will. "The term *intellect* (understanding) implies an intimate knowledge, for *intelligere* (to understand) is the same as *intus legere* (to read inwardly). This is clear to anyone who considers the difference between intellect and sense. Sensory knowledge is concerned with external sensible qualities; whereas intellective knowledge penetrates into the very essence of a thing since the object of the intellect is *what a thing is* (the whatness of a thing). Human knowledge, however, begins with the outside of things, and it is evident that the stronger the light of the understanding, the further can it penetrate into the heart of things."[4] Hence the intellect may be defined as the knowledge activity which knows the essences of things, both absolute and relative, and sees the relations between things, such as the relation of effect to cause, of means to an end. It forms universal concepts, judges, reasons, and by reasoning attains knowledge also of things that do not come under sense knowledge in any way, such as the first cause and the ultimate end. The will may be described as the power of loving, desiring, enjoying that which is apprehended by the intellect as good. Its sphere is coextensive with that of the intellect. The will is a high type of

---

[4] St. Thomas, *Summa Theologica*, II, II^{ae}, q. 1, a. I.

spontaneous striving on the one hand, and of deliberate choice and striving on the other. The will and intellect make man really a man, they raise him above the level of the brute animal.

Man is truly a man only in so far as he uses his power of understanding and his power of determination. Intellect and will constitute human personality, and make man the possessor of human rights as well as duties. Unless man has the powers of intellect and will, he can never possess rights nor have duties. Upon what would they be based? One cannot attribute rights to or impose duties on an animal. Whoever repudiates the true teaching of the origin of man, of his social nature, and of his ultimate end or goal, deprives himself of all necessary weapons to resist statal despotism, which robs him of his true dignity as a man and renders him a slave of the State motivated only by servile fear. But every human being is a proper personality, having a divine origin and a sublime end in virtue of which he becomes a sharer of time and of eternity. Therefore, it is a strictly philosophical axiom that while the State is created for time, the individual is created for eternity; that the State is not an end in itself but only a means toward an end. Hence the State is not a master but a servant bound to treat the individual as a free and responsible person, as a creature endowed with immortality. Only thus can the individual vindicate his personal dignity and the proper place which belongs to him in the natural order and in his social relations. In all other hypothesis, it is not only extreme temerity but an impossibility even to remind the State of its duties or to insist on an adequate cooperation from the State in order that the individual may attain his ultimate goal and his full moral and spiritual development. In relation to his ultimate goal man takes up an entirely special position. In this regard it is no longer the individual that must serve the State but the latter is bound to serve the individual because the State is made for time only, while the individual is created for eternity. If we deny a transcendental goal to the individual, he will remain inexorably only a cog in the machinery of the State, and the goal of the individual will always be subjected to the collective goal of the majority, which goal can be only temporal, or lasting only as long as a particular group or society exists. Hence it is that notwithstanding the illusion of progress we are gradually reverting to barbarism. Man's nature from a consideration of origin and end will be discussed at further length in the next part.

If a vigorous and immediate reaction against positivism in defense of man's rights is urgent, even more urgent is the spiritual and moral regeneration of the individual and society. It is imperative to halt the contagious mania of trying to reduce everything to a naturalistic level and to banish from life all moral and spiritual principles, as if true progress and true civilization were limited to the satisfaction of mere material wants. To accomplish this, man must be restored to his true position in the universe. By denying his soul its lofty aspirations, its intense, innate yearning for supreme happiness, man, instead of being elevated to the highest plane for which he was created, is debased to the level of the brute. The choice is inevitable; it is the choice between right or wrong, good or bad; between the ultimate goal or total failure; it is the choice between true culture, enlightenment, and civilization and barbarism, anarchy, and chaos. This choice is determined by one's conception of man. A materialistic, pantheistic conception of man has determined the world's present choice and with it has come today's ills and evils.

PART II

TELEOLOGY AND THE ETHICAL-JURIDICAL ORDER

There is finality in nature, in the universe, in man. Elsewise one could not speak of the ethical-juridical order. It would have no basis, no justification; it would be a mere illusion, a chimera. It is clear that pantheism, materialism, and positivism are powerless to explain the cosmic order or the finality in man. They cannot solve the origin, the nature, or the end of man. Christian philosophy with its teleological conception of man and the universe alone gives a thoroughly satisfactory solution to the momentous problems of life. This philosophy reveals to us our affinity to all things; indicates the profound unity of being, to whose hidden depths it opens the door; and directs man to his rational end.

1. THE FOURFOLD PRINCIPLE OF CAUSALITY

The term *cause* refers to anything having a positive influence of any sort on the being or occurrence of something. Aristotle distinguishes four categories of causes; namely, the *material*, the *formal*, the *efficient*, and the *final cause*. The *material cause* denotes the raw materials, or matter out of which the new thing is made, e.g., the marble or wood out of which a statue is made. The *formal cause* is that added to or done to the raw materials in order to make them into a new product. Thus of a statue marble or wood are the material cause; and the form (the word is used in its wider sense) making the raw material a particular statue, e.g., the statue of Apollo, is the formal cause. The latter actuates, determines, and specifies matter. The *efficient cause* is the action of the agent or worker who produces the new article or effects the change from raw material to the finished product. Thus the sculptor can be called the efficient cause of the statue. Finally, the *final cause* is the purpose or end for which a given fact is performed. It is the sculptor's idea or mental pattern according to which a shapeless block has been made to assume the special shape of Apollo. Strictly it is the idea, not as a mere picture in the mind, but in so far as the idea is actively guiding or influencing the action of the sculptor in making the statue. In this connection it is well to note that efficient and final causes pull together.

The following considerations will pave the way to our main thesis. Every being acts according to its nature. Since cosmic agents differ in nature, they aim at their ends in different ways. We may group all cosmic agents into three classes; inorganic, biological, and intellectual.

1. Inorganic or inanimate physical objects exist without change in the same state in which they are, unless acted upon by external influences. Having neither intellect, nor sense, nor internal principle of life, they cannot apprehend their end. They are moved to seek it by an intellect external to themselves.

2. Biological or animate beings, whether plants or animals, are not passive like the stone but possess a certain initiative of their own. They act not like blind machines but as a result of their own impulse to live and to grow. Stimuli moves them in the form of attraction or repulsion, depending upon whether it is such as to aid or hinder their life processes. The behavior of living beings is said to be teleologically caused, since they are urged either naturally or instinctively to their end.

3. Intellectual beings not only can apprehend the end but also can reason upon the means to attain it. They can appreciate both the suitability of the end to their nature and the aptitude of the means to obtain it. Being in virtue of their reason and will masters of their own acts, they proceed to their end by themselves.

We must distinguish here between the *proximate* and *remote* or *ultimate end*. The end is proximate when it is not desired for itself but only in so far as it is a step toward the attainment of an ultimate end. The end is ultimate when it is desired for its own sake.

2. THE TELEOLOGICAL CONCEPTON OF THE UNIVERSE

In the motion of the heavenly bodies, centrifugal and centripetal forces are so adjusted and regulated that an extremely difficult movement takes place regularly and without any disturbance. On our earth the ultimate particles of matter are of such number and variety and so distributed and mingled together that life and development of plant, animal, and man are possible. The lower forms of beings are so arranged as to satisfy the demands of the higher. Of the different kinds of living things each one has its own peculiar and artistic structure and conformation. The outer conditions of life are perfectly adapted to the need of each kind; and their activity is determined so as to suit the requirements of their preservation and propagation.

The closer we study nature the more evident appears the magnificence of finality in the field of mechanics and chemistry as well as in that of physiology and psychology. In other words, in nature there is an endless series of laws; general laws governing the world, particular laws governing and directing individual beings to their end; hence, there are physical, chemical, geometrical, physiological, and psychological laws, etc. In nature everything has a purposive end, everything is wonderfully coordinated according to a pre-established plan. There is finality in nature. By this we do not mean to attribute to the inorganic world itself conscious and intelligent finality, such as is revealed in human purposive activities, but to maintain that behind the universe there is our efficient cause, God.

a) Finality in Nature

If there were no finality in the universe with its grandeur, unity, and harmony, there would be none in man with the result that the ethicojuridical order would remain destitute of a stable and lasting basis. Right and morality would consist merely in the mechanics of human activities, and so-called human dignity would be an empty name. If the perfume of the flower has no purpose, neither have the leaves, nor the roots, nor the plant. One who denies finality to the universe must deny it to man.

Yet materialism denies finality to the universe, since for it the world consists only of atoms and space. This doctrine is not a specialty of modern times. It is as old as corrupted mankind itself. It extends from Democritus to Hackel, from Epicurus to Spencer and Santayana. Materialism, modern positivism, and theophobia repudiate cosmic teleology for the simple reason that it leads to God. "But" remarked a State university professor "you cannot admit a purpose in the universe because it leads to God." For this reason they try to explain cosmic order without an efficient cause or a creative mind. Materialism, however, contradicts itself by admitting, on the one hand, finality in nature and in life and by denying, on the other, the existence of a creative and directive intelligence; in other words, admitting the effect but ignoring the cause. Consistency demands that if you deny finality to the universe in its totality, you must also deny finality to its single parts. It would be nonsense to ascribe finality to the eye, or to the nose, or to the hand of man, if man himself had no end or purpose. If the whence, the what, and the whither of man is unknown, all other knowledge about man is to no purpose. Materialism must demonstrate, yet it cannot, why the teleological argument is invalid and unscientific, and why every conception that leads to God must be regarded as idiotic or nonsensical. True science is based neither on prejudice nor caprice. Now an *a priori* denial of scientific value to the teleological argument, which from the cosmic order proves God's existence, is certainly not based on logic and truth but rather on prejudice and error. Let us see now whether a general finality which cannot be explained by mechanism and evolutionism really exists in the universe.

Final cause may be considered as in rational and as in irrational beings. In rational beings it is a known and accepted end which determines their present acts. In irrational beings it is a controlling factor, a natural end to which they irresistibly tend. The philosophical argument may be stated as follows: All beings act for an end, and this end determines their activity. If an agent were not tending to a definite end, it would be indifferent toward acting in this or that way and consequently would never begin to act. The existence of final causes, thus demonstrated *a priori*, may equally be proved from experience.

There is little doubt that conscious beings act with an end in view. Moreover, it is due precisely to this end that an efficient cause produces a determined effect, that it operates in one way rather than another. A watch, for instance, has for its intrinsic end the measurement of time and necessarily presupposes a watchmaker. Obviously, the watch itself has no conscious finality because it lacks intelligence and will. The efficient cause, the

watchmaker, ordains and disposes the mechanism for this purpose. Now the watch presupposes a watchmaker as its intelligent
efficient cause, for still stronger reasons this is true in relation to
the finality governing the universe. Since the material universe
is unconscious of its end, it likewise requires an intelligent efficient cause to direct it to its end. The universe could neither be
a harmonious whole nor possess a specific end without an intelligent efficient Cause who reduces to unity the infinite number
of atoms and molecules, assigning to each of them a determined
end.

Both reason and common sense proclaim the presence of purposive finality in the universe to account for the orderly and
harmonious sequence of phenomena, and for the convergence
of diverse activities toward harmonious results. It is unthinkable
that the intricate parts of a microscope should have *happened*
and fitted themselves together by chance. And it is contrary to
right reason to suppose that the different materials out of which
the grand cathedrals of Europe are made, or the letters that
make up the *Iliad* or *Hamlet* happened to adjust and fit themselves together by mere chance. Yet that is what materialism
claims of the universe.

b) *Finality in the Organic World*

If the inorganic world clearly evidences purposive finality, the
organic world gives greater proof. "Every species follows its own
law of development. The organization of every creature struggles
on bravely and persistently until it has reached the summit of
the species. This persistent struggle reveals a plan stretching far
and wide beyond the present actual limits of nature. On every
step of the journey, from germ to blossom and fruit, new pos-
sibilities arise which are, nonetheless, wonderful because we
know the intermediate stages. The species, the manner of its
growth, and the certain law that governs it cannot be explained
by the slow process of development. No chemical or physical
force can give the organism an opposite tendency. All changes
affect the parts, not the form of the whole which endures after

the life of the individual. The germ forces the elements taken
from its surroundings to enter into certain combinations with
one another so as to produce a structure similar to itself. No
reason whatever can be given why living matter should assume
different elementary forms: why it should shape itself at one
time into leaves and twigs, blossoms, fruit, and thorns, and at
another into muscle, nerve and bone, hair and nail. Nor do we
know why these should blend with other groups of cells into a
harmonious unit. The biogenetical law, so much insisted upon
in the doctrine of descent, merely shows that one and the same
plan underlies the evolution of species and individuals. In this
very fact, so thoroughly in keeping with the general character
of the cosmos, we admire the Creator's wisdom in forming individuals and species according to the same idea, and in combin-
ing unity and variety for the same end.

"Many a caterpillar crawls from the tree to the ground or to
a wall to end there its chrysalis life. Then it passes a brief but
happy existence as a butterfly, and lays its eggs on a leaf. We do
not ask whence the living creature derived the power to do these
things. But we are bound to ask how comes it that the creature
invariably takes the right turn on an unknown road? How
comes it that it always attains to its end so surely, except when
some external obstacle besets its path? Are not necessity and
purpose here joined in the closest bonds of wedlock? Does not
this conformity to purpose, under the pressure of necessity, far
surpass the greatest efforts of human genius?"[5]

The above-mentioned laws and phenomena cannot be explained solely by mechanical forces. It must be borne in mind
that *mechanism and teleology do not exclude one another, rather,
they are in mutual agreement.* Without teleology there would be
no mechanism, but only a confusion of crude forces; and without mechanism there would be no teleology, for how could the
latter effect its purpose? The conception of mechanism is mean-

---

[5] Schanz, *A Christian Apology* (New York: Fr. Pustet and Co., 1902), pp.
251–253.

ingless without the idea of the end to which it is subservient
and the idea of the Designer who contrived it.

Again instinct, whether related to nutrition, growth, or preservation and its various activities, always reveals purposive finality.
For example, baby ducks without any training are instinctively
moved to seek water. With consummate art the spider spins its
web, the bird builds its nest, and the bee constructs its cell. All
these instinctive actions, which can be multiplied indefinitely,
are evident proof of finality. With fine acumen St. Thomas notes
that swallows build their nests always in the same manner and
that spiders spin their web always in the same way. They have
no power to act otherwise (in this instinct differs from reason).
St. Thomas points out that, on the contrary, all architects do not
build houses in the same way, because each one is capable of
devising a particular form for his work and of modifying it according to his proper plan. If from instinctive activities we pass
to automatic movements and reflexes, which are of a purely
physiological nature, the same conclusion is obtained. The
majority of physiologists readily admit that *directivity* or finality
is the characteristic note of such phenomena. The truth of this
finality is self-evident.

c) Finality in Man

The momentous question, and the really vital one consists in
determining man's ultimate end. This end cannot be something
transitory or subject to temporal or local changes, since it must
embrace the whole individual in relation to his social life and
activities. Without an understanding of the goal toward which
all human actions, thoughts, and volitions must tend, one will
never succeed in regulating his life in a proper manner or in
contributing in a positive way to the common good. Without a
definite and fixed purpose human life will lack orientation, it
will be a rudderless ship at the mercy of every wind, with no
hope of ever reaching a harbor. In order to be rational, man's
life must have an ultimate, immutable goal, a goal independent
of human will. This goal must encompass all men without dis-

stinction of sex, race, culture, or age. Since human nature is identical in all men, the supreme end must be identical for all. In any other supposition man's life would not reflect in itself a directive mind but rather disorder and anarchy. If the ultimate end of man depended on human will, then everyone could choose for his end idleness instead of work, vice and sensual gratification instead of virtue and sacrifice.

"What is this supreme end? We may say in the first place that it is my whole good or good in general. But such a statement would be incomplete, for one would go on to ask where this whole good or good in general is to be found. Here we are confronted with the theory of values. Concrete good things of many kinds lie within our grasp; pleasures of the body and of the mind, good health, fortune, friendship, and so on. All these correspond in a certain measure to our aspirations, but it becomes necessary to draw up a scale of their respective values, and this can only be done by the reason. Now our reason tells us that the *truly* human good ought to consist in that which will satisfy our specifically human aspirations, or, in other words, correspond to those faculties which are the highest we possess and which make us human, namely intelligence and will. Things other than the intellectual will be good only as supplementary, so to speak, and as controlled by reason.

"The happiness which corresponds to our mode of being will consists in *knowing* and *loving*. To know in a perfect way, to penetrate all the mysteries of the material universe and to dominate it, and to know in addition by means of His works the great Creator of them all, God Himself; then to love in the same perfect way, to delight in knowledge for its own sake, and to cast ourselves towards God our Creator — this will constitute philosophic happiness.

"It must not, however, be thought that the Christian excludes other good things, such as physical well-being, from human happiness. Rather these things are considered to contribute to happiness as a whole, and since man has a body, his body ought to share in happiness just as his soul, always on condition that these complementary good things remain in due subordination to the human good *par excellence*."[6]

d) *Solution of Difficulties*

It is vainly objected that man's knowledge of cosmic finality is limited, that he does not know whether this finality has always existed, whether it encompasses all the parts of creation, or whether the future might not be subject to change. That man does not possess a comprehensive knowledge of *all* the purposes working in the universe is quite obvious, but such knowledge is unnecessary. It is not necessary for man to know all the purposes of electricity before he harnesses it for the one purpose of his own utility. It is enough for man to know that there is such a force as electricity and to know some of its laws, so that he can apply them to his own purpose. Likewise, it is enough to know that the universe is regulated by innumerable laws, which manifest themselves continually by their imposing evidence. They cannot exist without a purposive finality. The closer we study nature the more evident cosmic finality becomes. The wonderful harmony of creation, the marvelous unity of action among elements so different in kind, the combinations of diverse tendencies to a common result, all show with unmistakable emphasis that a Divine Mind guides the universe and gives to all its elements their course and being.

In order to disparage the force of the teleological argument, some have recourse to certain exceptions. But such exceptions do not in any way destroy the general law of finality. "In spite of disorders which appear at the surface of the physical world, and in spite of moral evil, both of which result from the contingent and imperfect character of the world, the internal finality proper to each being in the universe leads up to another finality — which is external. The course of the stars, the recurrence of seasons, the harmony of terrestrial phenomena, the march of civilization, are all indications of a cosmic order which is not

---

[6] Maurice De Wulf, *Mediaeval Philosophy* (Cambridge: Harvard University Press, 1922), pp. 101–102.

the work of a single being — not even of man — but which proves the existence of a Supreme Ruler of all."[7] Furthermore, exceptions in the workings of nature need not cause alarm. Aquinas observes that although art operates in a purposive way, it nevertheless commits errors; the grammarian does not always write with purity of language and style, the physician does not always prescribe the proper medicine. From the fact, therefore, that there are defects or freaks in nature (they seem defects and freaks to us who do not know all the universal laws by which the Creator governs His universe), we are not justified in questioning the value of teleology. Moreover, if art did not operate in view of a specified end, errors would be impossible because its operations would be determined. As errors in art are evident indications of finality, so apparent errors and disorders in nature are anomalies which place purposive finality in greater relief.

3. The Nonteleological Conception of the Universe
a) Evolutionism

Finally we are confronted by evolutionism, which while rejecting purposive finality tries to explain cosmic order in terms of evolutionary processes. Unfortunately its advocates fail to furnish a single proof for their numerous hypotheses. Even if the world were the result of a slow evolution, that would demonstrate neither its efficient nor its final cause. A close study of the universe reveals a general plan which, as both experience and reason show, necessarily presupposes an architect. The doctrine which is in complete conformity with empirical facts is the Aristotelian doctrine of *act and potency*. Between these two extremes, lies *"the becoming." Potency* is *the undetermined;* act is *the determined.* To explain act, it is not enough to say that it follows potency, but it *is necessary to presuppose another entity which changes "potency" into "act."* Since an infinite regress is absurd, there is no other alternative but to admit a Perfect Being who reduces potency to act. Being, therefore, can be explained only

---

[7] M. De Wulf, *op. cit.*, p. 77.

through a being, since an effect can be explained only through a cause. Now if an effect manifests in itself evident traces of order, art, and intelligence, it must be attributed to an intelligent Cause which has acted in view of an end and with supreme Wisdom.

Even if the universe had followed an upward march from a lesser to a higher level of perfection, the following principle would not in any way be changed or modified: "the higher alone can explain the lower." The evolutionary hypothesis which tries to explain the higher by the lesser is essentially contradictory, for the contained can never be greater than the container, as the evolutionists themselves are forced to hold. It may be granted that the universe has, in the course of time, achieved a higher degree of perfection, but the realized perfection necessarily presupposes as its starting point another higher perfection, a God who explains both the universe and its evolution.

b) Kantian Subjectivism and Pantheism

Kant, though admitting the teleological argument, contends that it does not prove the existence of God. He saw in the principle of finality only a subjective norm for nature. The Kantian contention can be refuted simply by adhering to the self-evident empirical fact that there is an extramental world.

Kantian subjectivism finds its echo in pantheism which reduces all cosmic reality into one unique and absolute substance, and denies all transcendental value to the teleological argument. The pantheistic explanation of the universe denies the necessity of a cause distinct from and transcending the material world, and would postulate instead an immanent cause, one residing in the bosom of the universe. Thus while the existence of a living and personal God is implicitly denied, no hesitation is shown in proclaiming that everything is god. But if the teleological argument is founded in immanent or intrinsic finality (as *de facto* it is), and if the universe is composed of countless individual things manifesting specific forces wisely disposed and co-ordinated by a purposive final cause, then pantheism must necessarily be false.

Cosmic realities are distinct from, and not absorbed by, one another; each preserves its proper unity and individuality. This fact is confirmed by reason and experience. In the hope of strengthening their position many pantheists contend that cosmic teleology can be explained through impulses and activities inherent in nature. But how can these purposive impulses and activities be explained without recourse to an All-Intelligent Being?

Subjectivism as well as pantheism are purely *aprioristic* constructions and as such they are destitute of all scientific value. While it is true that no philosophical system is free from difficulties and that it contains certain irreducible and seemingly irreconcilable conclusions, nevertheless it is not true, as Kant erroneously believed, that such apparent inconsistencies destroy the value of the argument from finality. The important point in this connection is to distinguish apparent from real antinomies, evident and clear truths from vague, arbitrary guesses.

The existence of an Intelligent Cause is evident not only from the regularity and stability, from the predisposition and coordination which reigns in nature, but especially from the wonderful instincts which reign in the animal kingdom. To operate always in the same and in the best manner means to operate with an end in view; hence finality in brutes presupposes an intelligent being. Aquinas summarizes this proof in clear and precise terms: "Things lacking intelligence such as natural bodies, act for an end. This is evident from the fact that they act always, or nearly always, in the same way, and to obtain the best result. Hence it is evident that they achieve their end not by chance but by design. Now whatever lacks intelligence cannot move toward an end, unless it be directed by some being endowed with knowledge and intelligence; as the arrow is shot to its mark by the archer. Therefore some intelligent being exists by whom all natural things are directed to their end. This being we call God."[8]

---

[8] St. Thomas, *Summa Theologica*, I, q. 2, a. 3.

Dante in his *Divine Comedy* utters the same sentiment:

> Among themselves all things
> Have order; and from hence the form, which makes
> The universe resemble God. In this
> The higher creatures see the printed steps
> Of that eternal worth, which is the end
> Whither the line is drawn. All natures lean,
> In this their order, diversely, some more,
> Some less approaching to their primal source.
> Thus they to different havens are mov'd on
> Through the vast sea of being, and each one
> With instinct giv'n that bears it in its course;
> This to the lunar sphere directs the fire,
> This prompts the hearts of mortal animals,
> This the brute earth together knits, and binds.
> Nor only creatures, void of intellect,
> Are aim'd at by this bow; but even those,
> That have intelligence and love, are pierced.
> That Providence, who so well orders all,
> With her own light makes ever calm the heaven,
> In which the substance, that hath greatest speed,
> Is turned; and thither now, as to our seal
> Predestin'd, we are carried by the force
> Of that strong cord, that never looses dart,
> But at fair aim and glad.[9]

PART III

MAN'S PLACE IN THE UNIVERSE

Obviously, a rejection of purposive finality implies a negation of cosmic order, of human personality, and of God. In such a case, there would be no justification for subordinating the inorganic to the organic world, the animal kingdom to man.

---

[9] Dante Alighieri, *Divine Comedy* (tr. by H. F. Cary) (London: Dent, 1908), Canto I, v. 100–122.

Neither domestic nor civil society would have an objective and immutable end. Everything would be surrendered to the caprice of chance, that is, to a blind and irresistible impulse of physical forces. Man himself would be a purely material mechanism responding to certain biological and economic urges. To talk about inviolable human rights without admitting a soul and a creating God is to talk nonsense; we must recognize God and His moral law or else admit that might makes right and that we still live in the Hobbesian state of war of all against all. If there is no soul and no free will, it is foolish to talk of human rights and duties, or of human dignity and responsibility. Human personality acquires its intrinsic value and meaning only in a purposive conception of the universe, for in the materialistic and pantheistic scheme there is no purpose, no God, no personality, no valid moral laws, no order, no authority, no rights. Such are the inevitable consequences of the rejection of the theistic-teleological conception of the universe.

On the other hand, in Christian philosophy, man and society have a definite purpose and goal. In view of this purpose or goal, man is naturally moved to create a family and to live in society in order to satisfy his physical and spiritual needs. Man attains his perfection and his dignity by living in conformity with the moral and social order. Though the social nature of man demands the existence of a political organization, it also delimits civil powers and checks the arbitrariness of rulers. Once we grant that the human individual occupies the privileged place which belongs to him in society and in the universe, it follows that he cannot be regarded as a mere instrument or cog in the machinery of the State. In this light the moral order becomes a thing sacred and dear to life and not a caricature; it becomes an indissoluble bond between God and man, between heaven and earth, between time and eternity. The function of the State then is to help man attain his ultimate end. Hence the State is not an end in itself, but only a means to an end. Due regard must also be had to the various relations and concrete circumstances wherein man is working out his mission in life.

A proper evaluation of man must not ignore the dual element of which he is composed, i.e., body and soul. If man must be considered under a twofold aspect, material and spiritual, temporal and eternal, it follows that his material and temporal goal must be subordinate to his spiritual and eternal goal. No true analysis of human nature can overlook this important point. Therefore, though not concerned directly with the spiritual well-being of the individual, the State cannot remain indifferent to whatever belongs to man's moral and spiritual development.

On account of his sublime end man excels by far every sphere of political activity. Granting the necessity of its existence for happiness and for the common good of all, still the State has no right to absorb the individual or to hinder him from the attainment of his ultimate goal. It is this sublime end that secures to man his rightful place in society and guarantees him a proper sphere of activity independent of political will. Hence primary and fundamental rights do not spring from the State, because they are as old as humanity and are founded in the natural moral law. The State, therefore, cannot take away or modify those inalienable rights which belong to the individual as possessing a rational nature.

The ignorance of the ultimate end of man led ancients to improvise other ends for themselves, such as pastimes and pleasures. This purely materialistic view of human life is one of the tangible signs of Roman decadence. Pleasure having been made the supreme norm of conduct, everything became subservient to it, and in order to procure the maximum of pleasure, men did not hesitate to violate the rights of the weak and helpless, and even utterly to disregard the dignity of man as a person. Thus women, children, foreigners, and generally the humble classes were often reduced to slavery. This sad condition prevailed for centuries until Christianity announced to the world the true end of man, rightfully assigning to the spiritual part of man that pre-eminence which belongs to it. St. Paul makes this new doctrine clear and explicit: "There is neither Jew nor Greek: there is neither bond nor free: there is neither male nor female. For you are all one in Christ Jesus."[10] And again, "Here there is not 'Gentile and Jew,' 'circumcised and uncircumcised,' 'Barbarian and Scythian,' 'slave and freeman'; but Christ is all things and in all."[11] If these truths are denied, it will avail little to proclaim the rights of man on parchments, or to appeal to popular will and to national constitutions.

In spite of the triumphs achieved in every field of science, we have today lapsed into a pagan conception of life. Making material progress its ultimate purpose and highest aspiration, modern society has been led astray. It has confused the pleasurable and useful good, i.e., economic and material possessions, with the moral good. It is high time to proclaim the true and perennial principle that the only salvation for society and the individual is the practice of the moral good. Social and moral well-being depends absolutely on a thorough regeneration of the individual in morals and conduct. But a true moral and social reform without religion cannot be accomplished, since true religion alone with its eternal standard of right and wrong can solve the pertinent problems of life.

Since human society is created for time and the individual for eternity, it follows that the State cannot set itself up against the ultimate end of man. All social and political ends must be subservient to this primary end. Christianity alone vindicates the real worth of man, irrespective of race, sex, or fortune. It both delimits statal functions and furnishes political philosophy with the only true orientation which is in harmony with the needs of human nature. The true notion of personality, possessed by only a few sages of antiquity, has through Christian teaching become a common possession. In this light, man is no longer confounded with the citizen, nor society with the State; and the evangelical precept that we ought to obey God rather than men has been gradually accepted as the supreme rule of human conduct. This rule vindicates the dignity of man and assigns to him a rightful place in the hierarchy of beings. Man thus becomes a subject or

---

[10] Gal. 3:28, 29.
[11] Col. 3:8–11.

possessor of rights; the individual and his connatural needs become the primary justification for the exercise of political powers.

a) Slavery and Racism

As the State cannot create, neither can it abolish man's right to be treated as a person. This right is fundamental, inalienable, and inviolable. Any contract that would violate human dignity, subjecting the individual to another, is immoral, opposed to the natural law, and consequently incapable of ratification. No man can validly surrender his primary natural rights. Slavery, then, which considers man as a thing or a chattel, is repugnant to the moral law. It may be true that slavery at times does not interfere with, or hinder man's specific rights and the fulfillment of his duties, but the principle that it is wrong for a free and rational person to surrender his whole being to another in view of material interests remains unchanged. The words slavery and right are contradictory. It might be retorted that in the past, slavery was legally established. But mere legality does not constitute a true moral right. Slavery might have seemed justifiable and assumed the appearance of right because it had law and custom in its favor, but mere legality is no justification in matters which militate against human freedom and consequently against the personal dignity of man.

Today we are confronted with a political heresy which militates against personal rights and the ultimate end of man — racism. This heresy aims at subverting and destroying the unity of social order and at depriving man of his rightful place in the universe. It was ushered in by an exaggerated type of nationalism which engulfed practically all modern nations especially after World War I. Nationalism rests on the false notion or belief that one nationality is superior to another. Nationalism has its own creed, its own priesthood, its own ritual. Whole peoples have been systematically indoctrinated with the idea that every human being owes his first and last duty to his nationality, that nationality is the ideal unit of political organization as well as the actual embodiment of cultural distinction, and that in the final analysis all other human loyalties must be subordinate to loyalty to the national State, namely, to national patriotism. Nationalism is a modern substitute for religion and fully partakes of all the vehemence of elemental religious intolerance. The mania of grandeur is the outstanding feature of every nationalism, and has found its climax in the claptrap of racial myth, race purity, and race superiority.

Race prejudice has been achieved not through an appeal to reason or the higher faculties of man, but through an appeal to human passions and prejudice. Obviously, national pride often silences even man's natural instinct for truth. The majority of human beings are likely to despise their equals, since this attitude helps them to have a higher opinion of themselves. Race consciousness and race prejudices are in evidence everywhere, but especially in Nazi Germany. Race supremacy is upheld there, not only as a national but as a religious ideal as well. According to the Nazis, the German or Nordic race is superior to all other races; hence all members of this race should be united under one leadership throughout the world. This is the chosen race to which all other races must be subservient. The new Germany, therefore, must have for its object the ideal of blood consolidation. Race and blood are deified. A cosmic god, is identified with the universe. Equality of men before God is denied. None but the German may exercise citizen rights. For the realization of their blood community, war is necessary and regarded as the supreme national duty. In Germany, racism is closely associated with anti-Jewish persecution and propaganda. Arguments against the Jews are sought no longer in theology but in biology.

Racism is also gaining momentum in the United States, and though it has not as yet attained the highly developed form of Nazism, it possesses substantially the same elements. This fact is shown particularly in our attitude toward the Negro. The Negro is deprived of personal rights. He is restricted in educational, religious, and economic opportunities. Negro children attend dilapidated and overcrowded schools; Negro students are very often not tolerated even in Catholic colleges. The general tendency is to regard any colored people as inferiors and outcasts. For instance, in the Railway Brotherhood there are no Negro conductors, clerks, or freight checkers. This antagonistic attitude is also manifested against the Jews and southern European foreigners. Anti-Semitism is obviously on the increase. Moreover it is not uncommon to perceive a certain coldness and apathy in city dwellers toward country dwellers, in educated classes toward the uneducated, in the rich toward the poor.

Such prejudices and antagonisms bring about devastating divisions and rend asunder the unity of human society. Racism in one form or another is spread everywhere; it is an obvious outcome of modern paganism and materialism. In fact it is the worst kind of materialistic mockery of mankind, a philosophical absurdity, a pseudo-scientific nightmare, an insult to Christianity, and the worst kind of barbarism. It is a reeking vomit of moral degeneracy and mental atrophy. Racism is wrong, because it confuses the manifestly antisocial character of some Jews, of some Negroes, of some foreigners with the respective race or nation. This doctrine is clearly contrary to the philosophical principles we have been inculcating in this book, and contrary to the solemn teachings of Christ. It is, therefore, intrinsically immoral for a Christian to participate in anti-Semitism or racism. Christ taught not only the fatherhood of God, but also the brotherhood of men. Equality of individuals was the new principle the Church gave to mankind. In the new dispensation there is no distinction of races, and all may become members of the Church of Christ.

The doctrine of race supremacy can never be reconciled with the command of Christ to love one's neighbor as oneself. One soul is as precious to Him as another; and His voice pleads as well through the lips of His dark sons as those of His white. All are one in Christ. "So we, the many, are one body in Christ, but severally members one of another."[12] On account of the immortal soul that dwells in man, every true Christian and every de-

---

[12] Rom. 12:4.

cent person must regard all men, the colored and the white, as his brethren and fellow men. All are at least potential members of the Mystical Body of Christ. It is, of course, certain that the Cross of Christ will eventually triumph over the crooked cross; that His all-embracing love shall conquer the narrow gospel of pride and hate; and shall destroy the counterfeit religion of racism which is engulfing so many parts of the world today. In a letter of May, 1938, the Sacred Congregation condemned the following absurd dogmas of racism:

"1. The human races, by their innate and immutable character, so differ among themselves that the lowest of them differs more from the highest in the human stock than it does from the highest type of the brute creation.

"2. The vigor and blood purity of the race are to be preserved and cherished by every means possible; whatever, therefore, leads to this end is in itself honest and licit.

"3. From the blood in which the character of the race is identified flow all the qualities of man — intellectual and moral — as from their most powerful source.

"4. The principal end of education is to cultivate the character of the race and to inflame the soul with a burning love of its own race as its highest good.

"5. Religion is subject to the law of the race and must be adapted to it.

"6. The first source and highest rule of the entire juridical order is the instinct of race.

"7. Except the cosmos or the universe, nothing exists as a living being: all things, with man himself, are only various forms, through long ages appearing, of this universal living being.

"8. Individual men exist only for the "State" and on account of the "State"; whatever of rights may pertain to them are derived solely from the concession of the State."[13]

---

[13] *The Catholic Mind*, Jan. 8, 1939, pp. 507–508.

SELECT READINGS

Catholic Encyclopedia, arts. "Materialism"; "Pantheism"; "Teleology."

Cronin, M., *The Science of Ethics* (New York: Benziger, 1922), Vol. I, Ch. III.

Farrell, W., *A Companion of the Summa,* Vol. I, "The Architect of the Universe" (New York: Sheed and Ward, 1941).

Gilson, Etienne, *God and Philosophy* (New Haven: Yale Press, 1941).

Jennings, H. S., *Scientific Aspects of the Race Problem* (New York: Longmans, Green and Co., 1941).

Krzesinski, A. J., *Is Modern Culture Doomed?* (New York: The Devin-Adair Co., 1942).

La Farge, J., S.J., "Racism and Social Unity," *Catholic Mind,* Jan. 8, 1939.

Pius XII, *Unity of the Human Race.*

Ryan, J. A., "American Democracy vs. Racism and Communism" (New York: The Paulist Press), pamphlet.

Sheen, Fulton J., *The Moral Universe* (Milwaukee: The Bruce Publishing Co., 1936).

CHAPTER VIII

THE INDIVIDUAL AND THE STATE

IT IS of vital importance today to re-examine the traditional Christian teaching concerning certain fundamental rights of the individual which the State must protect and respect. The most important of these rights are embodied in the American Declaration of Independence: "We hold these truths to be self-evident: That all men are created equal; that they are endowed by their Creator with certain inalienable rights; that among these are life, liberty, and the pursuit of happiness. That to secure these rights, governments are instituted among men, deriving their just powers from the consent of the governed; that, whenever any form of government becomes destructive of these ends, it is the right of the people to alter or to abolish it, and to institute a new government, laying its foundation on such principles, and organizing its powers in such form, as to them shall seem most likely to effect their safety and happiness."

The right to life, to ownership of property, to a livelihood, to personal liberty, the right to choose a profession, to form labor unions, have been and are either ruthlessly violated or completely disregarded in practically all the modern states. Generally speaking, in totalitarian states "no rights exist save as grants or permissions; no sanctions of freedom rooted in a natural law anterior to and beyond the reach of State authority have any recognition whatever."[1] The State has gradually come to be regarded as a supreme source of all rights and as an ultimate end of all public activities.

The totalitarian State grants or limits at will the rights of

---

[1] Ross, Hoffman, *The Will to Freedom* (London: Sheed and Ward, 1935), p. 60.

men, even the right to life. The life of every citizen is at the mercy of the political clique or the State. "In Russia the bourgeois class has been suppressed; in Italy dissenting parties; in Germany even other races. . . . Political passion has led to the creation of special tribunals, concentration camps, deportation centres; the prisons are filled to overflowing; exiles may be numbered in hundreds of thousands, deportees cannot be counted, those arbitrarily killed are without number, and so are those of whose fate nothing is known. Nor are these exceptional measures confined to the moment of the revolution. The totalitarian State does not admit the existence of opponents. For eighteen years the Soviets have continued to shoot them, to send them to forced labor camps, or to deport them to Siberia."[2] And why not, if there is no real moral law? What can be expected when the State is regarded as an absolute will, a sort of divinity, and this in disregard and even in violation of natural rights?

Moreover, it is necessary to deal here with the right of private ownership, because, on the one hand, communists want the State to take over in their entirety the ownership and management of all businesses, and on the other, Fascists and Nazis, while not abolishing private capitalism, want to put private business under the absolute control and supervision of the State. Liberalism, too, allows those in power to do as they please, even when they wish to combine among themselves, but it leaves the workingmen, who are the underdogs, helpless and unable to combine in any way. Briefly, all systems that divorce politics from ethics are un-Christian, and their philosophies can lead only to loss of personal freedom, to chaos, and to servitude.

In this chapter we propose to show that the above-named rights belong to the individual, not merely in virtue of his citizenship, but in virtue of his status as a human being endowed with reason and free will; that they are possessed in virtue of the natural law, and are antecedent to any organization of men into civil society. Since the State exists for the sake of the members, it

---

[2] Luigi Sturzo "The Totalitarian State," *Dublin Review*, July, 1935.

clearly follows that it cannot take away or modify those inalienable rights. In consequence of this fact, the individual has a right to expect from the State protection and security.

PART I

THE RIGHT TO LIFE

The first and foremost inalienable right is that of life and physical existence. This primary right flows from the concept of person and the nature of man. No one, individual or State, may unjustly limit or take away this right to bodily integrity. The State is bound to guarantee life and physical integrity to its subjects, because without personal safety, order and peace, social and private well-being would be impossible.

1. SELF-DEFENSE

It is important to distinguish between the unjust and just taking of another's life. It is ordinarily not within the rights of any individual to take another's life. The right of defense against and the punishment for the violation of any rights rests with civil authority. In these matters no individual has authority over another; and no individual has a moral right to proceed personally against another even in defense of his own rights unless circumstances make it impossible to call in the aid of civil authorities. If in the latter case the defense can be accomplished only by taking the life of the unjust aggressor, one is permitted to do so. The homicide here is not the direct end aimed at, but the indirect though inevitable result of the just act of self-defense. The various conditions requisite for lawful killing in self-defense are: The killing must be done in the actual unjust aggression, and it must be necessary for the successful defense of self. No greater violence may be used in self-defense than is needed to avert the aggression. In other words, this right must always be exercised with the *moderation of a blameless defense.* The right of self-defense extends in justice not only to the protection of life but also to that of freedom, property, and the defense of others. Many moralists believe that a woman being criminally attacked may kill the aggressor if such is necessary to save herself from sexual violation. The right to life is founded and rests upon the theistico-teleological conception of the universe.

However, one may not kill another in defense of reputation or honor. Even the so-called "unwritten law" on the violation of marital fidelity is not an adequate reason for killing the guilty parties. In such cases the killing follows the act of violation, and is, therefore, not an act against aggression, but only too often one of revenge. Moreover, it is not a proportionate means of repairing the injured right. In the matter of honor or good name, the use of such means of retribution are strictly forbidden by the moral law. This matter will be discussed under dueling.

Every man has a purposive end to attain, an end which, spring-ing from a higher order, is independent both of individual and so-cial will. Every human being or person, then, has the right to attain in a befitting and rational manner his proper goal. Existence free from all unjust aggression and restraint is neces-sary to attain this end. Hence, whoever unjustly deprives another of his life violates the universal order as well as the moral laws regulating the existence and well-being of civil society. The right to existence is primary and the source of all other natural rights. Hence, every man has the inalienable right to be treated as a human being, or as a person in the true philosophical sense.

2. SUICIDE

Suicide is the direct killing of one's self on one's own authority. The suicide puts an end to the possibility of further service to society and of his own moral growth and perfection. Such an action is a deliberate challenge to the moral law, saying, as it were, to the latter: "So far and no further." For anyone who acknowledges the general obligation of the moral law, there can be no doubt as to the immorality of suicide. Its overt rejection of moral obligation and ethical values condemns it utterly. For the man who sees in the natural moral law an expression of the divine mind, suicide is a supreme act of rebellion against God Himself, since it is God who places the allotted span to each in-dividual life. For a person who denies the moral law, there is no telling argument against suicide, just as there can be no real ideal of true moral right or wrong of any kind. If the absolute obligatory force of the moral law is denied, not only suicide but any other action is justifiable.

In this connection it is well to note that in antiquity the pagans themselves, though having no true notion of the true end of man, of the universe, or of God, detested suicide. It was customary among the Greeks to cut off the hands of the suicide and to deny him the honors of public burial. Cicero states that Pythagoras expressly condemned suicide. In trials and adversities man ought to exercise the virtue of fortitude. If it is human to feel pain and sorrow, it is characteristic of a morally strong man to bear it with courage. If guilty of some transgression, a man of character will courageously expiate his guilt; if innocent, he will wait until his innocence is vindicated. To appeal to certain exceptional cases in justification of suicide is futile. True hero-ism should never be identified with moral cowardice. If in time of war a captain prefers to blow up his ship and to sacrifice his life doing it rather than to surrender to the enemy, no one will consider him guilty of suicide. Though his death is objectively contrary to the moral law, he has a moral end in view, that of the good of his country, or the good of all, and his act may be subjectively meritorious.

3. DUELING

Now if suicide is intrinsically unjust and immoral, the same is true of dueling. The direct end of a duel is, in plain words, bravado; the vindication of one's supposed honor or reputation is sought only indirectly — how can the crippling or killing of an adversary restore honor or reputation? If in order to avoid the imputation of cowardice one could be justified in endangering his and another's life, the offended person might just as well throw himself under a train or jump from a high precipice. The absurdity of such a remedy is plain. If the person whose rights to his good name have been violated is a man of character and conscious of human dignity, he will not challenge his adversary to a duel. Nothing can justify a duel; and nothing is more cowardly than to do through fear of being branded a coward an act contrary to conscience and reason, to say nothing of the positive law of God. The decisive factor in a duel is not right but strength, alertness, skill, etc., all means incapable of repairing the injury.

Dueling must be regarded as a violent and immoral struggle, which militates against the idea of a well-ordered and peaceful society and implies a manifest violation of social order. The State has a sacred right and duty to forbid such an immoral practice and to inflict severe penalties on every attempt against the life and bodily integrity of its citizens. An honest life is the best vindication of one's honor and good name. The Gospel precept that the best revenge is pardon is here very appropriate. One who instead of accepting the challenge to a duel pardons his adversary is a man of character, one deserving of esteem and praise. This does not mean that one must bear every insult or injury. A person whose rights have been violated has many moral and legal means for vindicating his honor.

Allied to the question of homicide is that of the mutilation of bodily organs. Here the same practical principle obtains as above. There can be no question of direct mutilation of any part of the body for its own sake. To be permissible mutilation must have a proportionately grave reason, one which is in full harmony with the moral law; in other words, a good effect of at least equal importance must result from the act of mutilation. Such would obtain, for instance, when amputation of a leg or arm is necessary to preserve life. In our day a new question has arisen in the practice of sterilizing criminal or mentally weak, where mutilation of the individual is advocated for the public good. This problem will be dealt with in the Appendix.

4. LYNCHING

Mob lynching of suspected or convicted criminals is always an unlawful act of homicide. Lynching is an act of open revolt against constituted authority, and all the more reprehensible be-cause in the heat of human passions and frenzy innocent people can and often have been killed. A mob action receives its im-petus, or at least its encouragement from the members of the mob, so to that extent the mere presence at a lynching renders one co-guilty of the act. It is a sacred duty of the State to enact and rigidly to enforce such antilynching laws as are necessary to extirpate this criminal and murderous practice.

5. EUTHANASIA

Another crying evil of the day is euthanasia or mercy killing. By this is meant the slaying of helpless invalids and of people in incurable pain. It is called mercy killing because it is prompted by the motive of relieving a person from suffering. Legalized mercy killing is advocated by many sentimentalists in practically every walk of life, and even by some ministers of religion. They claim that all objections to euthanasia are based upon the assumption that it is man's business to live; but that this is not so they allege is shown by the honor and respect paid to men who have preferred death to life. They also claim that the one who desires to die that his loved ones may be relieved of the misery caused by his own suffering should not be denied that privilege; that after all one's life is his own; that no one can determine for another what his duty is. The general conclusion of these sentimentalists is: Why should we by law prevent one from doing what we regard as an heroic deed?

This unnatural practice has been legalized in some countries. The present German government is said to be employing it to get rid of thousands of incurables. Bishop Von Galen of Munster in a sermon preached on August 3, 1941, testifies to this: "And see how the fifth commandment is ignored. 'Thou shalt not kill.' We see it violated under the very eyes of the authorities whose

duty it is to enforce respect for law and life, when they allow
the deliberate killing of innocent human beings, as well as the
sick, solely because they are unproductive, because they can no
longer contribute to the wealth of the world." Bills to permit
persons suffering from a painful incurable disease to apply for
merciful deaths are pending even in some of our states. Does
not this show that the world is forgetting the natural law, and
that sentimentalism is overcoming calm judgment?

Frankly, euthanasia or mercy killing is only a new and a very
polite term for wholesale murder or plain suicide. If legalized, it
will be but legal murder. Mercy killing is contrary to the natural
law because it is against human nature and, consequently,
against the dictates of reason. The strongest instinct in man is
the preservation of life. "The sole rational and general basis of
the duty to respect human life — the only principle that is ap-
plicable in all cases and suffices in each — is the *sovereign
dominion of God over man* or, to put it in another way, the
creaturely character of man, coupled however with the principle
of the fundamental equality of all human beings."[3] Therefore,
one who believes in God cannot question the ethical implications of mercy killing. For a Christian this question is not open
to debate, and no sane person can condone it. No private individual, not even the State, has the power of life and death over
their fellow man, unless the latter is an unjust aggressor, and
then only as last resort. Furthermore, no man can dispose of
his life as he wills. Life comes from God, the Author and
Supreme Dispenser of Life.

Moreover, if mercy killing were legalized, all kinds of abuses
would follow. If doctors were given power to kill patients whom
they cannot cure or whose conditions they cannot alleviate, the
doors would be opened to every kind of quackery. Every time
the doctor made a serious mistake, he could immediately cover it
up with homicide. It should be remembered that the duty of
doctors is to keep people alive, not to kill them. We all deplore

---

[3] J. Leclercq-Hanley, *Marriage and the Family* (New York: F. Pustet, 1942),
p. 44.

suffering; but the law of suffering is universal as far as the human race is concerned. It is natural to avoid suffering, but not to avoid it unlawfully.

6. CAPITAL PUNISHMENT

At the present time many people are opposed to the death penalty for any crime. They argue that life imprisonment suffices to prevent repetition of a crime. Others argue for capital punishment from the ease with which paroles are secured and escapes effected today. It is also a notorious fact that the most desperate class of criminals consists of discharged convicts. When imprisonment is not a sufficient guarantee for the safety of society, it must be admitted that civil authority possesses the right of putting men to death.

The traditional teaching is embodied in the following passages of Aquinas: "Every part is directed to the whole, as the imperfect to the perfect, wherefore every part is naturally for the sake of the whole. For this reason . . . if the health of the body demands the excision of a member through its being decayed or infectious to the other members, it will be both praiseworthy and advantageous to have it cut away. Now every individual person is compared to the whole community, as a part to the whole. Therefore, if a man be dangerous and infectious to the community because of some sin, it is praiseworthy and advantageous that he be killed in order to safeguard the common good.[4] It is lawful to execute an evildoer in so far as it is for the welfare of the whole community. Since the care of the common good is entrusted to persons of public authority, they alone, and not private individuals, have the right to put evildoers to death."[5] In conclusion we wish to state that civil authority must restrict the death penalty to extreme cases and make use of it only as a last resort.

---

[4] St. Thomas, *Summa Theologica*, II–II^{ae}, q. 64, a. 2.
[5] *Ibid.*, II–II^{ae}, q. 64, a. 3.

PART II

THE RIGHT TO PRIVATE PROPERTY

The individual not only has a right to life but also a right to the means needed to sustain life. This implies man's right to private ownership. The communists deny such a right and condemn all private property as unjust. The State, according to them, should own all wealth, direct all labor, and compel an equal (as distinct from equitable) distribution of all produce. However, as will be shown, private ownership is not only proper to but necessary for man and society. Just in itself, private ownership is a requisite for social order and justice.

1. THE NATURE OF OWNERSHIP

Here we are concerned with property or dominion over material objects, not with jurisdiction or dominion over persons. The term property in general implies an intimate and special connection of one thing with another; but in a special and juridical sense it implies a conjunction or bond between a thing and a person. For this reason ownership, considered concretely and in its fullest extent, comprises two elements: (1) the right to retain, use, and dispose of an object at will, and (2) the right to exclude others from the possession and use of the same object. We may then define ownership as *the exclusive right to the possession, use, or disposal of a material thing.* The right to own applies to one who has an exclusive right to the disposal of a thing; the right to use refers to one who has the temporary use or enjoyment of the advantages of property belonging to another. Ownership is private or public according as the property belongs to the individual or to the community. Private ownership does not extend to those things which are necessary to all and of which the supply is sufficient for all, like air, the heat and light of the sun, etc.

Ownership is the concrete expression of an instinct imbued by biological law and most necessary for human life. This acquisitive instinct is so deeply rooted and so manifest as to demand acknowledgment. Even the animal kingdom recognizes a mine and thine, not only as to individuals, e.g., young of a family, but also as to things, e.g., the bird who jealously guards her nest, or the dog who hides his bones. The acquisitive instinct is basically and primarily a native tendency, even though it owes much of its strength, development, and direction to custom and precept.

2. The Congruity of Ownership

It may be asked whether ownership is natural to man. "Everything created," St. Thomas replies, "can be considered either in regard to its nature or being or to its use. As to its nature it is not subject to human but solely to divine power; but the use of external things has been granted by God to men for their benefit in accordance with right exercise of reason and will; for the imperfect is always for the sake of the perfect. It is by this argument that the philosopher proves (*Pol.* I) that the possession of external things is natural to man."[6] Let us develop this argument.

Ownership is natural to man because it is founded upon his twofold nature of body and soul. Being material and spiritual, man needs external things both to live and to attain his ultimate goal. Hence, the innate right to external ownership is logically connected with the right man has to life and to the realization of his end. From the right man has to self-preservation follows the right and duty to the reasonable and necessary means for the attainment of his end. It would be absurd to impose a duty and bestow a right on man, and at the same time to deny him the necessary means for the fulfillment of the former and the exercise of the latter. But the physical life of man cannot be preserved without the possession and assimilation of external substances. Hence, private ownership is the natural and necessary corollary of the right of self-preservation.

---

[6] St. Thomas, *Summa Theologica*, II–II^{ae}, q. 66, a. 1.

Moreover, external ownership is a necessary condition for the realization of man's ethical end, just as physical life is an indispensable condition of man's moral life. As a matter of fact, man in his free tendency toward the good must be supported and guided by intellectual knowledge. But human intellect according to natural law cannot rise to the contemplation of a suprasensible world without the aid of the senses; nor can the senses function without the aid of sense organs. It is apparent, then, that the development of man's intellectual and moral life is rooted in and depends on his physical development. And since physical life and development demand material aids, it is clear that the natural right to external possessions is closely connected with the moral nature of man.

The right of private ownership is natural to man not only because of his composite nature, but also because of the order established by the Creator. Now the cosmic order is regulated by a twofold law, hierarchical and teleological. On the one hand, hierarchical law requires the less perfect to be subordinated to the more perfect, for instance, the mineral to the vegetal, the vegetal to the animal, and finally everything to man, the king of creation. On the other hand, teleological law requires that a rational being capable of self-determination and of acting for an end should bear toward irrational beings the relation of the end to the means. Thus, just as an end has a natural pre-eminence over the means, so intellectual faculties have a natural pre-eminence over material things. The right, therefore, to external property emanates from the natural relations man has to the universe.

The above consideration enables us to see why the process of appropriation and assimilation, which takes place also in plants and animals, becomes the manifestation of a right only in man. The obvious reason is this. The impulse to appropriate and assimilate external substances becomes a genuine right only in rational creatures who regard themselves as ends and material things as means. If that tendency were not directed by the intellect and moved by the will, it would remain simply a natural impulse or a blind instinct; it would not be a rational power such as is required by every right.

THE NECESSITY OF PRIVATE PROPERTY

The right of ownership is not only allowable but necessary. Its necessity is founded not in the nature of the thing possessed but in the actual needs of the individual and the welfare of society. St. Thomas, following Aristotle, advances the following arguments: "Private ownership is necessary to human life for three reasons. First, every one is more careful to look after what belongs to himself alone than after what is common to all or to many; every shirker of labor leaves to others what is a matter of joint concern, as happens where there are too many servants. Second, human affairs are more orderly handled, if each individual has the duty of managing something, whereas there would be nothing but confusion if everyone without distinction had the disposal of anything he chose to take. Third, by means of private ownership society tends to be kept at peace, every member being content with his own possession, whereas we see that frequent strifes occur among those holding things in common and in undivided ownership."[7] Our task will be to develop these three arguments in logical order.

1. PRIVATE PROPERTY NECESSARY TO MAN
a) *For Self-Development*

Deprived of property rights, man would be forced like the animal to live upon the uncultivated fruits of earth. Work itself would be inconceivable under such conditions. It is only because of the right of private ownership that man will bestir himself,

---

[7] St. Thomas, *Summa Theologica*, II–II^{ae}, q. 66, a. 2.

work and till the earth, accumulate and save the fruits of his
efforts and labor. "Private ownership is necessary for self-development, which is but another aspect of the law of self-preservation,
and constitutes one of the primary duties we owe to God; and,
except in certain contingencies where the duty of self-sacrifice
supervenes, the preservation and development of one's life is an
inherent right of the individual which the State may not infringe. But the development of man's life is governed by a certain internal necessity which no external authority can altogether control or direct. There are lines of thought and action
along which the individual must necessarily work, if he is to
get the best out of his life; nor are any two individuals ever
equal in their natural abilities and capacities. Any external coercion, therefore, which takes a man off his own lines is an in-
fringement of personal liberty, which only exceptional circumstances or the very existence of society can justify."[8]

b) For Human Freedom

Man is the natural proprietor both of his faculties and of
their activities, as well as of the legitimate effects resulting therefrom; for, according to ontological law the effect must be attributed to its respective cause. But to possess property and to
work in order that it may serve as means to an end for man, is
the effect of man's legitimate liberty exercised upon external
things. Consequently, the principle from which proceeds the
duty of respecting the legitimate liberty of others is also the
principle from which proceeds the duty of respecting what man
with free and legitimate efforts has conjoined to his person.
Such a principle is but the right of juridical independence,
which, while excluding the power of one over another, simultaneously imposes the duty of respecting other people's liberty
both in itself and in its legitimate effects. Remove this juridical
and natural duty of respecting what another with occupation

---

[8] Fr. Cuthbert, O.S.F.C., *Catholic Ideals in Social Life* (New York: Benziger,
1910), p. 80.

and labor has honestly acquired for himself, and you will be forced to profess more or less explicitly the absurd conceit: *To you the labor, and to me the fruits of your labor.*

This intimate relation between the respect due to man's liberty and the respect due to ownership is so evident as to be called a truth of common sense. Proprietorship in the genuine acceptation of the term denotes the freedom of possessing and disposing of things. Freedom implies ownership of self, of one's faculties, their functions and the effects of those functions. Therefore, a denial of private ownership is equivalent to a denial of human freedom.

Leo XIII writes: "It is surely undeniable that, when a man engages in remunerative labor the very reason and motive of his work is to obtain property, and to hold it as his own private possession. If one man hires out to another his strength or his industry, he does this for the purpose of receiving in return what is necessary for food and living; he thereby expressly proposes to acquire a full and real right, not only to the remuneration, but also to the disposal of that remuneration as he pleases. Thus, if he lives sparingly, saves money, and invests his savings, for greater security, in land, the land in such a case is only his wages in another form; and, consequently, the workingman's little estate thus purchased should be as completely at his own disposal as the wages he receives for his labor. But it is precisely in this power of disposal that ownership consists, whether the property be land or movable goods. The Socialists, therefore, in endeavoring to transfer the possessions of individuals to the community, strike at the interests of every wage earner, for they deprive him of the liberty of disposing of his wages, and thus of all hope and possibility of increasing his stock and of bettering his condition in life."[9]

2. PRIVATE PROPERTY NECESSARY TO SOCIETY

Man more than any other living being requires family life. But without private ownership, the sacred fire which keeps the

---

[9] Leo XIII, *Rerum Novarum* (The Condition of the Workingmen).

family spirit alive would soon die out; affection for the offspring would disappear; children would no longer see their parents as benefactors; the home itself would fall into ruin. There would be no comfort, help, or hope for the aged; no pleasant memories or family traditions for the young. Without private ownership domestic society would be entirely absorbed by the State; the sacred bonds of marriage would be impaired, since the doctrine of community of goods leads inevitably to the doctrine of community of women.

The abolition of all private property militates against justice, because it would deprive all citizens of the goods acquired by the free exercise of their activities, which in consequence are their own. It would, obviously, be an act of injustice to hand over to others without compensation lands and other external goods which one has acquired for himself. Hence a new distribution of these goods, according to the socialistic scheme, could not be effected without open theft and flagrant violation of justice. "Socialists," says Leo XIII, "working on the poor man's envy of the rich, endeavor to destroy private property, and maintain that individual possessions should become the common property of all, to be administered by the State or by municipal bodies. They hold that, by thus transferring property from private persons to the community, the present evil state of things will be set to rights, because each citizen will then have his equal share of whatever there is to enjoy. But their proposals are so clearly futile for all practical purposes, that if they were carried out the workingman himself would be among the first to suffer. Moreover they are emphatically unjust, because they would rob the lawful possessor, bring the State into a sphere that is not its own, and cause complete confusion in the community."[10]

In conclusion we may add that the perfect temporal equality for all men sought by the communists is both unnatural and socially impossible. It is unnatural because although men are equal in the abstract, namely, in so far as they are endowed with

---

[10] Leo XIII, *op. cit.*

the same human nature and have the same origin and the same end, yet in the concrete they are unequal, just as are the concrete natures from which they spring. Therefore, before the differences of classes can be abolished, it must be ascertained whether men's abilities in the concrete are equal or unequal; if they are unequal (and experience shows that men are endowed with various capacities and abilities), then the inequality of men's condition arises from the order of nature itself.

Communist equality, strictly speaking, is socially impossible. For society is constituted after the hierarchical form of an organic body, in which certain parts are superior and others subordinate. If all men were equal in the concrete, as communism maintains, the necessary gradation and subordination in society would be impossible. The following statement made by an observer and sympathizer of the Soviets will make our point clear: "The Soviet Union is fond of calling itself a 'classless' society. Classless society, my eye! The new aristocracy has a good government job, a high-priced American car to ride in, an apartment with several times the fifteen square meters per person the law allows and more luxury than they would dare show the masses of the people; a *datcha* or place in the country, and probably a pretty mistress. No classes? Watch a ragged, shrinking baggage carrier trotting along at the heels of an important Soviet official on a station platform!"[11]

Individual ownership is not only permitted but even intended by nature; it is necessary for mutual independence, for general tranquillity, for personal and social prosperity. A denial of this right would undermine domestic stability and destroy human personality. Private property has both a *personal* and *social* aspect.

In the last two arguments St. Thomas requires individual ownership as an indispensable element for social order, peace, and contentment. This implies that abolition of private ownership necessarily results in confusion and social disorders, culminating in political tyranny and widespread suffering. The ob-

---

[11] H. A. Franck, "Vagabond in Sovietland," *America*, Mar. 16, 1935.

servations regarding his own times and the preceding ones, upon which the argument rests, now have another seven centuries of further and decisive confirmation. The abolition of ownership is invariably followed by social unrest and upheavals, witness the French Revolution and more recently the Russian Revolt. Of course, socialists and communists will regard such uprisings as a struggle for freedom, because order for them is disorder for the world. The world, however, has always recognized and will always recognize in the establishment of the rights of property the realization of a profound and infrangible law of nature, and an indispensable condition for the life and progress of human society.

3. The Social Nature of Ownership

According to liberalism, man can be the owner and master of material goods in such a way as to disregard in their use every other end except his own advantage and pleasure. He may destroy or abuse such possessions regardless of the needs and interests of others. This theory ignores the social aspect of ownership and militates against the natural law. The right of property is not an absolute right; it is limited by moral law and by social welfare. Man is a social being and must behave as such. Hence, he has two rights in regard to the possession of material things. The one consists in the power to procure and dispose of them, and in this respect man is permitted to possess things as his own. The other concerns their use, and in this respect man ought not to hold his possession privately but as common property, so that he will share them freely with others in their need. Pius XI emphatically points out that ownership of riches should be not only for one's own advantage, but also for the common good. "We reassert in the first place the fundamental principle laid down by Leo XIII, that the right to property must be distinguished from its use. . . . This follows from the twofold character of ownership, which we have termed individual and social, that men must take into account in this matter not only their own advantage but also the common good. To define in detail these duties, when the need occurs and when the natural law does not do so, is the function of the government."[12]

The sharing of possessions with the needy is not a matter of choice but an obligation of the natural law. By natural law earthly possessions are intended to satisfy the needs of all men, and private ownership cannot go counter to it. "The institutions of human laws cannot digress from the natural or divine law. According to the natural order established by Providence, earthly goods are ordained to the end that out of them, the needs of men may be relieved. . . . Therefore the things that some men have in superabundance are claimed by the natural law for the support of the poor. . . . Secretly to take for use the property of another in a case of extreme need cannot properly be called theft, since what one takes for the support of his life becomes his through such necessity."[13]

Riches are not identical with the end of man, but subservient to the main purpose of the *good life*. They are withal an instrumental good, and that only in so far as they minister to man's life. To look upon riches as the ultimate goal of human life is to pervert the natural status of things.

Leo XIII has written wisely on the right use of riches: "Whoever has received from the Divine bounty a large share of blessings, whether they be external or corporal, or gifts of the mind, has received them for the purpose of using them for perfecting his own nature, and at the same time, that he may employ them, as the minister of God's Providence, for the benefit of others. . . . True, no one is commanded to distribute to others that which is required for his own necessities and those of his household; nor even to give away what is reasonably required to keep up becomingly his condition in life; for no one ought to live *unbecomingly*. But when necessity has been supplied, and one's position fairly considered, it is a duty to give to the indigent out of that which is over. 'That which remaineth, give alms.' It is a duty, not of justice (except in extreme cases), but Christian

---

[12] Pius XI, *Quadragesimo Anno* (The Reconstruction of the Social Order).
[13] St. Thomas, *Summa Theologica*, II–II^{ae}, q. 66, a. 7.

Charity — a duty which is not enforced by human law. But the laws and judgment of men must give place to the laws and judgment of Christ, the true God; who in many ways urges on his followers the practice of almsgiving — 'It is more blessed to give than to receive'; and who will count a kindness done or refused to the poor as done or refused to Himself."[14]

PART IV

THE STATE AND OWNERSHIP

1. STATE AND POVERTY

The State not only has the negative duty of prohibiting what ever may be detrimental to the life or bodily well-being of its citizens, but also the positive duty of rendering its services to the community according to the needs and social conditions of times and places. For this reason the State is obliged to secure and maintain an adequate and effective protection of the life and health of the workingman. This duty is very urgent because the laborer is too often unable to help himself because of circumstances entirely beyond his control. We must, however, guard against falling into paternalism, the other extreme. In the diagnosis as well as in the cure of a disease, it is necessary to follow the right method since either excess or lack might prove detrimental. In the enactment of laws regarding public and private welfare, the State must never lose sight of the natural and acquired rights of the individual. With this end in view and within its proper limits, a State faithful to its high mission will effect a social program more in harmony with the present needs and altered conditions of social and economic life. Only in this manner can the right to one's own existence and attainment of one's own end be strengthened and integrated in all its amplitude.

---

[14] Leo XIII, *op. cit.*

The State is bound in a special manner to protect the needy and the weak against the greed, selfishness, and arrogance of the privileged. "Civil power," wrote Leo XIII, "is more than a mere guardian of law and order. While it is true that a just freedom of action should be left to individuals and families, it must be remembered that this principle is valid only as long as the common good is secured and there is no injustice. . . . It is in the power of a ruler to benefit every order of the State . . . and in a particular way the *interests of the poor;* and this by virtue of its office, and without being exposed to any suspicion of undue interference. Let it not be feared that solicitude of this kind will injure any interest; on the contrary, it will be to the advantage of all, for it cannot but be for the good of the commonwealth to rescue from misery those on whom it so largely depends."[15] And to continue "Rights must be religiously respected wherever they are found; and it is the duty of the public authority to prevent and punish injury, and to protect each one in the possession of his own. Still, when there is question of protecting the rights of individuals, the poor and helpless have a claim to special consideration. For the richer class have many ways of shielding themselves, and stand less in need of help from the State, whereas the mass of the poor have no resources of their own to fall back upon and must chiefly depend upon the assistance of the State. For this reason wage earners, since they mostly belong to that class, should be especially cared for and protected by the government."[16]

By his right to existence, man is entitled to such physical nourishment as is necessary to lead a life on a normal human level. Obviously, the right to one's existence would be frustrated if a human being could not provide what is absolutely necessary for a decent human existence. The duty to relieve those who are in dire need and incapable of helping themselves is incumbent first on the family, parents, and immediate relatives, then, if these are incapable of assisting, on the municipality, and

---

[15] Leo XIII, *op. cit.*
[16] *Ibid.*

finally on the State. The solicitude of the State for the needy blends with the work of Christian charity which the Church has preached for centuries. Although inspired by diverse motives, the cooperative work of Church and State finds its justification in the right that the individual has to existence, and in the evangelical precept which commands us to love one another as brethren of the same heavenly Father. Both societies have the same end in view, with this difference, that the love of neighbor goes beyond the limits required by justice; it does not wait for, but knows even how to anticipate the need. Thus the duty of justice is completed by the duty of Christian charity. The State then is juridically bound to provide the means of subsistence to him who is in want and cannot provide for himself.

But the State must not invade the sphere reserved to the Church in this matter. While the latter encompasses all the duties which are imposed by the precept to love our neighbor as ourselves, the State has a more restricted field of action which is limited by juridical duties. It is well to note that State intervention should not be employed except as an extreme resource, e.g., in times of public calamities. This does not weaken in any way the general principle that the State must provide an opportunity for all who are willing to earn this sustenance without having recourse to public aid. The individual who can help himself is bound to earn the necessities of life, but where work cannot be had because of economic conditions, maladjustments, or mislegislation, then the State must take care of its needy and provide for their necessities.

2. THE DIGNITY OF LABOR

In pagan antiquity, work, especially manual labor, was despised as unworthy of a free citizen and only fit for slaves and menials. Christianity has a loftier conception. "As regards bodily labor," says Leo XIII, "even had man never fallen from the state of innocence, he would not have been wholly unoccupied; but that which would then have been his free choice, his delight, became afterward compulsory, and the painful expiation of his sin."[17] That manual labor is honorable was shown us, above all, by the divine example of Christ Himself. Unfortunately modern industrialism has degraded labor to the subhuman level of a commodity, subject in value to a mechanical law of supply and demand, and has exploited it in an inhuman and barbarous system. Pius XI denouncing the abuses of industrialism wrote: "Bodily labor, which was decreed by Providence for the good of man's body and soul has everywhere been changed into an instrument of strange perversion; for dead matter leaves the factory ennobled and transformed, while men are there corrupted and degraded."[18] Christian tradition has always defended the idea that human labor has a *personal* value which raises it above the level of lifeless things and forbids the fixing of its price according to a heartless law of supply and demand.

We may now inquire whether man has a positive or a natural right to work. From the right that man has to existence it follows that he has the right and duty to exercise his bodily and spiritual faculties necessary for the proper functioning of life. Every human being has the right to utilize his powers and abilities as he pleases, provided he respects and does not interfere with the rights of others. The said right is based on the duty that one has to work, that is, to use his native and acquired abilities in order to gain a livelihood. To live is to work, or as Pius XI says "Man is born to labor as the bird is to fly." There is no such a thing as a right to idleness; St. Thomas gives four reasons why all men must work. First, man must obtain the means of livelihood; work is the means intended by nature itself to accomplish this. Second, work helps man to avoid the evils that accompany idleness. Labor has a moral value in that it keeps man out of mischief and arms him against the external enemies of his soul. Third, work exercises a strong check on the evil tendencies in fallen human nature which run counter to man's reason and which only too quickly assert themselves when man is idle. Work is the best means of subjecting the lower part

[17] *Ibid.*
[18] Pius XI, *op. cit.*

of man's nature, not at all evil in itself, to the control of reason: work is, in other words, the gymnastics of virtuc. Finally human labor has a social purpose to fulfill. It contributes to the welfare of the community in which man lives. St. Paul in his letter to the Ephesians pointedly remarks: "but rather let him labor, working with his hands the thing which is good, that he may have something to give to him that suffereth need."[19]

No one can deny him the right to work, nor interfere with its exercise provided he makes use of lawful and proper means. One is not justified in making use of means which belong to another, for in so doing he would exceed his proper sphere of action, violate the rights of others, and sin against distributive justice. For instance, from the principle that the rich ought to give of their superfluities to the poor and indigent, it does not follow that the latter have the right to coerce the former to do so in this way rather than in another. The workingman cannot legally use means that are not his, unless first an agreement is made with the owner. In the absence of an agreement, or in case the agreement is vitiated, the contract is null and void. While man has the duty and right to work, this right must be understood in a negative sense. It may be exercised only within the legal sphere of action and no one may hinder a man from getting work or deprive him of the work necessary for a decent human existence.

The right to work further implies that in times of public calamities, of economic crises, the State has a duty to provide opportunities for work. When the State is faced with the alternative of relieving the needy either directly by dole and charity, or by work, the latter course should be pursued. Such public help or relief, however, should not be considered as a specific and permanent right of the workingman, but only as a provisional measure in certain circumstances demanded for the preservation of the social order itself. Such a line of action cannot be interpreted as favoring anarchic or socialistic programs; it is a prudent provision of the State for safeguarding its own exist-

[19] Eph. 4:28.

ence. However the State must not supplant but merely aid and stimulate individual initiative. In normal times the individual worker has no right to demand to be given work by the State as socialists and communists claim. Of course, in their scheme of things the State gobbles up everything, not only industries and utilities but even the homes and the individual, and so there could be no alternative.

The right to work according to the socialists means that the State has at all times the duty to give employment to every man. This is false for the result of such an interpretation of the right to work would not be the actualization of a natural right but of a new social order in harmony with communistic principles and aspirations. The right to work in the socialist sense leads logically to anarchy, revolution, and ruin of the social order.

3. THE FACTORS THAT DETERMINE A JUST WAGE

In this connection it will be well to sum up the teaching of Leo XIII and Pius XI. According to Pius XI, (a) it is untrue to say that all products and profits except those required to replace invested capital belong to the workers. They belong also to the partnership of brain, spirit of enterprise, and management. (b) It is wrong to maintain that all the returns belong to capital, and that the workingman is entitled "to the barest minimum necessary to conserve and restore his strength, and to ensure the continuation of his class." (c) One class may not exclude the other from the advantages of wealth and property. (d) Before deciding whether wages are fair, many things should be taken into consideration, especially the following three factors. (1) The earnings of the workingman must be sufficient to support himself and his family. (2) The condition of the employer's business. (3) What is imperative for the common good.

The earnings of the workingman "must be sufficient for the support of himself and of his family." Fathers of families must receive a wage sufficient to meet adequately normal domestic needs. "Reforms should be introduced without delay which will guarantee such a wage to every adult workingman." "Ample sufficiency should be supplied to the workers." "Such economic and social methods should be adopted as will enable every head of a family to earn (as a minimum) what according to his station in life is necessary for himself, his wife, and for the rearing of children and this under pain of grave injustice, and of the greatest sin." "Workman and employer can make a perfectly free agreement about wages, but there is a dictate of natural justice more imperious and more ancient than any bargain between man and man, namely, that wages ought to be sufficient to support a frugal and well-behaved wage earner."[20] Pius XI does not enter into detail, attempt to specify in terms of money what wage would be in accordance with the principles he has laid down. For this varies with the different classes of workers, just as it depends on the real value of money and on the wealth of each country and its general standard of living.

However, for a well-balanced view of the papal teaching on the living wage for the individual or the family, it is necessary to remember that the Popes explicitly state that the members of the family as well as its head are obliged to contribute according to their ability to the joint maintenance of all. As regards the help of the junior members of the family, great care should be taken not to place them in workshops or factories until their bodies and minds are sufficiently developed.

Regard must be had to the conditions of any particular business. It is unjust to demand wages so high that an employer cannot pay them without disastrous consequences to his business. But if the struggling plight of an industry is due to bad management, or out-of-date methods, this is not a valid reason for reducing wages. When a crisis is apprehended, the Pope counsels employers and their men to come together, and in a spirit of human sympathy and good will remove obstacles and settle their differences. If conditions are flourishing, it would be only fair and equitable to give workers a bonus above what is due to them in strict justice.

---

[20] Pius XI, *Casti Connubii* (Christian Marriage).

PART V

THE RIGHT TO PERSONAL LIBERTY

The individual's right to existence goes beyond and implies more than mere bodily well-being. For man is before and above all a moral being, endowed with free will or liberty. This characteristic radically distinguishes him from the animal. Unlike the brute, man knows his end and can attain it by conforming his actions to the precepts of the natural moral law. He is bound to co-ordinate his activities in such a way as to reach his ultimate end; to act otherwise would be to rebel against the moral order. Positive law intervenes to check an unlimited use of liberty, for otherwise the preservation of the moral order as well as the realization of human ends embodied therein would be impossible. Liberty is limited by the rational ends of man and the ends provide adequately for the exercise of both individual and social liberty.

The right to liberty may also be taken in a more restricted sense to denote the personal security which the State is bound to guarantee to its citizens. Though liberty in this second acceptation is applied to a less elevated sphere than that of moral and religious liberty, its importance cannot be minimized. The State must guarantee the individual against any attack on his personal liberty. On this point there is unanimous agreement. The sense of personal liberty has made such progress that today the arrest of a citizen is hardly possible without a warrant. In well-regulated States an individual cannot be deprived of personal liberty unless he has violated another's rights. In practically all civilized countries, up to the present time, the law condemns and punishes every action directed against personal liberty such as seizure or rape of a person. In this restricted acceptation, then, personal liberty cannot be limited except for motives foreseen by the law, and only after a warrant for arrest has been issued. Of course, there are certain exceptional cases previously referred to in which the State can interfere without a warrant. It is a general principle that whatever may be the motive for depriving an individual of his personal liberty a public hearing and a regular trial of the person indicted must be instituted as soon as possible. If his innocence is vindicated, his personal freedom must be immediately restored.

The right to personal liberty has been held so sacred that almost all governments have extended it to the domicile or home. One's home with its surroundings and accessories is the sanctuary of the individual's activity, the shrine of human personality and family. Hence it is not without reason that the home is regarded as an integral part of that autonomous sphere within which a human being is responsible only to God and his own conscience. For this reason the home is inviolable. This inviolability is admirably expressed by the motto "my house is my castle." Every violent or clandestine intrusion into another's home is equivalent to an unjust aggression against the human person himself. Nevertheless the invasion of one's home without a search warrant may be justified when public order demands it, e.g., to uncover the substantial and fundamental facts of a crime, or to estimate in what measure certain suspicions are founded. In such cases the search may not only be useful but necessary. This State right, however, must not derogate in any way from the respect due to human dignity and to the rights of the citizens.

1. CHOICE OF A PROFESSION

Another basic right of the individual is his freedom to choose a profession or vocation. No one, not even the State, has the right to force an individual to follow one profession rather than another. Man is a free being; any coerciveness in the selection or in the practice of a profession is repugnant to human dignity. If civil legislation can do little or nothing to change the environment or to modify the numberless circumstances that accompany the individual from birth and exercise a decisive influence on his physical and intellectual formation, the State has no right to hinder any one who wishes to change his environment or aspires to a nobler profession than that followed by his ancestors. Every-one is free to develop his faculties by choosing that profession which best harmonizes with his talents, character, and ability without distinction of class or privilege. This does not deprive the parents of their duty to exert themselves with all authority and influence in order to prevent an unfortunate and premature decision. It is necessary to watch and properly to direct the first inclinations of children and to enhance in every way their intellectual and moral development. Only in this manner will young men or women succeed in making a wise and fortunate choice.

Choice of one's profession is of supreme importance both for the individual since his future in a great measure depends upon it, and for the social well-being. A good choice of a vocation, the one best suited to his talents and inclinations, will further his success. The function of the State, therefore, is to foster and promote all the means calculated to facilitate a good choice. The right to existence presupposes man's ability to procure those means without which a life befitting a human person would be impossible. Such means, as a rule, consist in the practice of a special profession, in the choice of which the individual must enjoy full liberty. This liberty will be better appreciated if we consider the fact that professional life with its joys and sorrows exercises a profound influence on the individual. Lastly, if man in view of his ultimate end and in harmony with his ability is bound to cooperate in the general welfare, it is an indication that he must have a free choice of a vocation in conformity with his conscience and inclinations.

Finally, the spiritual and material well-being of society requires division of labor into classes and professions. Here we are confronted by the dilemma: either the State must be empowered to assign to each citizen a particular profession for the care of social needs; or, realizing that not all will pursue the same vocation, must allow each one to make his own choice.

The first view, advocated by collectivism, would encounter in-surmountable difficulties. Nothing in fact is more difficult than to estimate with precision the ability, conscientiousness, and diligence of each individual. It would, moreover, be equivalent to a most complete subservience of the individual to the State, and of private well-being to a supposed common well-being. On the contrary, the principle which respects professional liberty is in full harmony with the concept of human dignity. However, it would be wrong to regard professional liberty as an absolute and unlimited right, for it is clear that no one can follow a pro-fession detrimental to another's personal liberty. Again, this liberty of action like all other rights is limited by the norms of morality. There is no such thing as a right to perform actions opposed to morality. Furthermore, as the general well-being comes before the individual well-being, the State has a right, in the measure demanded by the general welfare, to set limits to individual liberty. Besides this there are other limitations of a juridical nature such as the natural and contractual relations of dependence, e.g., the relations of children to their parents, of minors to their guardians, of wife to husband, and of servants to their masters. Another limitation of particular importance is the one imposed by custom or by certain practices resulting either directly or indirectly from the moral law. Thus it would not be in conformity with the customs of certain countries for a woman to engage in politics or other professions unsuited to her nature and her high mission. Professional freedom, however, should not be the privilege of some fortunate few. If all men are equal before the law, all should be free to select that pro-fession which harmonizes with their ideals and native abilities. We shall now consider briefly the liberty of association.

2. LABOR UNIONS

Man is moved to live in society by his countless needs. But if man is social by nature, it is natural for him to form groups and associations for the gaining of intellectual, moral, and economic ends that cannot be attained by individuals acting singly. Liberty of association is an important factor in self-development. Not only the family and the State but also many other groupings and associations are natural to man in the sense of according with his nature. The latter not only harmonizes with man's nature but in many circumstances they become an obligation for men for the attainment of the common good. This applies in a special manner to labor unions. The philosophy of liberalism and individualism denied this obvious truth. The events of the recent past show that labor unions were outlawed in almost every country in the world. Those in power were allowed to do as they pleased, even when they wished to combine among themselves, but the workingmen were left helpless and unable to combine in any way. That is why Leo XIII sounded the call so strongly for workingmen's unions declaring that men have a natural right to form such unions and that no State may justly deny that right. "For to enter into a society of this kind is the natural right of man; and the State must protect natural rights, not destroy them; and if it forbids its citizens to form associations, it contradicts the very principle of its own existence, for both they and it exist in virtue of the same principle, viz., the natural propensity of man to live in society. . . . We may lay it down as a general and perpetual law, that workmen's associations should be so organized and governed as to furnish the best and the most suitable means for attaining what is aimed at; that is to say, for helping each individual member to better his condition to the utmost in body, mind, and property."[21]

Pius XI says in this regard: "At that period rulers of not a few nations were deeply infected with liberalism and regarded such unions of workingmen with disfavor, if not with open hostility. While readily recognizing and patronizing similar corporations amongst other classes, with criminal injustice they denied the innate right of forming associations to those who needed them most for self-protection against oppression by the more powerful. There were even Catholics who viewed with suspicion

---

[21] Leo XIII, *op. cit.*

the efforts of the laboring classes to form such unions, as if they reflected the spirit of Socialistic or revolutionary agitators."[22]

Fortunately, labor unions, once prohibited as conspiracies in this country, and later harried and hounded by conscienceless managers, are now recognized as a normal part of our industrial life. Only a small number of employers will decline to admit the right of collective bargaining. The above pronouncements alone suffice to show the Church's genuine interest in the cause of the workingman, and her determination to use every means to protect his rights. Here we have a very definite rebuke to those who want to prevent employees from joining labor unions. The State should encourage and protect labor organizations, for the right to such unions is a natural one and necessary for the common good. The State, however, should not try to do everything that can be done by "smaller and lower bodies," but realize that its first duty is to abolish conflict between classes, for class warfare is as harmful to the good of mankind as is unbridled competition. Nothing of value to human life can be attained in this regard except on the principle of mutual cooperation between both individuals and associations, which principle must rest on the firm foundation of Christian justice and charity.

It must not be forgotten that the right of association is like a two-edged sword, which can be beneficial as well as detrimental to social welfare. As certain medicines taken without a doctor's prescription will harm instead of help a sick person, so liberty of association if it deviates from its legitimate sphere, will be injurious to society. With all due respect for liberty and within the limits demanded by the common good, the State has the right and duty to watch lest liberty of association degenerate and endanger the State itself. Such a right can be exercised only when the common good demands it. Those who deliberately shun the light and seek darkness in order to carry on their pernicious work, cannot but arouse suspicion. Truth has no secrets but fearlessly asserts itself in the open. To tolerate a

---

[22] Pius XI, *Quadragesimo Anno*.

secret society whose activities are concealed is like tolerating a hidden cancer. Confronted by the nefarious work of secret societies the State cannot remain indifferent, for its very life is at stake. The abolishment of such societies would be a real blessing for the common good, and an assurance of peace and prosperity. On the other hand, the State should foster and protect those societies which unfold their activities in the open and within the boundaries sanctioned by the general welfare. In the words of Leo XIII: "There are times, no doubt, when it is right that the law should interfere to prevent association; as when men join together for purposes which are evidently bad, unjust, or dangerous to the State. In such cases the public authority may justly forbid the formation of association, and may dissolve them when they already exist. But every precaution should be taken not to violate the rights of individuals, and not to make unreasonable regulations, under the pretense of public benefit. For laws only bind when they are in accordance with right reason, and therefore with the eternal law of God."[23]

[23] Leo XIII, *op. cit.*

SELECT READINGS

Cahill, E., S.J., *The Framework of a Christian State,* Ch. XI.
Catholic Encyclopedia, arts. on "Suicide"; "Duels"; "Euthanasia"; "Labor Unions."
Husslein, Joseph, *The Christian Social Manifesto* (Milwaukee: The Bruce Publishing Co., 1931).
Leo XIII, *Rerum Novarum* (The Condition of Labor).
Michel, V., O.S.B., *Christian Social Reconstruction* (Milwaukee: The Bruce Publishing Co., 1937).
—— "St. Thomas and Today"; "Human Rights" (St. Paul: Wanderer Press, 1936), pamphlets.
Pius XI, *Quadragesimo Anno* (The Reconstruction of the Social Order).
Ross, E. J., *A Survey of Sociology* (Milwaukee: The Bruce Publishing Co., 1932), Ch. VII.
Ryan, J. A., *Distributive Justice* (New York: The Macmillan Co., 1927).
Sullivan, J. F., *Special Ethics* (Boston: Holy Cross Press, 1931).

CHAPTER IX

LIBERTY AND EQUALITY

THE magic word, *liberty*, is upon the lips of everyone. It is a word which inflames human hearts and thrills human breasts; a word which symbolizes the dream of nations and consti- tutes their most precious heritage. Liberty is the apex of earthly glory and happiness; the mainspring of social activities and progress. For liberty, men suffer and die; from that word the poet, the hero, and the saint draw courage and inspiration. As light reflects and diffuses itself into the most variegated colors in prismatic hues, so too liberty. Hence the phrases: liberty of thought, liberty of speech, liberty of the press, liberty of con- science, to mention a few.

Yet, the vast majority of mankind fail to understand the true meaning of liberty. For the anarchist, liberty means absolute freedom from any and every law, human or divine; for the socialist, liberty means freedom from economic slavery; for the liberalist, and the freethinker, liberty means a complete divorce from the objective moral order to which every man should con- form. For too many, liberty is confused with license, and count- less crimes are and have been committed in its name.

By a curious paradox, the most blatant devotees of freedom are, generally speaking, the most intolerant of the liberty of others. The communists and Nazis loudly demand absolute liberty for themselves and the complete emancipation of man from any and every restraint. Yet in practice as exemplified by Soviet Russia, the communists not only deny the maximum but even the minimum of liberty to their subjects. In free-thinking Russia and Germany, academic freedom is practically unknown; teachers and professors must refrain from expressing unorthodox views in their lectures and writings, even when they teach such apparently noncontroversial subjects as biology and mathematics. There is no such thing as freedom of speech or of the press, and hardly any freedom of thought. The Soviets have abolished religious freedom, yet encourage and subsidize atheistic propaganda. The Nazis, while making war on Christianity, permit ample freedom and grant financial aid for the dissemination of the new religion of racism and blood. These countries are not content to dominate the outer world and leave man's inner life to religion, they want also to take over the whole man, body and soul. In other countries bigotry and prejudice are rampant, and constant attacks are made on religious freedom, especially of the Catholic church.

In view of this alarming situation it is well to re-examine the traditional doctrine of liberty, and to arouse sleeping and enslaved humanity to a realization of its innate and inalienable rights. The Christian principles so forcibly enunciated by Leo XIII will guide us. The Pope defines true human liberty in the following memorable words, which we quote at length because of their importance:

". . . The true liberty of human society does not consist in every man doing what he pleases, for this would simply end in turmoil and confusion, and bring on the overthrow of the State; but rather in this, that through the injunctions of the civil law all may more easily conform to the prescription of the eternal law. Likewise, the liberty of those who are in authority does not consist in the power to lay unreasonable and capricious commands upon their subjects, which would equally be criminal and would lead to the ruin of the commonwealth; but instead the binding force of human laws lies in the fact that they are to be regarded as applications of the eternal law, and are incapable of sanctioning anything which is not contained in the eternal law, as in the principle of all laws. . . . If, then, by any one in authority, something be sanctioned not in conformity with the principles of right reason, and consequently is hurtful to the commonwealth such an enactment can have no binding force of law as being no rule of justice, but certain to lead men away from that good which is the very end of civil society.

"Therefore, the nature of human liberty, however it be considered, whether in individuals or in society, whether in those who command or in those who obey, supposes the necessity of obedience to some supreme and eternal law, which is no other than the authority of God, commanding good and forbidding evil. And, this most just authority of God over men far from diminishing, or even destroying their liberty, protects and perfects it; for the real perfection of all creatures is found in the prosecution and attainment of their respective ends. But the supreme end to which human liberty must aspire is God."[1]

PART I

LIBERTY

1. LIBERTY OF THOUGHT

Although no physical force is strong enough to imprison thought, since it is a spiritual activity, one cannot speak of absolute freedom of thought. No one is free to think whatever he pleases, for everything in nature is subject to law. In mathematics we are not free to think that twice two is five; nor in geometry to think of a square circle or of a hexagonal right angle, for such notions are contradictory and absurd. In history we must admit the existence of Alexander the Great and Napoleon; in architecture we must comply with the laws of statics; in painting with the laws of perspectives, and so on. The sphere of intellectual liberty is indeed limited.

We are free to think of this or that object only according to the laws of reality and consistency. The occurrence of the fact

---

[1] Leo XIII, *Libertas Humana* (Human Liberty).

that I am witnessing is true and I am not free to deny it. I must believe it, now and always, to be consistent, to be truthful to myself. As the good is the proper object of the will, so the true is the proper object of the intellect. The human mind is determined by its proper object to think in this rather than in another way; in other words, truth imposes itself on the mind. The mind does not create truth; human reason simply perceives and discovers it. Reason is not free to declare certain things true or false, but must conform to evidence. It is well to note that this limitation of liberty or intellectual dependence on truth, does not degrade but ennobles human thought.

Liberty of thought, understood in the sense that man is free to think whatever he pleases, is a false doctrine militating against the most elementary principles of logic. Every contingent being is subject to a law which in harmony with its nature directs it to a proper end. The inorganic world is governed by physical and mechanical laws; the vegetative kingdom is subject to botanical laws; and the animal kingdom to zoological laws. Finally, man is governed by psychological laws, by the laws of reason and will. While the physical and mechanical laws operate upon the inorganic mass, as it were, transiently and from without, the biological principle, or the vegetative soul, organizes its activities immanently or from within. Plant life assimilates from its surroundings, and by this means evolves and realizes its natural plan, the plant itself being the agent. For stronger reasons the same applies to animals. Lastly in man, the biological and sensory activities are co-ordinated and dominated by a single directive principle, the rational soul.

In virtue of his rational and volitional endowments man tends to his ends freely and not under the impulse of external or internal coercion. However, the essence of freedom of will does not strictly consists in the power of doing evil, but in the fact that man has the power of choosing means suited to the end proposed, for he who can choose one thing out of many is master of his actions. This characteristic distinguishes human actions from all others. Freedom of will constitutes the dignity of

rational beings and should be enjoyed by man without any undue interference from the State.

True freedom demands that man's actions be controlled by
reason, and not by impulse and passion. The good sought after
by the will must be the moral good. An action is morally good
when it is subservient to, and in conformity with man's ultimate
end. Yet it often happens that man instead of choosing the moral
good chooses an apparent good. "A man" says Cardinal Mercier,
"chooses evil under the guise of apparent good. Such an unfortunate action is possible on account of his possession of many
faculties each of which has a different proper object; what is
the real good of one is not necessarily that of another — as is
manifest in the case of the higher and lower appetites, where
what is truly the pleasure of the lower is sometimes not at all
the good of man, as he is a rational being. When the will seeks
an inferior good in place of what is upright, it violates the law
of its nature, thereby acting inconsistently with right order and
abusing its liberty. Hence a moral evil is called a defect, un-
righteousness, a fall."[2]

The human individual has an innate right and duty to exercise his energies and intellectual faculties in the solution of the
great problems confronting the philosophical and scientific
world. Hence man should be free (and the State should respect
this freedom) to devote his life to the study of the universe and
its laws, to scrutinize nature, the oceans, and the vast expanses
of space. He should be free, if he so desires, to dwell in isolation
from the world, to dedicate himself to God in a special manner;
free in the laboratory to carry on his microscopic or bacteriolog-
ical observations and analyses. Scientific truth is so precious a
jewel that it should be sought after by everyone according to
his capacity, and the State has a duty to foster it in every possible
way. The State would certainly fail in its mission by placing on
scientific research any absurd and unworthy restriction depriving
it thus of its legitimate freedom. Here it will be well to bear in

---

[2] Cardinal Mercier, *A Manual of Modern Scholastic Philosophy* (London:
Kegan, 1919), Vol. I, p. 274-275.

mind the impressive words of Leo XIII: "Liberty is a power perfecting man, and hence should have truth and goodness for its
object. But the character of goodness and truth cannot be
changed at option. These remain ever one and the same, and
are no less unchangeable than nature herself. If the mind assents
to false opinions, and the will chooses and follows after what is
wrong, neither can attain its native fullness, but both must fall
from their native dignity into an abyss of corruption. Whatever,
therefore, is opposed to virtue and truth, may not rightly be
brought temptingly before the eyes of man, much less sanctioned
by the favor and protection of the law."[3]

2. LIBERTY OF SPEECH

Liberty of thought is closely connected with liberty of speech.
Now liberty of expressing one's thoughts should be limited to
the manifestation of truth, order, and justice. Otherwise the
doors would be opened to intellectual and moral anarchy. While
some would inculcate the duty of giving to each one his own,
others might teach that theft is morally lawful, or that calumny,
adultery, and murder are praiseworthy and commendable. Again,
while the former would proclaim obedience to legitimate authority, the duty of love of one's country and of defending it in
need, the latter might encourage rebellion, treason, and desertion. It is clear that to countenance such freedom is equivalent to
sacrificing social order upon the altar of false liberty. Therefore,
it is essentially wrong to advocate an absolute freedom of thought
and speech. On the other hand, no hindrance should be placed
to the manifestation of thought in conformity with truth. If
truth were merely a creation of the mind, a product of our
thought, it would be hard, if not impossible, to distinguish it
from error and vice versa. But truth is objective and immutable;
for instance, the truth of the proposition that two times two is
four does not depend upon the human mind. Whether the
human mind perceives it or not, truth is what it is. Therefore

----

[3] Leo XIII, *Immortale Dei* (The Christian Constitution of States).

freedom of thought or speech cannot be absolute; it is limited by what is true. In the interest of truth and of social order the Church condemns this absolute freedom which is only another word for license. Man as a rational and moral being is not free to think or to do as he pleases. His thoughts must accord with truth and his actions conform with the moral and natural laws.

Even more absurd is the attitude of those who, while proclaiming the dogma of absolute freedom of thought and speech, bitterly oppose every teaching not in harmony with their own ideals. Such an attitude is obviously not inspired by the sacred principle of liberty but by hatred, a hatred which condemns whatever is not in harmony with atheistic, naturalistic, and liberalistic views. The so-called freethinkers deny Catholics freedom to think and act according to the latter's professed beliefs. A liberty of thought more contradictory than this can hardly be thought of: they proclaim to the four corners of the globe an equal liberty to all except to those whose mission has been for 1900 years to teach order, justice, charity, and fraternity. They advocate liberty for vice, but not for virtue; liberty for spreading seeds of corruption, but not for diffusing the light of truth.

"We must now consider briefly liberty of speech, and liberty of the press. It is hardly necessary to say that there can be no such right as this, if it be not used in moderation, and if it pass beyond the bounds and ends of all true liberty. For right is a moral power which it would be absurd to suppose that nature has accorded indifferently to truth and falsehood, to justice and injustice. Men have a right freely and prudently to propagate throughout the State what things soever are true and honorable, so that as many as possible may possess them. But lying opinions, than which no mental plague is greater, and vices which corrupt the heart and moral life, should be diligently repressed by public authority lest they insidiously work the ruin of the State. The excesses of an unbridled intellect, which unfailingly end in the oppression of the untutored multitude, are no less rightly controlled by the authority of the law than are injuries inflicted by violence upon the weak. And this all the more surely, because by far the greater part of the community is either absolutely unable, or able only with great difficulty, to escape from illusions and deceitful subtleties, especially such as flatter the passions. If unbridled license of speech and of writing be granted to all, nothing will remain sacred and inviolate; even the highest and truest mandates of nature, justly held to be the common and noblest heritage of the human race, will not be spared. Thus, truth being gradually obscured by darkness, pernicious and manifold error, as too often happens, will easily prevail. Thus, too, license will gain what liberty loses; for liberty will ever be more free and secure, in proportion as license is kept in fuller restraint. In regard, however, to any matters of opinion which God leaves to man's free discussion, full liberty of thought and of speech is naturally within the rights of everyone; for such liberty never leads men to suppress the truth, but often to discover it and make it known.

"A like judgment must be passed upon what is called liberty of teaching. There can be no doubt that truth alone should imbue the minds of men; for in it are found the well-being, the end, and the perfection of every intelligent nature. Therefore nothing but truth should be taught both to the ignorant and to the educated, so as to bring knowledge to those who have it not, and to preserve it in those who possess it. For this reason it is plainly the duty of all who teach to banish error from the mind, and by sure safeguards to close the entry to all false convictions."[4]

3. LIBERTY OF CONSCIENCE

True liberty consists primarily in the natural duty to conform one's conscience with the supreme norm of morality. This norm is promulgated to man by the light of reason, but conscience applies the principles of the moral law to individual acts. Conscience is not, as is falsely believed, a purely subjective affair; it is not a synonym for caprice or arbitrariness. Conscience is an

---

[4] Leo XIII, *Libertas Humana* (Human Liberty).

intellectual judgment based on implicit or explicit, actual or habitual deliberation, comparison, and reasoning. As every judgment, so every dictate of conscience or moral judgment, must, in order to be justified, conform to the supreme standard of truth and goodness. For this reason the notions of good and evil, of justice and injustice, of virtue and vice, as well as the concepts of truth and falsehood are the basic notions embodied in moral judgments, or conscience. Now as there is a possibility of erring in matters of conscience but no right to error, so we may speak of a psychological possibility of maintaining erroneous opinions in moral matters but no right to maintain them.

A man cannot be compelled to act contrary to his own conscience, no more than a son can be constrained to love his father. Conscience and intrinsic human liberty are not subject to physical force. The attempt to induce someone by coercive means, for instance, imprisonment, fine, or torture, to perform an action against his will might make martyrs or hypocrites, but no more than that. As a rule every attack on man's conscience is by that very fact an attack on his personal dignity and liberty, which must be respected by all and in a manner befitting a rational being. Though the State has no right to interfere with an individual's private life or to coerce his conscience, it undoubtedly has a right to restrict personal liberty within certain limits demanded by the common good. The common good, however, must include the maximum of freedom that is compatible with the safeguarding of proper opportunities for all.

4. LIBERTY OF RELIGION

Religion is a necessary presupposition of all morality. Without religion neither moral obligation nor a sound social order can exist. All true religion must embrace the following beliefs; that there is a God, the Creator and Lord of all things, that nothing, not even a secret thought, can escape His all-seeing eye; that every man must render to Him a strict account of every word and work, of every thought and affection. The powerful and beneficial influence of this belief on individual and social life, cannot be questioned. With the repudiation of this belief all control over egoism and passion is removed. "God is dead" cries Nietzsche "everything is permitted."

Though the practice of religion is outside the competence of the State, still the latter cannot act as if God and religion did not exist, or at least were none of its business. The State must recognize the existence of a Supreme Being though it has no right to coerce its citizens to worship this Supreme Being in one way rather than in another. By its very nature the State cannot be atheistic for the simple reason that one cannot scorn, ignore, or blaspheme publicly the Lord of heaven and earth, without disparaging civil authority which comes from Him.

Religious errors as such are not subject to civil punishment, but religious errors must be distinguished from crimes against religion. Even those who believe that the Catholic Church is the only true Church established by Christ, will, out of respect for a false liberty, tolerate certain crimes which are being daily perpetrated against God. It is strange, indeed, that while other public offenses against civil rulers are severely punished, there is no punishment for crimes against God Himself, the founder of all moral and social order, the source of all right and authority. One example will suffice: daily, perjury is committed in our courts; it is openly proved to be perjury, yet how seldom if ever is it punished? Perjury is the calling upon the Supreme Being to witness to a lie, and branding that lie with His Name. It is a crime against God and religion. It is not only an individual's crime, but the crime also of the State which tolerates such blasphemy. A State that tolerates perjury daily in its courts is not only on the downgrade, but has already reached the depths of infamy. Reformation should begin in the law courts at once, and perjury should be punished to the full extent of the law. Once the sanctity of the oath is destroyed, man has no basis for trust in his fellow man. Once that trust and fidelity is destroyed, law courts cease or become a farce. Witness Russia! "No God — No Civil Court."

It is necessary not only to preserve but also to integrate and cement whatever good there is. Modern legislation condemns many actions simply because they offend or scandalize certain people. But unfortunately the same modern legislation, under the false mantle of liberty of the press and education, allows in public schools, colleges, and universities crass materialism, agnosticism, atheism, and even communism to proceed on its victorious march without let or hindrance. In this manner the State, instead of suppressing, contributes indirectly to the spread of unbelief and atheism, and thereby paves the road to its own destruction.

We shall return to the question of religious freedom in a later chapter; here it is enough to indicate how civil power should act in regard to individual liberty, and to what extent the State must guarantee individual freedom in matters of religion. Everyone should enjoy the liberty of professing and practicing a belief, provided the practice of that belief does not interfere with or hinder the rights or religious principles of his fellow men, and provided one is not spreading subversive doctrines dangerous to the social order and general tranquillity. The principle of religious freedom should regulate social relations between citizens belonging to diverse sects and religious beliefs. "Even where the State does not profess any particular religion it should do everything possible to advance the spiritual welfare of its subjects. This embraces the censorship of the Press and of the theater, regulation of amusements, gambling, liquor traffic, and the protection of the young and weak from temptation. Most modern states err on the side of too much liberty, which is taken advantage of by the vicious and criminal element. The European war has familiarized us with censorship, free speech and a free press have been variously limited through the exigencies of national necessity. And while peace brought us a return to former customs, the right of government to limit freedom has been clearly recognized."[5]

---

[5] John Elliot Ross, *Ethics* (New York: The Devin-Adair Co., 1938), pp. 322–323.

5. LIMITS TO LIBERTY

So-called free thought aims at the subversion of all moral and social order; repudiates the principles of truth and justice, and establishes the worst kind of intellectual tyranny. In assigning to freedom its proper limits we do not in any way circumscribe free scientific research, nor oppose any social and economic betterment, nor the progress of culture and enlightenment. These limits refer to false freedom, to the denial of sound logic and reason. Human freedom must be restricted; and the first restriction comes from the natural moral law through man's conscience. And conscience is that stern monitor in every human soul that can never be silenced. The natural moral law is in complete harmony with man's rational nature, because it directs man to his ultimate end, to perfection and happiness. The natural moral law, then, by restricting human freedom does not hinder or destroy true liberty; it rather enlightens this liberty and protects it from the allurements of evil. This regulative law of liberty is an indispensable condition for a rational development of human conduct. Without it man is free only in slavery to error.

Personal liberty is also limited by the very nature of civil society. Without a limited human liberty a stable society of families is unthinkable. This limitation is imposed by the social functions and ends. Hence the individual is free to do not what pleases him, but what is beneficial to the community. If everyone could exercise his liberty arbitrarily the preservation of the moral and social order and the realization of social ends would be impossible. The actualization of social ends must take place according to the divine plan and man's rational nature: that is, it consists in the observance of the natural moral law which is the ultimate norm of human conduct. From this fountainhead human action draws its specific value. In the light of this principle the individual must be free in order to fulfill all his duties toward his fellow men. The State has no right to force its citi-

zens to comply with individual duties, or to prescribe directive
norms for their private conduct. The sanctuary of private life
is outside the competency of the State, and in this the individual
has an inalienable right to a free sphere of action. Man must
tend to his end freely; he is the architect of his own happiness
or ruin.

Liberty must also be subservient to another limitation, imposed
on it by public morality. Without morality no true earthly good
is possible. Morality is the only safe basis for justice, loyalty, fortitude, temperance and other virtues demanded by a well-ordered
social life. A people that despises virtue is already in the stage
of decadence and decomposition. The State, just as much as the
individuals constituting it, needs virtue for the practice of its
profession, since earthly happiness and true social good depends
upon it. As physical health is necessary for the growth and development of the individual, so virtue is necessary for the general
welfare. As a condition of national happiness Aristotle enumerates justice, prudence, fortitude, and temperance. Universal
history teaches that virtuous peoples have always been powerful
and happy, and that on the contrary, depraved nations have
rapidly disintegrated. Even the most enlightened pagan nations
such as Rome and Greece bear witness to that fact! If morality
is necessary for the general welfare and if the function of the
State consists in promoting the common good, then public authorities cannot remain indifferent in view of the ever increasing
deluge of evil. Some States have already sanctioned severe penalties against public indecency, adultery, divorce, incest, and other
vices which threaten the life of the nation.

But it is not enough that civil power cursorily represses public
vices, it must extirpate the evil by the roots. There is nothing
more unfortunate than weakness or indecision in matters of such
importance. And when the evil is spreading swiftly, prompt action is required as any delay may be fatal. As contagious diseases
threatening the physical welfare of society are promptly attended
to and checked by civil authorities, so the moral and social
maladies that threaten the purity of morals, the sanctity of

marriage, or the belief in the hereafter, must be immediately checked, and if possible, prevented. Selfishness and greed, more than indolence, are very often the greatest obstacles to moral reforms. The necessity of social and moral reforms is vividly felt; we see juvenile delinquency on the increase, drunkenness alarmingly prevalent even among high school children, political graft and corruption undermining the whole social structure, our press and movies openly flattering and catering to the lowest passions in man for the sake of monetary gain. If we compare the tone of our daily press with the indecent literature that our fathers shunned, we can see at a glance how fast we are drifting into moral rottenness and degeneracy. If a vigorous reaction against such evils calls for sacrifice there is no reason for losing courage. As long as vice is held up to honor publicly, few have the moral courage to resist it. Hence it is the duty of the State to do all that is possible to repress every offense against public morality. In this laudable and noble campaign the State should have the support of every honest man. The work of legislation cannot attain its goal without the cooperation of all citizens, and the majority of them are honest, decent, and upright. Everyone must make his contribution in this important matter since he owes it to himself, to his family, and to his country. This principle is of great value especially when there is question of reacting vigorously against vice and corruption, and of correcting public opinion, and of carrying to success the work of social, moral, and economic restoration. Difficulties and obstacles must be overcome; and the lofty purpose should inspire all, citizens and public authorities, with a true spirit of patriotism to cooperate to the best of their abilities. Civil authority supported and strengthened by joint public cooperation will be able to check the flood of licentiousness which corrodes the human heart.

Finally, the modern immorality of greed, selfishness, and sensual pleasure leads to a morality without God, to a morality bereft of duty and obligation. A morality divorced from its fountainhead loses all its value and meaning, being identified with the whims and fancies of each individual. Law will then be confounded with coercion, capable of compelling but not of obliging. But without the character of obligatoriness moral order loses all its efficacy and becomes an empty word. Modern culture with its liberty of thought, of conscience, of speech, of the press, and of worship; with its theories of divorce, of free love, has openly and remorselessly contributed to the breakdown of family life, to the triumph of might over right, to the spread of skepticism and to the general moral perversity. Moreover, we have reached such a stage of mental degeneration as to confound truth with falsity, justice with injustice, the good with evil. All possible means have been employed to render these ideas ever more uncertain and vague. The unhappy result of all this is that modern man having emancipated himself from God and from traditional morality remains now a victim of his own egoism and passions. It is the duty of the State and of men of good will to seek a remedy for this unfortunate situation. The opportunities for a joint cooperation in this holy crusade are plentiful. Hence such laws should be enacted as to safeguard public morals, the sanctity and stability of marriage, and the preservation of domestic and social order. Should civil authority be slow or indifferent in this regard, then the duty falls on competent Christian writers to make their influence felt through the daily press, reviews and periodicals; thus, they will exercise a kind of magistracy over the masses and public opinion. If such means are so cleverly employed by the forces of evil, why should they not be utilized for nobler purposes by the forces of good? The question of public morality should be the first and the foremost concern of all good citizens; all are expected to contribute their share in order to re-establish the kingdom of justice, of goodness and of truth.

6. CRIMINAL PROPAGANDA

Anarchists advocate not only an absolute freedom of thought, but also an unrestricted freedom of propaganda. Anarchy, according to the *Manifesto* published at the Congress of Geneva in 1882, declares itself the enemy of masters, of private owners, of industrialists, of civil laws, and of God Himself. It rebels against every principle of authority and social order. Such ideas undermine the principle of obedience due to legitimate authority; arouse class hatred, contempt and scorn for all law. Once the principle of truth, order, and justice are set aside, the disastrous consequences for the social order are evident. Anarchic and communistic propaganda is essentially antisocial and hence highly criminal. The State has a sacred right and duty to repress such propaganda.

The fear that the State in pursuing such methods might violate the principle of liberty is devoid of serious foundation. To tolerate anarchial and communistic propaganda is equivalent to saying: "Let the State and social order perish as long as liberty is saved." Collectivism has so many points of affinity with anarchy that it is hard to draw a line of demarcation between them, except that anarchy comes out with the whole truth of its desire to overthrow all order, while communism quibbles with half-truths.

Religion and communism are incompatible. "Religion," according to Marx, "is the opiate of the people." Communism has in view the abolition of private property by a state monopoly of the means of production. Contrary to all laws of marital fidelity, morality, and religion, it advocates free love and companionate marriage. Consistently with its *Manifesto*, communism proclaims the dictatorship of the proletariat secured by armed force, and the socialization of the great agricultural estates and of the means of production and distribution. But equally consistently has it wrought havoc upon all classes in Russia where it has been given a fair trial. It began the liquidation of the rich until there were no more rich; and then began the liquidation of the peasants, "the kulaks." The workers whom Communism was to free are now more enslaved than were the serfs of Czarism. The experience of the past few years proves that these ideas materialize into actual facts. Once the proletariat is convinced that capital is unjust, property a theft, every bourgeois a robber, tactics soon appear quite legitimate. Communistic propaganda is a real conspiracy against the social order, and all the more insidious because it plays upon the passions of man by exaggerating the abuses of the present-day social order, and completely ignoring the inherent goodness of society as such. As long as there are men on earth there will be abuse of the gifts that God has given, but this abuse does not destroy or take away the inherent good of the gifts themselves. The social order is one of these gifts. Communism and anarchy would do away with this gift.

Atheistic and materialistic propaganda is also criminal because social order based on atheism is impossible. In fact, positive law draws its obligatory force from the natural moral law. The penalties with which civil power threatens the transgressors of the law will be of little avail if subjects lack a sense of duty. A profound conviction that obedience to legitimate authority is necessary will engender in the citizens respect for authority. Hence it is that the obligatory character of juridical laws cannot be justified without an appeal to natural right which is prior to, and the basis of, positive right. The same conclusion flows from the concept of authority. Even though at times popular will is the proximate cause of civil power, yet the end of civil society remains independent of the popular will; this end, as it was shown, is essentially inherent in society itself and founded in the natural moral law. Without natural right there can be neither true positive rights nor true human authority. Now the existence of natural rights logically presupposes a supreme Legislator from whom all law ultimately draws its obligatoriness.

The belief in a true, living, and personal God and in a here-after is the cornerstone upon which the whole moral and juridical order rests. In the absence of this principle, a practical norm tracing a clear demarcation between good and evil, justice and injustice, will no longer be possible. Everything becomes relative, subjective, and changeable. It is of supreme importance, therefore, that this truth be well understood and impressed on the minds of citizens. The State has a sacred duty to prohibit all propaganda, oral or written, which tries to undermine these basic principles upon which the social order and common welfare rest.

PART II

EQUALITY

Equality is a word as magical and inspiring as that of liberty. Like liberty equality is too often misinterpreted and misapplied. There is a juridical equality in that all men are equal before the law, civil or moral, positive or natural. And then, too, there is an equality in that all men have an equal right to the protection and aid of society in attaining their temporal and eternal ends. However to argue, as collectivists do, from a juridical equality to an economic is fallacious and absurd. Every individual has an equal right to a sufficiency of material goods — but equal here does not imply a qualitative or quantitative identity. Finally, there is equality as to education; an equality which is not absolute but relative to the individual.

1. JURIDICAL EQUALITY

All beings of the same class are fundamentally alike in the general essential characteristics of that class. Hence all men, as far as they are men, are endowed with the dignity of human personality. From this it follows that in all there is a basic equality of rights, namely, all men are fundamentally alike and therefore equal. The triumph of this sublime doctrine must be ascribed to Christianity which teaches that before God there is no respecting of persons, whether rich or poor, learned or ignorant, master or slave, but that all men are equal. For a Christian there is no distinction between the Roman citizen and the barbarian, between the Jew and the gentile, between the slave and the master; all men are equal because all are brethren and children of the same heavenly Father.

Today the principle of equality is generally upheld by modern legislation, for in theory at least all citizens are equal before the law. However there are notable and infamous exceptions to this rule. Nazi Germany excludes Jews and others from enjoyment of civil rights. Soviet Russia deprives entire classes of their civil privileges. Our own southern States pay but lip service to the equality of our colored citizens. Because of juridical equality public offices are no longer a monopoly of certain classes but are accessible to all. In spite of humble birth, a deserving citizen can rise to the highest positions in public service, in the army, in legislative assemblies, and in the government of the commonwealth. In the political field we have universal suffrage; something which was unheard of in former days. The juridical order of the State must recognize and guarantee this equality of rights before law. Juridical protection as well as legal sanctions must be equal for all, otherwise it would be nonsense to speak of equality of rights.

2. ECONOMIC EQUALITY

In the present social order, and especially in the field of economics there are vast differences and injustices. The aristocracy of blood has been replaced by an aristocracy of capital, and there is an impassable gulf between the vast fortunes of the rich and the poverty of the poor. These conditions have been graphically depicted and vigorously condemned by recent Popes. "Every sincere observer," wrote Pius XI, "is conscious that the vast differences between the few who hold excessive wealth and the many who live in destitution constitute a grave evil in modern society. . . . The immense number of propertyless wage earners on the one hand, and the superabundant riches of the fortunate few on the other, is an unanswerable argument that the earthly goods so abundantly produced in this age of industrialism are far from rightly distributed and equitably shared among the various classes of men. . . . The wealthy were content to abandon to charity alone the full care of relieving the unfortunate, as though it were the task of charity to make amends for the open violation of justice, a violation not merely tolerated, but sanctioned at times by legislators."[6]

a) Collectivistic Solution

So, in spite of the modern proclamation of equality of all before the law, the abyss separating capital from labor is becoming wider and more pronounced. These facts are, of course, recognized by all. How remedy the situation? The only effective remedy according to communism is a State monopoly of all the means of production and distribution; this alone, they say, will establish a true equality of citizens both in the political and economic domain. In practice, however, communism merely substitutes one governing class for another, and the power and wealth it takes from the capitalists is given to the few or one at the head of the communist State; hence the evil instead of being ameliorated is aggravated. This has been amply proved both in Germany and Russia in the past few years. Hence, State control of wealth is not the answer to the problem. Leo XIII wrote the answer in glowing letters on the pages of history in his *Rerum Novarum,* but the people of the world and their leaders paid no heed, and so economic chaos now stares them in the face.

Not satisfied with legal equality, collectivism insists on an economic equality which would abolish all differences between rich and poor, between capital and labor. Such a theory is false and practically unsound, for as pointed out in an earlier chapter, no two men are equal in ability, industry, resourcefulness, talents, or skill. Given equal opportunity one would starve while another would prosper. Thus, the socialistic dream of absolute economic equality is doomed from the very nature of things. These differences are not admitted in the socialist theory, hence whenever they actually crop up in practice the only answer collectivism has been able to give to date is *liquidation.*

Socialism aims at the abolition of all individual private property. Private ownership presupposes the right to dispose one's

---

[6] Pius XI, *Quadragesimo Anno* (The Reconstruction of the Social Order).

goods, by selling, buying, or by making a will. These rights necessarily lead to differences in the distribution and possession of goods. Thus while some increase their possessions, others waste and squander them. Such being the case it seems quite clear that we cannot seriously speak of an equality of men in the concrete. Again, the above-mentioned differences in talent, ability, health, enterprise, saving, engender inequalities in social relations. All this conclusively proves that an absolute equality in actual social life is impossible. "Thus it is clear" says Leo XIII, *"that the main tenet of Socialism, the community of goods, must be utterly rejected;* for it would injure those whom it is intended to benefit, it would be contrary to the natural rights of mankind, and it would introduce confusion, and disorder into the commonwealth."[7]

Diversity of work and of profession enhances man's energies and exercises a decisive influence not only in the economic but also in the intellectual, scientific, esthetic, and cultural spheres. No matter how perfect or extensive, a society will always include the learned and the ignorant, masters and pupils, the rich and the poor. Harassed by innumerable ailments and maladies, human society must have its physicians, surgeons, and pharmacists. But during the brief span of life no single individual, no matter how intelligent or industrious, can gain proficiency in the various professions or trades. Diversity of professions or vocations give rise to a diversity of rights and duties. Many socialists themselves admit the impossibility of destroying professional differences. Thus, Engels sought to delimit the concept of equality only to the abolition of classes. To go beyond these limits is to expose oneself to insurmountable difficulties.

Furthermore, it is impossible to conceive a well-regulated society without a common authority, that is, without relations of dependence and subordination. Like any other society, civil society consists of rulers and subjects. A common authority is, therefore, necessary for compelling the stubborn and the indo-

---

[7] Leo XIII, *Rerum Novarum* (The Condition of the Workingman).

lent to comply with civic duties. So great and so profound are
social differences that the socialist leveling scheme is an absolute
impossibility.

In the socialist scheme, there is no room for any real rights or
duties, since according to them, the struggle for existence is the
fundamental factor in the social order. All means conducive to
that end are justified. Hence the right to existence resolves itself
into the right of the strongest. In such a system we shall have
brute force in place of equality; servitude in place of liberty;
anarchy in place of social order. In the words of Pius XI: "Communism deprives man of freedom, robs human personality of
all its dignity, and removes all moral restraints that check the
eruption of blind impulses. There is no recognition of any right
of the individual in his relation to collectivity; no natural right
is accorded to human personality which is a mere cogwheel in
the communist system."[8]

b) Christian Solution

Every man by virtue of his birth into this world, and simply
because he is a man, possesses certain definite and inalienable
rights, which no State can take away or modify. In the first place,
man has a right to existence, and this right carries with it a right
to the means necessary to maintain an existence fit and proper
for human beings. The right to live as a human being, therefore,
means the right to the material necessaries of life and living
conditions, as will support life becomingly and free from inor-
dinate worry in regard to these necessaries. The following consideration shows that this right is grounded in the natural law.

The purpose of material goods is to serve human happiness.
"Man," says St. Thomas, "has natural dominion over external
goods, because by reason and will he can use external goods for
his own benefit, as if they were made for him. For the less perfect
things are always for the sake of the more perfect."[9] This means
that material goods are for the benefit of all men to the exclu-

---

[8] Pius XI, *Divini Redemptoris.*
[9] St. Thomas, *Summa Theologica*, II–II&ae;, q. 66, a. 1.

sion of none. Therefore, whatever makes it impossible for some
men to obtain necessary material goods offends fundamentally
against the law of nature.

According to St. Thomas and Christian teaching, all men are
equal in their right to a virtuous life and a sufficiency of goods
necessary for such a life, to their ultimate end and personal dignity. All have the same right to life, bodily integrity, health,
honor, the rational development of their spiritual and physical
faculties, and to whatever is necessary for the attainment of these
rights. Any attack on, or hindrance to, the proper and free exercise of these rights is a violation of the natural law and an in-
fringement of personal freedom.

The State has not only a right but a positive duty to take an
active part in the regulation of economic life so that all men
may attain the purpose of civil society. If the established conditions of life are such that men with the best of will are by force
of circumstances excluded from attaining the purpose of civil
society, then the State most certainly has the duty and right to
interfere in these conditions, to use its full power toward setting
up and regulating conditions in such a way as to make
possible for all the attainment of the good life. "Whenever the general interest or any particular class suffers, or is
threatened with evils, which can in no other way be met, the
public authority must step in to meet them."[10]

The State should encourage and promote a wider diffusion of
private property. This is the crying need of the hour. In the
words of Leo XIII, the law should favor ownership and its
policy should be to induce as many people as possible to become
owners. There are four beneficial results of such a policy: (1)
Property will thus become more equitably distributed. (2) As a
further consequence of the wider diffusion of property, a greater
abundance of the fruits of the earth may be confidently an-
ticipated. (3) People will cling to the country in which they were
born, and to the land watered by the sweat of their brow. Thus

---

[10] Leo XIII, *op. cit.*

the undesirable drift to the towns will be stopped or checked. (4) People will have the assurance that at their death there will be some provision for their dependents. Obviously, the realization of this plan would not abolish but greatly diminish class inequality.

3. EQUALITY IN EDUCATION

When we say that every man has a right to a suitable education, we do not mean that every man must be taught the same things, or that he must follow the same curriculum. Just as communism of material goods is theoretically false and practically impossible, so also is an absolute equality as applied to education. A true equality in education implies that the State should offer educational facilities to all its citizens according to their ability and needs. For instance, it would be preposterous to demand that an expert in agriculture should be also an expert in medicine, in banking, or in music. Diversity of professions requires that instruction should be suited to the various needs of society. Thus in all ranks, from the highest professional man, to the humblest mechanic or laborer, there will be competent persons in the various fields. In regard to education, the State is bound to assist especially the poorer classes. This can be accomplished without interfering with the free choice of one's profession.

Liberty and equality are based on the right that man has to his existence, to his physical and moral development. These rights within their proper limits must be respected and protected by the State. By nature all men are equal, have the same physical and spiritual faculties, are subject to the same laws, and are destined to an immortal life. But, notwithstanding these equalities, the State is made up of diverse elements, which give rise to a manifold diversity of activities. By destroying these inequalities the State would also destroy men's natural incentives to labor.

Socialism is impotent to solve the great problems of life. It has no message of real value for the poor and indigent, no encouragement for those who fail in the journey of life. On the other hand, the poor, the oppressed, and the afflicted find in Christianity comfort, hope, and encouragement. Belief in immortality and a future reward is the best safeguard of all for true liberty and equality. In denying this transcendental end of man, positivism and radicalism destroy the pedestal upon which the social order rests. The proponents of absolute freedom and equality should be consistent and allow the same rights they claim to the Church. She should be left free to proclaim to the masses the sanctity of marriage, the parental right to the education of children, free to preach to the working classes social justice, temperance, brotherly love, economy, and honest work; free to admonish the rich of their duties of justice and charity toward the needy; free to remind the wealthy of the moderate use of their possessions; free to instill in the hearts of men Christian resignation in times of sorrow.

The disastrous consequences that flow from a wrong concept of equality do less harm to the Church, which is inured to constant struggle against odds, than to civil order and social security. While waiting for their utopias, the champions of absolute equality would do well to direct at least a part of their activities to the equalization and moderation of human covetousness, greed, and pride.

In every society there always were and always will be inequalities. No legislation can change human nature and destroy the inequality of talent, health, physical and moral traits which characterize single individuals. No two trees are alike, no two grains of sand are alike, likewise no two single individuals in the universe are alike. Life is beautiful because of its variegated features. Without inequalities man would be deprived of private initiative and liberty which are the greatest factors of progress and well-being. The true equality preached by Christianity does not beget division and hate, but rather tries to unite in the bonds of true brotherhood all nations, making of the whole humanity a single happy family.

SELECT READINGS

Catholic Encyclopedia, art. "Toleration."

Donat, Joseph, S.J., *The Freedom of Science.*

Kologriwof and Ambruzzi, *God, Man and the Universe* (London: Coldwell, 1937).

Leo XIII, *Libertas Humana* (Human Liberty); *Rerum Novarum* (Christian Constitution of States).

Maritain, Jacques, *Freedom in the Modern World* (New York: Scribners and Sons, 1936).

Pius XI, *Divini Redemptoris* (Atheistic Communism).

Sheed, F., *Communism and Man* (New York: Sheed and Ward, 1938).

Sheen, Fulton J., *Freedom Under God* (Milwaukee: The Bruce Publishing Co., 1940).

—— *Liberty, Equality and Fraternity* (New York: The Macmillan Co., 1938).

Tawney, R. H., *Equality* (London: Allen and Unwin, 1931).

CHAPTER X

THE FAMILY AND THE STATE

IN THIS un-Christian and materialistic age we are witnessing the breakdown of many age-old institutions. Even the family, the oldest and most basic of natural institutions, has not been spared. Family life is fast disappearing and divorce is rampant. Under the influence of individualism, the family is becoming entirely subject to individual whims and fancies. Such an attitude gives rise to the so-called pleasure family of today. Many marry merely for the pleasure and fun they can get out of it. When the fun ceases the family disappears. Many try marriage to see how they are going to like it.

Moreover, sacred and inviolable marriage and parental rights have been disregarded and ruthlessly violated in practically all countries. Russia, and to some extent other totalitarian states, endeavor to supplant Christian marriage with sexual license; to destroy childhood's natural relationship to parents; to replace the pleasures, duties, and the sacrifices of parenthood by the inanimate and machinelike State. The Communists and the Nazis prescribe in the minutest detail how children are to be reared. According to them the child belongs to the State as does his education, his character formation, his choice of vocation, his purpose and end. All this violates the fundamental unity of the family, and destroys the inviolability of consummated marriage between qualified persons.

Such teachings and practices which are intended to shatter the Christian idea of marriage, which make it as easy to separate from one's wife or husband as from some chance traveling companion, which deliberately undermine the institution of the family are repugnant to Christian teaching, to the natural law, and become a national curse and scourge. It is then a sacred duty of every Christian man and woman to defend and protect family rights and parental rights of education, the indissolubility of marriage, and the position of honor and dignity to which Christianity has elevated woman.

The Catholic Church has always attached supreme importance to the institution of the family, and carefully guarded the sanc- tity of marriage. Her teaching demands fidelity and equality be- tween husband and wife, love and obedience of children toward their parents. Furthermore, she teaches that the sound condition of the State depends on the sound condition of the family. There indeed is a crying need for social reform, but if this reform is to succeed at all it must begin with the family. The nucleus of society must be reformed first.

The family is prior to the State both in the order of time or existence, and in the order of thought. It has a special claim upon civil authority for protection against public dangers. In the words of Will Durant: "The family has been the ultimate foundation of every civilization known to history. It was the economic and productive unit of society, tilling the land to- gether; it was the political unit of society, with parental author- ity as the supporting microcosm of the State. It was the cultural unit, transmitting letters and arts, rearing and teaching the young; and it was the moral unit, inculcating through coopera- tive work and discipline, those social dispositions which are the psychological basis and cement of civilized society. In many ways it was more essential than the State; governments might break up and order yet survive, if the family remained; whereas it seemed to sociologists that if the family should dissolve, civiliza- tion itself would disappear."[1]

---

[1] Will Durant, *The Mansions of Philosophy* (New York: Simon and Schuster, 1929), pp. 395–396.

PART I

THE FAMILY

1. The Nature of the Family

The family which forms the cell of the social organism comprises the husband, wife, children, and their servants. Through it and in it humanity perpetuates itself. Though demanded by nature for the conservation of the human race, the family is, nevertheless, a free society in so far as each individual is free to create or not to create it. There is no obligation upon each individual to marry — there would be in case the human race were threatened with extinction. The family is a necessary society for without it the individual could not attain his physical, moral, and intellectual development. Man naturally aspires to progress and culture. This tendency in man would be incomprehensible, if he could not transmit to his descendants the fruit of his experience and his moral and intellectual heritage. The family is necessary, for the child must be trained from his earliest years in the ways of goodness, virtue, and sacrifice. The school undoubtedly can be of great help in the training of the child, but a complete and well-balanced education begins in the bosom of the family, it is regulated and controlled by the parents. The infinite patience, the spirit of sacrifice, the true and sincere love which the proper education of the child requires are found above all in the family. Though the family is not a perfect society, it is a natural one, neither an arbitrary institution dependent on human will nor an artificial one resulting from progress and civilization. It is based on and anchored in the social nature of man, and is demanded by and required for the human ends embodied in the moral order. Without the family, there can be no society, no State, no mankind. For this reason the enemies of society are also enemies of the family, directing their most vicious attacks against it. Communism is a sufficient proof of this.

By its condemnation of infanticide, infidelity, divorce, concubinage, etc., the Church raised the family to heights it had never reached before. The so-called Reformation attacked the sanctity of the family as well as other Christian teachings. Luther degraded marriage to a merely civil contract. "Marriage," he said, "and all that pertains to it is a temporal thing and does not concern the Church at all." This process of secularization has continued and the dignity of the family has progressively faded from the minds of men outside the true Church. In the past century the theory of organic evolution propounded by Darwin was transferred by sociologists from biology to the domain of social institutions. The family such as we know it today, which is monogamous, that is, the union of one husband with one wife lasting for the lifetime of either of the parties, came to be explained in purely naturalistic fashion as the product of an evolution from a primitive condition of sexual communism or promiscuity through group marriage, that is, unrestrained sexual intercourse within the same tribe or group, and polygamy which has two forms: (a) polyandry, the simultaneous union of one woman with more than one man; (b) polygyny, the simultaneous union of one man with more than one woman. Such teachings degraded the character of the matrimonial contract and opened wide the doors to divorce and to disruption of the family. Up to the present time the monogamous family, which is the cohabitation of only one man with one woman, is recognized by society as lawful.

Recently, however, extensive sociological and anthropological investigations have completely overthrown the evolutionistic theory. Men of the highest authority in their field, such as Peshel, Westermarck, Katzel, Starke, and many others have unanimously rejected the original promiscuity hypothesis as gratuitous. For instance; in the introduction to his *The History of Marriage,* Westermarck acknowledges that he undertook this work with the conviction that primitive man was given to sexual promiscuity, and with the confidence that he would find in the customs of the present-day man some still surviving evidences of primitive promiscuity. Before long, his findings forced him to reject entirely his former belief in the hypothesis of promiscuity.

In his massive three-volume work, after painstaking examination of facts, Westermarck comes to the conclusion that: "The hypothesis of a primitive stage of promiscuity not only lacks all foundation in fact, but is utterly opposed to the most probable inference we are able to make as regards the early condition of man."[2] Again: "It is not, of course, impossible that among some peoples the intercourse between the sexes may have been almost promiscuous. But the hypothesis according to which promiscuity has formed a general stage in the social history of mankind, instead of belonging — as Giraud-Teulon puts it — to the class of hypotheses which are scientifically permissible, is in my opinion one of the most unscientific ever set forth within the whole domain of sociological speculation."[3] With regard to the theory which claims that mother-right everywhere preceded father-right he says: "Those who advocate a primitive stage of mother-right without paternal rights and paternal duties are faced by the formidable fact . . . that among the lowest savages, who chiefly or exclusively subsist on game and such products of nature as they can gather without cultivating the soul or breeding domestic animals, the family consisting of parents and children is a well-marked social unit, with the father as its head and protector."[4] "Whatever might have been the case in earlier times, it is a fact beyond dispute that among the great bulk of existing savage tribes children are in the power of their father, though he may to some extent have to share his authority with the mother."[5]

Nor can it be maintained that monogamous marriage origi-

[2] E. Westermarck, *The History of Human Marriage* (London: The Macmillan Co., 1925), Vol. I, p. 38.

[3] *Ibid.*, p. 336.

[4] *Ibid.*, pp. 45, 46.

[5] E. Westermarck, *The Origin and Development of the Moral Ideas* (London: The Macmillan Co., 1906), Vol. I, pp. 598–599.

nated from the so-called group marriage, for Westermarck in his works conclusively shows that there is no clear case of the actual existence of such group marriages or group relations anywhere, and that the hypothesis of group marriage has no more support than that of sexual communism. Even if evolutionism could prove that promiscuity existed or that it still exists among certain tribes such as the aborigines of Brazil, the Fuegians, Bushmen, and several low tribes of Australia and India, that alone would not render the fact general, but would only indicate certain exceptions which usually serve to prove the rule.

Whoever carefully studies the history of those peoples that left deep traces of their culture, must admit that the history of marriage, instead of manifesting a progressive evolution from the lower to the higher forms, manifests very often a regressive process. In the legal books of Hammurabi (about 2250 B.C.) matrimony is regarded expressly as a juridical institution indicating that the monogamous form was the most common one. Although polygyny was not openly prohibited by the Greeks, it was nevertheless regarded as a degraded practice in relation to the commonly accepted monogamous form. This concept was also prevalent among the Romans. The exceptional cases of polyandry are explained by the scarcity of women. It goes without saying that such a circumstance cannot justify polyandric practices, because the latter would make paternity uncertain, and tends to produce sterility in the woman, thus restricting the birth rate.

Polyandry cannot but exercise a sinister influence upon the matrimonial bond, on the affection due to the children, and on the respect due by the children to their parents. Polyandry is against the natural law for it militates against the primary as well as the secondary ends of marriage. The same may be said of polygyny which, though not absolutely opposed to the specific end of marriage, is, nevertheless, not in harmony with the secondary ends. Such unions give rise to suspicions, jealousy, hatreds, to the great detriment of the children and of the whole family. Again, polygyny by its very nature tends to destroy domestic order and tranquillity as it stimulates human passions by odious preferences. Polygyny is also repugnant to the principle of equality which is the proper characteristic of matrimonial contract. In such a marriage the woman would intimately and exclusively be united to one man, the latter could be united to several women; this obviously destroys equality among the spouses. Hence the woman will no longer be a real mate called to share equally the joys and sorrows of marriage, but only a slave, a mere means of insuring offspring, an instrument of pleasure. Marriage, therefore, from the viewpoint of its primary and secondary ends must be monogamous.

2. THE RELATION OF THE FAMILY TO THE STATE

The end and function of the State is to provide for the common welfare of its citizens. Between the State and the family there exists a moral bond of mutual rights and duties, that is, both parties have the moral power to demand certain things of each other coupled with the moral obligation to do certain things. The family has rights and duties relative to the State, and the State has rights and duties relative to the family. In the first place, the State must respect the right of its citizens to marry and to have a family. Every man has the strictest right to enter into marriage with a partner, to establish a family, and to enjoy all the ordinary benefits and pleasures of family life. This right man possesses not by any grace or concession on the part of the State, but by reason of his being a human person. In regard to marriage the State has purely directive powers, that is, its activities must harmonize with the natural moral laws which are the cornerstone of the family and society.

Between the State and family there are quantitative as well as qualitative differences. The State embraces numberless individuals, the family only a few. The family, unlike the State, is a compact and closely knit association. Any attempt to reduce State unity to the level of family unity would be destructive of the State itself, just as any attempt to reduce family unity to the level of physical individual unity would be destructive of the family. Furthermore, the end and functions of the State and of the family are vastly different. The State has in view the common well-being, that is, its task is to provide indirectly those opportunities that will enable all its citizens to attain their earthly welfare without unjust distinction. The family aims directly at promoting this welfare and at satisfying the various needs. Family relations are limited to the parents, to the offspring, and to the servants; whereas State relations extend to numerous families and to larger organizations. Family duties and obligations differ vastly from State duties and obligations. Thus, while family activities are regulated by the reciprocal duties of love, of piety, and commutative justice; State functions are regulated by the duties of legal justice (implying the relations of the citizens to the State) and by the duties of distributive justice (implying the relations of the State to the individual). In the family, authority belongs to the parents and primarily to the father who is the natural head of the family. The form of family government is essentially monarchic, whereas the form of State government may be monarchic, aristocratic, or democratic. Moreover, the authority of State rulers may be more or less extensive, more or less absolute, according to the constitutional provisos; parental authority is always the same because its nature is immutable.

So much for the differences between State and family. We may now inquire what is the position of the family in society, and what rights are necessary for the family for the fulfillment of its duties and for the realization of its ultimate end. First and foremost the family must be free from State interference in the realization of its goal, which is inherent in the moral order. However, it would be a great mistake to confound true freedom with license. In order to be true and genuine, man's freedom of activity must be directed to his ultimate end. Obviously the State is incapable of engendering true conjugal love of sacrifice for the welfare of their offspring, or of inspiring the children with sentiments of love and gratitude toward their parents. All this is outside the sphere of political functions. There are, however, many other activities which come within the competency of civil power. Since the State is based on the family, and not the family on the State, the State must contribute in a positive way to family welfare so as to enable it to attain its full development. Moreover the State must guarantee whatever is necessary for the exercise of family prerogatives, otherwise the State would be no longer a benefactor of the family but a tyrant. Legislators then must realize and remember that the existence as well as the end of the family, being determined by nature and independent of human will, cannot be subordinated to political caprice and fancy. Whatever hinders the free and rational development of the family is a real menace to its very existence.

PART II

INDISSOLUBILITY OF MARRIAGE

The element of permanence in conjugal society is necessary for the proper education of children and is in accord with sound reason. Divorce militates against the essential purpose of marriage, and for that reason civil authority has no moral right to dissolve the marriage bond. Furthermore, the disastrous effects of divorce both on family and social life should be sufficient reason for the State to uphold the matrimonial bond.

The Gospel has secured to woman liberty, education, and many civil rights. The Gospel has made of the slave a queen; it has lifted her from a state of shameful bondage or licentious liberty to a place of respect and influence. The dignity of woman established, the indissolubility and unity of marriage flowed naturally from it. The principal curse of modern society is divorce. It is the destroyer of nations and is a sure mark of social decay. For fifteen centuries after Christ divorce was unknown among western Christians. But with the revolt of man against

God and His holy Church in the sixteenth century, divorce was made lawful.

The human race is preserved and perpetuated through marriage. Now if the preservation of the human race is the primary end of marriage, it follows that the marriage bond cannot be surrendered to the arbitration of the contracting parties and much less to the arbitrariness of the State. As foundations cannot be undermined without endangering the superstructure, so the indissolubility of the marriage bond cannot be attacked without undermining the family and thereby the social order itself. The very purpose and goal of the family makes marriage indissoluble; and this indissolubility is in perfect accord with the true dictates of human conscience and the universal consensus of human reason. Without permanency marriage would no longer be a stable union of a man and a woman, but only a brutal and bestial intercourse between sexes, repugnant to right reason and to the lofty aspirations of the human heart. Because of the vehemence of passion and the instability of man's emotions, the marital bond must be permanent and lasting and not temporary or transient.

A child is born into the world helpless and weak. He must be fed, clothed, guarded, and protected for many years. This cannot be the work of one but must be of both parents. Divorce deprives the child of the love and care of either or both parents. What is the child's by right ought not to be taken away by the will of the State or his selfish parents.

Moreover, unity and stability of wedlock is required for the education of the offspring. This education requires the cooperation of both parents. The mother contributes primarily to the molding and refinement of the heart, the father to the development and growth of the intellect. Divorce almost always annuls the work of one party, if it does not completely destroy the combined efforts of both. Divorce greatly impedes or completely frustrates the education of the child. On this account unity and permanence are essential properties of marriage.

1. DIVORCE

According to the natural law marriage is intrinsically indissoluble in the sense that marriage, unlike other contracts, may not be dissolved at the pleasure of the contracting parties. Such dissolubility would militate against the essential purpose of marriage, the propagation of the human race and the education of children. Marriage is also extrinsically indissoluble for civil authority has no right to dissolve a valid marriage. Such an act is directly forbidden by the original Divine positive law: "What therefore God has joined together, let no man put asunder."[6] The State has no more power to declare a marriage dissolved than it has to prevent people from marrying. When a marriage has been validly contracted, it can be dissolved by no human power. Instead of making divorce easy, it is the State's duty and to its interest to protect the inviolability of the marital bond.

Since marriage is a sacrament, the State has no immediate or direct power to declare whether or under what conditions its citizens may marry for Christ entrusted the ministration of the sacraments to the Church alone. However, since the authority of the Church is not universally recognized, the State may and must set down conditions and restrictions upon marriage as are demanded by the natural moral law and are necessary for the maintenance of the social order. For example, it may and must forbid the marriage of insane persons or those in close degrees of kinship.

Nor can the contracting parties dissolve their marriage. Ordinarily contracts are dissolved by the agreement of both parties concerned; this is true of material contracts among men, but not of the marriage bond. In contracting marriage the parties must not only consent to the contract but also to all the conditions required by the general welfare; but the general welfare demands that the marriage contract should not be broken except by the death of one of the parties. Even the modern civil codes

---

[6] Matt. 19:6.

regard civil marriage as a unique institution deserving special caution and consideration, and this in view of the fact that there is a profound difference between the marriage and other contracts since the end, the rights, and the duties of marriage are determined by nature and not by the will of the State or of the contracting parties.

We distinguish between *absolute divorce* which implies the dissolution of the marriage bond, and *limited divorce* which leaves the marriage bond intact and implies only separation from bed and board. According to Catholic doctrine, there can never be an absolute divorce from a Christian marriage at least after the marriage has been consummated. Separations from bed and board are allowed for various reasons.

It has been retorted that divorce under certain circumstances, as in cases of adultery, desertion, etc., serves as a suitable means for restoring peace and happiness to the family. True, divorce may obviate a great many inconveniences, but this cannot be a guiding criterion for lawmakers who before all else must take into account the moral lawfulness of an act as well as its consequences. Divorce does at times avoid certain evils, but as a general rule it opens wide the doors to greater and numberless other evils. As in all other human affairs and institutions, so in marriage there will always be certain inconveniences; but these inconveniences can under no circumstances be a justification for the breakdown of the family. Furthermore, in cases of necessity there is the possibility of separation from bed and board, and hence the above objection becomes groundless.

The so-called arguments against the indissolubility of marriage are sophistries devoid of value and tending to foment sinful passions and to legalize conjugal infidelity. Once legalized, divorce will accomplish its nefarious task. Neither legislator nor magistrate will succeed in saving the family and society from utter disintegration. Even if divorce were limited to certain cases, as for instance, to adultery, insanity, or an incurable disease of one of the parties, the remedy would be worse than the evil it seeks to cure. If certain sins or violations of the divine and hu-

man laws are required by law to obtain a divorce, the party who
wants a divorce will not hesitate to commit them and thus
supply the law with its pound of flesh. A breach in the indissolubility of marriage will inevitably lead to the abolition of marriage itself. Divorce does not, as it is often asserted, indicate an
advance in culture and civilization, but rather a retrogression to
barbarism and immorality. Instead of cementing, it dissolves
conjugal union; it engenders new wounds without healing the
previous ones; it does not enhance, but menaces the sanctity of
the nuptial bed.

In his encylical on "Christian Marriage," Leo XIII graphically
sums up the evil consequences of divorce: "It is hardly possible
to describe the magnitude of the evils that flow from divorce.
Matrimonial contracts are by it made variable, mutual kindness
is weakened, deplorable inducements to unfaithfulness are supplied, harm is done to the education and training of children,
occasion is afforded for the breaking up of homes, the seeds of
dissension are sown among families, the dignity of womanhood
is lessened and brought low, and women run the risk of being
deserted after having ministered to the pleasures of men. Since
nothing has such power to lay waste families and to destroy the
mainstay of kingdoms as the corruption of morals, it is easily
seen that divorces are in the highest degree hostile to the prosperity of families and states, springing as they do from the depraved morals of the people, and, as experience shows us, open-
ing a way to every kind of evil-doing in public as well as in
private life.

"Further still, when divorce has once been tolerated, no restraint is powerful enough to keep it within the bounds marked
out or surmised. Great indeed is the force of example, and even
greater still the might of passion. With such incitements it must
needs follow that the eagerness for divorce which daily spreads
in devious ways, will infect the minds of many like a virulent
contagious disease, or like a flood of water bursting through every
barrier. These truths, doubtless, are clear in themselves. But they
will become clearer yet if we call to mind the teachings of

experience. No sooner has the road to divorce begun to be made smooth by law, than at once quarrels, jealousies, and judicial separations largely increase. Upon this so great a shamelessness of life follows as to make even those who previously had favored the divorces repent of their action lest, if a remedy is not sedulously sought by repealing the law, the State itself might come to ruin.

"The Romans of old are said to have shrunk with horror from the first examples of divorce, but ere long, all sense of decency was blunted in their soul. The meager restraint of passion died out, and the marriage vow was so often broken that the statement would actually seem to be true — women used to reckon years not by the change of consuls, but of their husbands.

"In like manner Protestants at first allowed legalized divorces in certain but as yet few cases. With the occurrence, however, of circumstances of a similar kind, the number of divorces spread to such extent in Germany, America, and elsewhere, that all wise thinkers deplored the limitlessness of the laws as simply intolerable. Even in Catholic States the like evil existed. Wherever at any time divorce was introduced . . . many applied their minds to contriving all kinds of fraud and devices, bringing accusations of cruelty, violence, and adultery merely to feign grounds for the dissolution of the matrimonial bond. . . . Thus we clearly see how foolish and senseless it is to expect any public good from divorce. On the contrary, its obvious tendency is the certain destruction of society."[7]

Many prominent modern writers, such as Rousseau, Bentham, Hume, Montesquieu, De Bonald, Comte, Hobbes, Wallace, Hegel, Treundelenburg, Tolstoi, though avowed enemies of the Church, were openly opposed to divorce, certainly not for theological reasons, but because divorce militates against the good of the State and the dignity of human personality, because it is destructive of family peace and prosperity and most injurious to the education of children. Even the popular modern writer, Will Durant, after an exhausting analysis of the breakdown of mar-

---

[7] Leo XIII, *Arcanum* (Christian Marriage).

riage concludes: "The last word, however, must be for mono-
gamy. The lifelong union remains the loftiest conception of
human marriage; and it is still the goal which the perfect lover
will set himself when he pledges his troth. There is something
cowardly in divorce, like flight from the field of war; and something unstable and superficial in one who flits from mate to
mate. Men and women of character will solve these difficulties
as they arise, knowing that difficulties as great would meet them
on any other battleground. Their reward comes when the hard
years of mutual readjustment are over, and a steady affection
tenoned and mortised in the care of children and the sharing
of a thousand vicissitudes has supplanted the transitory ardor
of physical desire, and made two minds and two hearts one.
Only when that test of the soul has been passed will they know
the fulness of love."[8]

2. THE SACRAMENT OF MATRIMONY

Christ raised the marriage contract to the dignity of a sacrament. Marriage is now something sacred; it is blessed and enriched beyond our human means, and raised from the level of
something natural to the plane of the supernatural. The sacramental grace enables the married to resist the assaults of con-
cupiscence, to use marriage for its proper purpose, and to bear
the burdens of their state in life.

In the sacrament of matrimony the husband and wife take
each other "to have and to hold, from this day forward, for
better, for worse, for richer, for poorer, in sickness and in
health, until death do us part." Christ Himself emphatically declares that marriage is *indissoluble:* "And some Pharisees coming up asked Him, testing Him, 'Is it lawful for a man to put
away his wife?' But he answered and said to them, 'What did
Moses command you?' They said: 'Moses permitted us to write
a notice of dismissal, and to put her away.' But Jesus said to
them, 'By reason of the hardness of your heart he wrote you that

---

[8] *Op. cit.*, p. 231.

Commandment. But from the beginning of creation God made them male and female. For this cause a man shall leave his father and mother, and shall cleave to his wife, and the two shall become one flesh. Therefore now they are no longer two, but one flesh. What therefore God has joined together, let no man put asunder.' And in the house, His disciples again asked Him concerning this. And He said to them, 'Whosoever puts away his wife and marries another, commits adultery against her; and if the wife puts away her husband, and marries another, she commits adultery.' "[9] St. Luke also records the words of Christ against divorce. "Everyone who puts away his wife and marries another commits adultery; and he who marries a woman who has been put away from her husband commits adultery."[10] In like manner St. Paul: "But to those who are married, not I, but the Lord commands that a wife is not to depart from her husband, and if she departs, that she is to remain unmarried or be reconciled to her husband. And let not a husband put away his wife."[11] In these passages the indissolubility of marriage is affirmed. This divine positive ordinance confirms and ratifies the stability of marriage for the whole human race.

3. ARTIFICIAL BIRTH CONTROL

Another widespread plague which threatens death and destruction both to the family and to the State is birth control. Our present birth-control movement goes back to the "Essay on the Principle of Population," written by Robert Malthus in 1798. Malthus advocated birth restriction by postponement of marriage and by marital continency.

Today the modern naturalist upholds the use of artificial devices, called contraceptives, for preventing conception. Many advocate not only unrestricted sexual intercourse within the married life, but also outside the marital state. They extol the naturalness of the sexual urge in man, become eloquent about

---

[9] Mark 10:2-12.
[10] Luke 16:18.
[11] 1 Cor. 7:10, 11.

the harmful effects of its frustration, and speak of contraceptives as the means of saving man from the tortures inflicted by traditional morality.

For man any sort of artificial birth control is not only unnatural but gravely sinful. The Catholic doctrine on this matter is clearly stated by Pius XI in his encyclical letter on "Christian Marriage" (1930): "No reason, however grave, may be put forward by which anything intrinsically against nature may become conformable to nature and morally good. Since, therefore, the conjugal act is destined primarily by nature for the begetting of children, those who, in exercising it, deliberately frustrate its natural power and purpose sin against nature and commit a deed which is shameful and intrinsically vicious. . . . Any use whatsoever of matrimony exercised in such a way that the act is deliberately frustrated in its natural power to generate life is an offense against the law of God and of nature, and those who indulge in such are branded with the guilt of grave sin."[12]

Birth control is not merely an individual problem, it is a national problem, for it harms the individual, physically and morally, and menaces public morality by undermining the State. In this connection it is well to remember that the State does not legislate on or interfere with the purely private actions of individuals, but as soon as any action has social consequences it comes within the competency of the State, and this from the standpoint of its relation to the moral law. Medical authorities agree that most contraceptives are physically harmful. Besides, who can adequately estimate the harm contraceptives have on the human spirit, on society, and on future generations? The use of contraceptives does violence to human nature, sometimes making for biological sterility in the woman using them. It makes for nervousness, nervous affliction, and neurosis. Again, man is a rational animal consisting of body and spirit. The marriage act in its true nature is a spiritual union as well as a physical one. Moreover it has its moral side — that of accepting

---

[12] Pius XI, *Casti Connubii* (Christian Marriage).

or avoiding full natural responsibility for what one does. All these aspects are excluded when by the use of contraceptives the marriage act is reduced to the purely biological level.

Birth control has a bad effect on private and public morality. The dissemination and knowledge of contraceptives is a powerful agent making for looseness of sex morality and profligacy. It encourages laxity and immorality among the married as well as among the unmarried. This is a well-known fact as testified to by Dr. W. Gerry Morgan, of Washington, D. C., at one time president of the American Medical Association, in his statement before the Committee on Ways and Means, House of Representatives, May 20, 1932 (Hearings, pp. 74–77); as well as by Dr. Howard Kelley, of Johns Hopkins University, testifying before the same committee. Statistics also show that marriages in which birth control has been practiced are most likely to end in divorce. Many doctors claim that the use of contraceptives is not more than 60 per cent successful. This is taken to explain why abortions have been on the increase despite the enormous spread in the use of preventives.

Birth control finally exercises a pernicious influence on civil society and produces economic decay. As an illustration of this we appeal to past as well as present events. This vice prevailed in the days preceding the decline and fall of ancient Greece and Rome. The disaster which has overtaken France was due in a great part to this nefarious practice. It dates from before the Franco-Prussian War and has been most prevalent for the past twenty-five years. In many European countries just prior to the present war, men of all shades of religious and political creed have been endeavoring to counteract the evil effects of birth control as evidenced in static and decreasing birth rates.[13]

In order therefore to protect both the individual family and

---

[13] For up-to-date statistics, cf. *Marriage and the Family. A Study in Social Philosophy,* Jacques Leclercq, translated from the French by Thomas R. Hanley, O.S.B. (New York, 1941); Raymond W. Murray, C.S.C., *The Birth Rate and Birth Control";* and Frank T. Flynn, *Social Problems* (New York, 1938), Part III "Population, Growth and Decline"; Raoul de Guchteneere, *Judgment on Birth Control* (New York, 1931).

society, the State should forbid and impose penalties on the dissemination of birth control literature and the sale of contraceptives. Thus it will contribute positively to the good of the family without interfering with its inner life. On the other hand, the State would really interfere with the freedom of the family, if it adopted the recent proposal of Mrs. Sanger who would have a law passed making it necessary for married couples to obtain special permission from the State in order to bear a child. Moreover, the granting of such a license would hold for one child only, and the couple would have to renew their request for each additional child.

PART III

EDUCATION

The welfare of the individual and of society depends upon the proper education and training of children. The education of the child, if it is to be more than mere instruction or injection of crude elements of knowledge, must be such as to equip him for a full realization of life, and to put him in the most favorable conditions possible for profiting by life's opportunities, avoiding its dangers, and so attaining its true and proper end.

Every man has a right to a suitable education or a proper bringing up. A suitable education is one that enables a man to take his proper place in life. It includes a strict right to all the knowledge needed for living a moral life and for facing successfully the ordinary conditions and situations of adult life. The right to education also includes the right to preparation for whatever profession or vocation one is best suited.

Having a social nature, every man also has the strictest right to an education that fits him for social life, that makes him capable of proper social relations with others and willing to cooperate with his fellow men in every way. He has, moreover, the strictest right to enter into all kinds of cooperative activities with his fellow men, to join different kinds of organizations or associations for social intercourse, or industrial organizations for the betterment of his conditions of life or of work, or mutual benefit societies of different kinds.

On the important question of education there are today two mutually conflicting systems. On the one hand, state totalitarianism holds: (1) that education primarily and properly belongs to the State; (2) that the schools belong to the State; (3) that the child belongs to the State; (4) that the State has no religion, or has a religion of its own invention as in Germany with its return to ancient idolatry and also worship of the State, and Russia with its theophobia; (5) that the formation of national character belongs to the State; (6) that the formation of the teachers belongs to the State; (7) that no one shall teach the people except by patent of the State.

On the other hand, the traditional Christian teaching maintains: (1) that the children of Christians have a right by divine law to a Christian education; (2) that Christian parents have a twofold right and duty, both natural and supernatural, to guard this inheritance of their children; (3) that Christian children are not the sole property of the State; (4) that the formation or teaching and training of children as Christians, is of higher moment than all secular instruction and may not be subordinated nor exposed to the risk of being lost; (5) that in the selection of teachers to whom their children shall be entrusted, Christian parents have a right and a duty which excludes all other human authority. These two systems are mutually exclusive. We have to choose between them. Pius XI, in unison with the teaching of his predecessors, states emphatically, that: "first of all education belongs pre-eminently to the Church, by reason of a twofold title in the supernatural order conferred exclusively upon her by God Himself: absolutely superior therefore to any other title in the natural order."[14]

---

[14] Pius XI, *Providentissimus Deus* (Christian Education of Youth).

1. State Monopoly of Education

State monopoly of education militates against man's natural freedom of teaching and man's freedom of acquiring knowledge. For in virtue of the natural law of self-development and sociability every man possesses, antecedently to and independently of any positive right, the inalienable right of communicating truths to others and of acquiring them from others, provided he observes the laws of justice and of charity toward others and himself. One of the chief means for self-development is freedom of thought and of speech. Obviously this freedom of thought and of speech does not consist in the pursuit of mendacity and sin but in the pursuit of truth and justice. "There can be no doubt," says Leo XIII, "that truth alone should imbue the minds of men; for in it are found the well-being, the end, and perfection of every intelligent nature. Therefore nothing but truth should be taught both to the ignorant and to the educated, so as to bring knowledge to those who have it not, and to preserve it in those who possess it. For this reason it is plainly the duty of all who teach to banish error from the mind, and by sure safeguards to close the entry to all false convictions."[15]

In the light of these sound principles every one has a natural and inalienable right to express his thoughts. Neither the State nor anyone else can limit the exercise of this right to a few persons, for such would be clearly opposed to the principle of the equal right of all; in other words, it would deny freedom of thought and of speech.

Teaching is nothing else than the manifestation of our thoughts to those who are willing to listen to them; it is one of the means of exercising the freedom of thought and of speech. Teaching is not only a natural right, but a natural action which clearly ratifies the naturalness of this right. Whenever a discussion on some important topic takes place, he that knows more about the subject is always teaching; it has been the principal

---

[15] Leo XIII, *Libertas Humana* (Human Liberty).

means for preserving traditions, usages, customs, and the first laws of peoples. The spoken word alone has enacted the laws of paternal government in the domestic society which is the foundation of every other society. The word is the perennial instrument of the origin and progress of civilization; it is the most ancient and perpetual pledge, the outward expression of internal light of the eternal truths revealed to man. No government nor anyone else, however powerful, has the right to impede the oral imparting of true knowledge.

The situation is even more tragic when the State compels parents to entrust the teaching and training of their children to teachers appointed by the civil authorities. The usurpation of this parental right leads straight to socialism and statal despotism. It deprives parents of the liberty to choose between public and private education, between useful and useless or harmful teaching. In monopolistic institutions children often are imbued with doctrines opposed to religion, sound morality, and good customs. If the State possesses an exclusive right of teaching, it can for stronger reasons claim and take over the administration of family material goods, and arrogate to itself all other parental rights. It should be apparent to everyone that of all earthly possessions children are the most precious; hence the right and duty of educating them is a greater parental duty than the administration of their material goods. The State has no right to prescribe what, when, and how we shall eat. Neither has it the right to prescribe intellectual food for our minds. Hence:

1. A monopoly of education whereby the State reserves to itself alone the right of operating schools is unjust and contrary to natural rights.

2. Laws of any State which, contrary to the dictates of their Christian conscience, or even contrary to their legitimate preferences, force parents to send their children to government schools, are unlawful and opposed to the natural rights of man.

3. Such a statal system directly deprives the parents of their inalienable rights and inevitably leads to socialism. For if the State can *justly* assume the rights of education, why not the ad-

ministration of the goods of the family and other parental rights?

4. The State has the duty to protect and respect the natural rights of parents to control the education of their children.

5. State monopoly of education would moreover entail the following results: "(*a*) The end of all educational freedom; (*b*) the establishment of a bureaucratic control of our schools; (*c*) the death of private initiative in education; (*d*) the introduction of politics into the schools system; (*e*) increased expenditures of public moneys with little or no increased efficiency in education; (*f*) multiplication of jobs and officeholders in the school system — a direct menace to political freedom; (*g*) arbitrary educational rules, policies, and laws issued by a central bureau; (*h*) interference with the rights of parents and children in matters of conscience; (*i*) the school would be used as a means of propagating political theories acceptable to those in power; (*j*) partisanship in politics would control education, in a word the schools would be sovietized."[16]

State monopoly of education is also opposed to the function and purpose of the State. The government has the duty of promoting the general welfare by fostering and aiding private activity and initiative, and by refraining from whatever would hinder or eliminate it. But such a monopoly, not only would hinder but would also exclude private initiative and activity in the educational field to the great detriment of education, since free competition between public and private educators stimulates progress and advancement. It is interesting to know that the apostles of educational monopoly are the very ones who insist on absolute freedom of the press and association as inalienable rights of every man. Hence the pertinent question: Why should there be freedom of teaching through the medium of the press and no freedom of teaching through the medium of the spoken word? Why should this freedom be extended to all private associations and denied only to private schools? If it is permissible to teach

---

[16] *A Catechism of Catholic Education* (N.C.W.C.), p. 68.

through the artificial medium of the press, why not through the natural medium of the living word? Likewise, it is an open contradiction to uphold freedom of association and at the same time to deny this to private schools. If people may form associations for social or economic purposes, parents should be free to erect and maintain schools for the education of their children.

2. THE RIGHTS OF THE CHURCH TO EDUCATION

The right of the Church to maintain schools is implied in the commission of her Divine Founder: "All power is given to me in heaven and in earth. Going therefore, teach ye all nations; baptizing them in the name of the Father, and of the Son, and of the Holy Ghost; teaching them to observe all things whatsoever I have commanded you; and behold I am with you all days, even to the consummation of the world." The office of the Church instituted by Christ is to teach all nations. This commission authorizes the Church to teach the truths of salvation to every human being, whether adult or child, rich or poor, private citizen or public official. But this divine commission given to the Apostles and through them to their successors, the Bishops of the Church, cannot be carried out effectively without the establishment and maintenance of schools.

In virtue of her supernatural mission through sharing in the divine teaching authority of Christ and by reason of the fact that she generates, nurtures, and educates souls by means of her sacraments and her doctrine in the divine life of grace, the rights of the Church in education are pre-eminent. Her right to freedom in teaching is inherent and inviolable. "The Church is independent," writes Pius XI, "of any sort of earthly power as well in the origin as in the exercise of her mission as educators, not merely in regard to her proper end and object, but also in regard to the means necessary and suitable to attain that end. Hence, with regard to every other kind of human learning and instruction, which is the common patrimony of individuals and society, the Church has an independent right to make use of it, and above all decide what may help or harm Christian education.

And this must be so, because the Church as a perfect society has an independent right to the means conducive to its end, and because every form of instruction, no less than every human action has a necessary connection with man's last end, and therefore cannot be withdrawn from the dictates of the divine law, of which the Church is guardian, interpreter, and infallible mistress."[17]

3. THE RIGHTS OF THE FAMILY TO EDUCATION

Furthermore, children belong to the family before they belong to the State. It is then apparent that education begins even with the birth of the child. The training at this early age is the foundation, the basis of all that the child's later development in more advanced education, and even his application during the whole course of his life, will receive. Plutarch in a treatise on the education of children makes this appropriate remark: "It is necessary to use every care in order to make a good choice of the nurses entrusted with the children's early education. In a word, if it be necessary to mold the limbs of children immediately after their birth that they may not contract any natural defect, *we cannot too soon form also their disposition and their manners.*" The mind of a child is like plastic clay, which receives without resistance any form that we wish to give it — once strengthened by age it bends with difficulty. As seals impress themselves quickly on wax, so precepts imparted to young minds easily become imprinted and leave deep traces there.

This duty of the parents to provide for the education of their offspring is expressed clearly and emphatically in Canon 1113 of the Code of the Canon Law. "Parents are under a grave obligation to see to the religious and moral education of their children, as well as to their physical and civic training, as far as they can, and moreover to provide for their temporal well-being."

To guide the child's intellectual and moral efforts is the sacred right and duty of parents. Only when left in control of

---

[17] Pius XI, *op. cit.*

the rearing and education of the children can the family do its work properly. Therefore, except in cases of inability or culpable neglect on the part of parents, the State usurps the authority and the rights of the family when it removes children from the influence of parents or compels them to attend prescribed schools. In view of the almost universal hypernationalistic pretensions as to the education of children, it is gratifying that our government formally recognized the prior rights of the family in the famous United States Supreme Court decision of June 1, 1925, on the Oregon School Case, which reads: "The fundamental theory of liberty upon which all governments in this Union repose excludes any general power of the State to standardize its children by forcing them to accept instruction from public teachers only. The child is not a mere creature of the State; those who nurture him and direct his destiny have the right coupled with the high duty to recognize, and prepare him for additional duties." This is a clear recognition of the prior right of the family to the education of the child.

Since the family is prior to the State, the latter cannot claim the exclusive right of education without subordinating the family to itself, that is, a primary end to a secondary end. Indeed, whenever education becomes an exclusive State function, the former thereby is made completely subservient to the latter. Such a view utterly denaturalizes the family and ignores or pretends to ignore the profound distinction between the purpose or end of the family and the State. These important distinctions were already pointed out in the beginning of this chapter.

It is, therefore, the duty of the State not to usurp this right of education, but to aid the family in the bringing up of the children by supplying those necessary educational facilities which the means of individual families are incapable of furnishing. "Paternal authority can neither be abolished by the State nor absorbed; for it has the same source as human life itself." Children are in some way part of the father, and as it were, the continuation of the father's personality. Strictly speaking, the child takes its place in civil society not in its own right, but in its quality as a member of the family in which it is begotten. And it is precisely because 'the child belongs to the father, that before it attains the use of free will, it is in the power and care of its parents' (St. Thomas, II*, II*°, q. 10, a. 12). The socialists, therefore, in setting aside the parent and introducing the providence of the State, act *against natural justice,* and threaten the very existence of family life."[18] Such a priority of rights on the part of the Church and of the family in the field of education does not in any way infringe upon the true and just rights of the State in regard to the education of its citizens.

4. THE RIGHTS OF THE STATE TO EDUCATION

Although parents have an inherent, direct, and natural right to educate their children in accordance with their religious beliefs, the State has certain jurisdiction of its own in this matter. The State, however, has not a natural or direct right. The State has a right and duty to provide facilities for the training of youth, since a proper education is necessary for social well-being. This general welfare constitutes the primary concern of the State. Hence we are justified in drawing the following conclusions.

1. Schools are a means of assistance to the family. If circumstances prevent parents from educating their children, others may perform this duty.

2. It is a duty of the State to protect the prior rights of the family and of the child in regard to education. It must protect the child if the parents are wanting either physically or morally.

3. The State must encourage the Church and the family and supplement by its own schools their work when this falls short of what is necessary. The State has ample means to assist and it is only right that it uses these means to the advantage of the contributors.

4. The State can exact and take measures to secure all citizens such knowledge of civic and political duties as is needed for the common good.

---

[18] Leo XIII, *Rerum Novarum* (The Condition of the Workingman).

5. In promoting education the State should respect the rights of Church and family concerning Christian education and not usurp or unjustly interfere with them.

The functions of the State in regard to education are clearly outlined in the Pastoral Letter of the Bishops of U. S. A. 1919 "The State has a right to insist that its citizens shall be educated. It should encourage among the people such a love of learning that they will take the initiative and, without constraint, provide for the education of their children. Should they through negligence or lack of means fail to do so, the State has the right to establish schools and take every other legitimate means to safeguard its own vital interests against the dangers that result from ignorance. In particular, it has both the right and duty to exclude the teaching of doctrines which aim at the subversion of law and order and therefore at the destruction of the State itself. The State is competent to do these things because its essential function is to promote the general welfare. But on the same principle it is bound to respect and protect the rights of the citizen and especially of the parents. As long as these rights are properly exercised, to encroach upon them is not to further the general welfare, but to put it in peril." Therefore the State, the Church, and the family each have vital interests in the child, and these must be protected and respected mutually. The State must see to it that the child is properly trained for citizenship, and the Church must see to it that her children are adequately trained for membership in the kingdom of heaven.

From the above considerations it is clear that a State monopoly of education is opposed to parental rights. It is expedient now to consider education particularly as affecting the rising generation. It is universally admitted that the primary purpose of education is not a wholesale turning out of poets, orators, scientists philosophers, etc., but to make men acquainted with their rights and duties, with morality and religion. Instruction is inseparable from education just as the intellect is inseparable from the will, just as mental activities are inseparable from volitional activities.

5. EDUCATION, MORALITY, AND RELIGION

It is difficult to think of any branch of knowledge that does not imply a direct or indirect reference to some moral or religious principle. How, for instance, can history avoid or ignore the question of man's origin? How can geography, an indispensable ally of history, be studied without reference to the origin of the earth, of the sun, and of the stars? Then other questions present themselves: Is there a revealed religion or not? What are the primary concepts of morality? Is there no difference between Nero and Titus; between Nero killing his mother, and Titus contributing to the happiness of the human race?

Among subjects of higher learning, which make up the so-called secondary education, may be mentioned philosophy, physics, chemistry, and advanced history. Here the questions present themselves: What systems of philosophy and ethics should be inculcated? What conclusions can be drawn from such systems? Should Christian religion be regarded as true or false? Is the morality taught in such schools in harmony with sound reason and prolific of individual and social good? What is the explanation of the forces that govern the world? Are biblical events and facts regarded true or false?

The primary purpose of higher education is the study of the ultimate causes of things and their finality. Should theism or atheism be its subject matter? Is the existence and immortality of the soul affirmed or denied? Is divine Providence upheld, or blind evolution advocated? What are the views of the educators about marriage, divorce, and birth control? Who has the right to determine what kind of teaching shall be imparted to the youth? Who is bold enough to maintain that parents have no right to educate their offspring in institutions which they consider most beneficial for moral and intellectual development? Finally, why must parents be compelled to send their children to the so-called educational institutions where innocent minds are imbued with false doctrines and where pure hearts are corrupted?

Freedom of education is the sole measure for preserving parental authority and the parents have a right to insist on this freedom. It would be tyrannical to deny it. When there is no freedom of teaching, when education and instruction are the exclusive prerogatives of the State, parents who regard such teaching
as immoral are confronted by the cruel alternative either of
sending their children to a school that is sometimes evil or of
depriving them of an education; and in such an alternative the
choice of Christian parents cannot be a matter of doubt; they
must prefer to see their offspring deprived of the unwanted kind
of instruction and remain in ignorance. For while ignorance may
sometimes lead to immorality it is better to be ignorant of some
facts than to be indoctrinated with immorality and false principles; in the first instance there may be a great danger of falling into the abyss, but in the second, the fall has already taken
place, to emerge from which is, humanly speaking, impossible.

SELECT READINGS

Catholic Encyclopedia, arts. "Family"; "Marriage"; "Divorce":
    "Education"; "Right to Educate"; "Duty of Parents."
Cronin, M., *The Science of Ethics* (New York: Benziger, 1922),
    Vol. II, Chs. XIII and XIV.
Haas, F. J., *Man and Society* (New York: Century Co., 1930),
    Ch. VI.
Joyce, G. H., S.J., *Christian Marriage.*
Leclercq, Jacques, *Marriage and the Family* (tr. by Thomas R.
    Hanley, O.S.B.) (New York: Pustet, 1941).
Leo XIII, *Arcanum* (Christian Marriage).
Noll, J. F., *Our National Enemy No. I: Education Without
    Religion* (Huntington: Our Sunday Visitor Press, 1942).
Pastoral Letter of the Bishops of U. S. A., 1919.
Pius XI, *Casti Connubii* (Christian Marriage); *Providentissimus
    Deus* (Christian Education of Youth).
Ross, E. J., *A Survey of Sociology* (Milwaukee: The Bruce Pub-
    lishing Co., 1932).

CHAPTER XI

THE CHURCH AND THE STATE

THE PROBLEM of the relation between Church and State is an important one, especially in these days when there is so much opposition to and persecution of the Church. Recently we have witnessed a bloody persecution of the Church in Mexico and, during the late civil war, in Spain. For more than twenty-five years communism has not only rejected religion in general and Christianity in particular, but has made open war against the very idea of God. Religion, in the words of Marx, is the opium of the people.

Religion and communism are incompatible, both in theory and in practice. The theory of historical materialism, say the communists, has demonstrated that the very idea of God and of the supernatural powers arises at a definite stage in human history, and at another definite stage begins to disappear as a childish notion. Man, in their view, controls natural forces not because of his faith in God and in divine assistance, but in spite of that faith. A communist who rejects the commandments of religion and acts in accordance with the directions of the Party ceases to be one of the faithful. On the other hand, one who, while calling himself a communist, continues to cling to religious faith, ceases thereby to be a communist. One cannot be both Christian and communist.

According to communism the Church must be entirely separated from the State and its property confiscated; religion must not be taught in the schools, and the Church must have no power over education. Propaganda against religion is essential. This propaganda is being disseminated by the powerful Union of the Militant Godless of Moscow, and in this country militant organized atheism is carried on by the American Association for the Advancement of Atheism. Atheism in the United States has so far advanced that, as Monsignor Sheen says, if Moscow were to fall, the center of communism would be transferred to New York City.

Of course, the persecution of the Church is not an exclusive trait of communism. In fact all the totalitarian States must sooner or later come into conflict with Church teaching and consequently with the Church itself. Thus in Nazi Germany the terms of the Concordat between the Third Reich and the Vatican have been ignored and openly violated. Nazi leaders urge Catholics to abandon their faith; they are constantly disparaging the Church and clergy. The National-Socialist press is relentlessly attacking the hierarchy and other Church leaders. The Catholic publications are disappearing one by one. Preaching has been curtailed. In some places it is only permitted after being censored by the State police. Dissolution of Catholic organizations and the almost obligatory enrollment of youth in the Hitler Youth Movement is in evidence everywhere. Moreover, there is a gradual suppression of religious and confessional schools; the latter, one of the most influential forces in old Germany, are being liquidated.

In this religious persecution thousands have been imprisoned, exiled, sent to concentration camps, and murdered, simply because they are faithful to God and to their own consciences. The Nazi persecution of the Church extends far and wide: it includes Poland, Belgium, Holland, Austria, and other occupied countries. Monasteries are closed, Church property is confiscated by the State. Religion is made an object of ridicule; the Commandments of God are openly violated; monks and nuns are despoiled and expelled from their houses. In the place of the one, true eternal God, the Nazis have created according to their own good pleasure false gods — Nature, the State, the people, or the race. According to the *National-Sozialistische Monatshefte* of September, 1938, "It is said that the body belongs to the State and the soul to the Church or God. This is no longer the case.

The whole man body and soul belongs to the German Nation and to the German State. The latter has also taken all matters of faith under its control." Needless to say, this attitude toward the Church is but the result and actualization of the philosophical teaching of Hobbes, Spinoza, Hegel, etc., who contended that the State is a projection or manifestation of divinity, the source of all right, and that consequently religion itself is subject to the statal will.

Again, here in the United States there is a great deal of intolerance and persecution of the Church. Catholic institutions are constantly attacked; they will probably continue to be assailed in the future as they have been in the past. No other Christian body incurs so much public hate and obloquy, nor are its members so openly discriminated against socially, economically, and politically. This attitude, no doubt, is due to prevailing false views on the relation of Church and State. Too many people are profoundly ignorant of the Catholic doctrine on this subject. It is, therefore, necessary to throw some light on this important question.

PART I

THE CHURCH

1. A Divine Institution

Besides the family and the State there is another society, perfect and universal, founded on positive divine right, the Church of Jesus Christ. The first two belong to the natural, and the third to the supernatural order. Each has proper limits assigned to it by the eternal law and a proper sphere of activities determined by the specific end of each. The respective end or goal of these societies being established by nature cannot be destroyed or modified; nor can they be antagonistic to one another for they are mutually perfective.

Since the goal of religious society, being the eternal happiness of man, is in direct relation with God, it is superior to and necessarily governs the goals of the other two societies which, being the temporal happiness of man, are in indirect relation with God.

Christ divinely instituted the Church and determined its nature and organization. "And Jesus spoke to them saying, 'All power in heaven and on earth has been given to me. Go, therefore, and make disciples of all nations, baptizing them in the name of the Father, and of the Son, and of the Holy Spirit, teaching them to observe all that I have commanded you; and behold, I am with you all days, even unto the consummation of the world.' "[1] The mandate could not have been more explicit. In virtue of His divine authority, Christ commissioned His Apostles to teach and to guide all nations in the way of holiness and truth; He appointed them as His ministers and representatives in this important concern. As if this were not enough, He makes His command even more explicit: "He therefore said to them again, 'Peace be with you. As the Father has sent me, I also send you. . . . Receive the Holy Spirit; whose sins you shall forgive, they are forgiven them; and whose sins you shall retain, they are retained.' "[2] The efficacy of this new mission is complete. "He who hears you, hears me; and he who rejects you, rejects me; and he who rejects me, rejects him who sent me."[3] "Go into the whole world and preach the gospel to every creature. He who believes and is baptized shall be saved, but he who does not believe shall be condemned."[4]

Thus the Christian family, the Church, or the visible body of Christ is organized. The organization which Christ established was to be a teaching organization, consisting of rulers and subjects. Some are appointed to teach, to govern, and rule, namely, the pastors or bishops; others are to listen and obey, namely the faithful. This organization embraces all the faithful without distinction of race, rank, fortune, sex, or age.

---

[1] Matt. 28:18–20.   [3] Luke 10:16.
[2] John 20:21–23.   [4] Mark, 16:16.

This organization of the Church became complete when Christ made Peter the head of the apostolic college, and gave to him the power of the keys: "And I say to thee, thou art Peter, and upon this rock I will build my Church, and the gates of hell shall not prevail against it. And I will give thee the keys of the kingdom of heaven; and whatever thou shalt bind on earth shall be bound in heaven, and whatever thou shalt loose on earth shall be loosed in heaven."[5] And again: "Feed my lambs; feed my sheep."[6] In the Church we have the hierarchy which teaches and rules in virtue of a mandate obtained from God. They have the right and the power to teach and govern the faithful; to enact and promulgate laws; to threaten transgressors with punishment. On the other hand, we have the faithful or laity who obey and respect the teachings of the Apostles.

The Church then is a visible society founded by Christ and intended by Him to be the means for redemption and salvation of men. It consists of a supreme head, the Pope, the bishops, who are successors of the Apostles, the priests, and the faithful. In other words, the Church may be defined as an organization or congregation of all who profess the faith in Christ, partake of the same sacraments, and are governed by the visible head of the Church, the Pope, and their lawful pastors. In spite of accidental differences of place and time the Church is today essentially the same as in apostolic times; its teachings, its sacraments, and its hierarchical organization are the same.

2. A PERFECT AND NECESSARY SOCIETY

Like the State the Church is a perfect and necessary society. It is a society perfect in its origin because it is a divine institution in the strictest sense of the word; it was founded directly by God. It is perfect and sublime in its goal, which surpasses every temporal and earthly goal, having for its object the eternal happiness of man. It is perfect in its hierarchical form and completely independent of any created authority; it is perfect in its

---

[5] Matt. 16:19.
[6] John 21:17.

universality, having in view the expansion of its kingdom to all the peoples of the earth without distinction of tongue or race, regarding all men as children of God; it is perfect in its duration, not being circumscribed by time but destined to carry on its work of spiritual regeneration and social reconstruction until the end of the world. It has the assurance of Christ's lasting assistance: "Behold, I will be with you until the consummation of the world." The Church is therefore a supremely perfect society. In carrying out and executing its mission, the Church does not depend upon any earthly authority; for it possesses in itself all the necessary means and all the rights which are required for the attainment of its end; namely, the sanctification of souls and eternal happiness. The Church has a system of beliefs and a code of morals peculiarly its own; a full legislative authority of binding and loosing. Briefly, it possesses all the requirements for being what it is, a truly perfect society.

The Catholic Church is also a necessary society. If men had been left free to accept or to reject the word of God; free to embrace or reject the faith and its practice, the Church would have from its very beginning been exposed to the danger of disintegration. Christ commanded the Apostles to preach the Gospel to all nations; but He, likewise, willed that men should accept and believe the Gospel under pain of everlasting punishment, and that they should make use of the means of sanctification entrusted by Him to the Church.

3. JURIDICAL PERSON

The Catholic Church, being a necessary society, is a juridical person. It is a juridical person in the true sense of the word, because it possesses all the characteristics which belong to a person; namely, individuality and a proper sphere of juridical action determined by its goal or end. The Church does not derive its personality from ecclesiastical law, because the latter does not antedate but follows its institution; neither is this personality conferred upon her by civil law, for the Church being a sovereign society is independent of the State.

The element of jurisdiction inherent in the Church cannot be ignored even by unbelievers. For twenty centuries the Church has exercised its divine mission in the world, fully conscious of its rights in conformity with which it enacts laws and exacting complete obedience and submission to its teaching. Down through the ages millions of her faithful children, irrespective of tongue, nationality, and culture, of economic and social distinctions, have recognized the authority of the Church; have professed her doctrine, and frequently have died for their faith. All this entitles the Church to a juridical status, even though she is universal or supranational. Therefore the Church, with her robust and powerful organization, with her immemorial traditions, with her canonical code, with her profound influence in the intellectual and moral order, cannot be compared to, and placed on the level of a private association created for private ends — an association that can be modified or destroyed.

From the beginning and through twenty centuries of uninterrupted existence, the Church presents herself as an independent juridical organization. She exists and operates by her own virtue; she needs no benevolent concessions of human legislators. Her end or goal is the true, supreme, and supernatural good of the mind and heart. The attainment of this good or happiness demands an absolute unity of faith and moral doctrines. Her doctrines and teaching are suited for all times, all conditions, and all men, because they were given to her by the maker and molder of human nature, her divine Founder, who knows better than any human legislator what is best for the governance of men and nations. The Church refuses to substitute for these principles expediency as a rule of conduct; she is unquestionably the greatest moral power at work in the community today. Her aim is to strengthen the foundations upon which our whole civic fabric rests and to re-enforce respect for law and order, the only sure guarantee for the perpetuation of our free institutions.

From the above considerations it should be quite evident that the Church is a juridical person not only nationally but also internationally. Church and State are two organisms essentially independent. Millions of Catholics dispersed on the face of the earth are united under the supreme head, the Pope. As head of the Church and of the ecclesiastical hierarchy, the Pope is a subject or person of international right. Such juridical prerogative belongs only and exclusively to the Roman Catholic Church. This colossal organization includes not merely individuals and families but entire peoples and nations, and invites all without distinction to enter its fold. Century after century, with renewed zeal and energy, the Church sends forth into every part of the globe her messengers of truth and true culture; everywhere she erects her tents, unfurls her banner, promulgates her laws which are a fountain of spiritual, social, and physical well-being for all. Since the Church, apart from and independent of, any benevolent concessions on the part of civil power, determines her proper status of being, establishes a government and a hierarchy of her own, enacts and promulgates her own laws, she possesses and exercises a true and sovereign jurisdiction.

Exactly because the Church is a juridical person both in the national and international sphere, she becomes like all sovereign societies entitled to the privileges of diplomacy. From the fact that Catholics are simultaneously subject to Church authority in spiritual concerns and to civil authority in temporal matters, certain questions often arise which must be settled by a mutual accord between the two powers. Hence it becomes necessary for the Church to enter into treaties with the civil authorities and to conclude diplomatic compacts or concordats. The Church's right of diplomacy is necessary for the assurance and preservation of peace between her and the secular powers, and for the advancement of the spiritual and temporal welfare of their subjects. The Church has for centuries exercised this right, and this right is generally recognized by all modern States. Justly, then, the Church has been establishing diplomatic legations in and relations with practically all modern States. It would be a flagrant contradiction, if a society entitled to diplomatic activities, should be deprived of the right of exchanging representatives with other States. Such a right is recognized even by many writers bitterly hostile to the Church. All this proves that the Church is a juridical person in the international domain.

In this connection it might be objected that since her members are subject to many particular States, the Church herself cannot be regarded as a sovereign society vested with the character of an international personality. However, from the material point of view the Church has a wider expansion than any State. Her kingdom is not limited by mountains and oceans; it embraces all men converted to the faith. It can then be said with good reason that *materially* the State is within the Church rather than the Church within the State. But even from a formal point of view it is false to assert that the Church is within the State in the same manner as a part is in the whole, or an inferior part in a superior. Even if the Church were territorially circumscribed by State boundaries, we could still compare such an inclusion to the union or inclusion (metaphorically speaking) of the soul in the human body. Now, just as the soul though circumscribed by the body, is immensely superior to the body, so the Church is higher than the State. The Church can never either *de jure* or *de facto* become a subject or member of any particular State; for in her own sphere of action she is essentially an independent and sovereign organization. We may add that the Church shows and proves her independence by the energetic manner in which she protests against all unjust statal intervention in ecclesiastical matters.

PART II

THE CHURCH AND THE STATE

1. RELATION OF STATE TO RELIGION

What attitude must the State take toward religion? As first things should come first, it is obvious that duties toward God are the most important; hence they should occupy the first place in private and public life. In this regard the natural law obliges the State to render to God a true worship; that is, to profess a true religion. Under the present dispensation this true religion is no other than the positive religion revealed by Christ. The public profession of religion by the civil authorities basically demands that the State on certain occasions and in its public capacity should exhibit acts of adoration, of thanksgiving, and petition; that it should punish crimes against religion; that it should positively promote and cherish public worship. This thesis is directed against the liberalistic attitude of today which divorces politics from ethics and considers religion as a purely private affair.

Our first debt and duty is the recognition of our dependence on God, as our Creator and Preserver. Religion is only the discharge of that duty of justice. God is the Author both of the individual and of civil society itself; hence the worship of God is incumbent on both. "Nature and reason," observes Leo XIII, "commanding every individual devoutly to worship God in holiness (because we belong to Him and must return to Him, since from Him we came), bind also the civil community by a like law. For men living together in society, no less than individuals, are under the power of God; and society, no less than individuals, owes gratitude to God. It is He who gave it being and maintains it, and whose ever bounteous goodness enriches it with countless blessings. No one, then, is allowed to be remiss in the service due to God, while the chief duty of all men is to cling to religion in both its teaching and practice — not such religion as each may prefer, but the religion which God enjoins and which certain and most clear marks show to be the one and only true religion. Whence it follows that men commit a public crime in acting as though there were no God."[7]

Unquestionably religion is the highest good of man on earth, having a direct bearing on social order and well-being. These blessings depend essentially on religion for the latter is the

---

[7] Leo XIII, *Immortale Dei* (The Christian Constitution of States).

foundation of morality. Nothing is more potent to incite people
to an honest life than religious teachings. It cannot be repeated
too often that God is the ultimate basis of the moral order, that
there is no moral order without God, and no morals without
religion. Hence since the State has not only a right but a positive
duty to promote whatever is conducive to the common well-
being, it has an equal right and duty to promote religion.

Moreover, the State is bound to protect and preserve the basic
principles upon which its superstructure rests. But the cornerstone of the civil edifice is religion. When citizens are guided not
by religious principles, but by materialism and atheism, the
civic virtues such as reverence for authority, public peace and
tranquillity, justice and honesty, are doomed to destruction, as
social upheavals so clearly prove. In an atheistic society there
can be no true moral authority in the rulers; laws cannot engender true obligation in conscience, nor can they possess a valid
sanction; there can exist no true brotherhood of men, no mutual
loyalty and veracity, no consolation in misfortunes; pleasure and
utility, self-interest and expediency, in a word, rugged individualism, can be the only rule of individual and social
conduct; the only right is might, the only defense of the weak
is dissimulation, fraud, and treason.

2. THE RIGHTS OF THE CHURCH MAY NOT BE IGNORED BY THE STATE

As a perfect society the Church has certain rights which may
not be ignored, interfered with, or violated by the State. The
teaching of the Church contains nothing that is incompatible
with the dignity and well-being of the State. She recognizes and
confirms whatever belongs to the nature and function of the
State, and proclaims the independence and supremacy of the
State in its own sphere. She teaches that both State and Church
are sovereign organizations, absolutely distinct from each other;
that they differ essentially in so far as the State is a natural society, whereas the Church is a supernatural society. The Church
also rightly insists that their goals or ends are different, the

State having for its ultimate aim the temporal well-being of its citizens and the Church having for the ultimate goal the spiritual and eternal happiness of the children. In addition these two powers must employ different means for the attainment of their respective end; the State employs physical coercion; the Church employs prayer, preaching, and the sacraments.

The State violates the rights of the Church by interfering in purely ecclesiastical affairs, and the Church violates the rights of the State by interfering in purely civil matters. The paradox of such an interference is thus described by one political leader: "How grotesque a council of cardinals would be which busied itself with the calibre of cannons or the tonnage of cruisers! A ministerial cabinet would be just as ridiculous if it decided to legislate in matters of theology or religious dogma. A State that does not wish to spread spiritual disturbance and create division among its citizens must guard against any intervention in matters which are strictly religious. . . . The duty of the State does not consist in trying to create new gospels or dogmas, in overthrowing the old divinities in order to replace them with others which are denoted by blood, race, Nordism, and so forth."

3. RELATIONS BETWEEN CHURCH AND STATE

The Catholic position concerning the relation between Church and State may be summarized as follows: In mere civil matters the State is independent of the Church, but in moral and religious questions the Church is independent of the State. In those things which pertain both to ecclesiastical and civil power, the supreme decision must eventually rest with the Church. This introduces the question of joint jurisdiction.

"The principal matters that provoke controversy concerning the mutual limits of jurisdiction of the two societies, are marriage and education. According to Catholic doctrine, marriage is not merely a civil contract; it is also a sacrament. Since its sacramental character, being a spiritual entity, is higher than its civil character, the matrimonial contract must be conceived and regulated in harmony with its spiritual nature and purposes.

oped—

The Church cannot sanction or recognize a marriage which is contrary to either the revealed or the natural law. Therefore, she lays down conditions for the validity of the matrimonial contract, conditions which are necessary to safeguard its spiritual and sacramental character. A disagreement with the State arises whenever the latter independently attempts to regulate the validity of the contract.

"According to the Catholic position, the State has no right to make laws affecting the validity of marriages of baptized persons. . . . [The Church] recognizes, indeed, that the State may properly impose certain regulations which do not affect validity, but which are necessary for the common good, and therefore morally binding upon the persons concerned. Such are the requirements of residence, an official license to marry, the registration of the marriage by the officiating clergyman, and many others. But the Church maintains that none of these conditions is of sufficient importance to justify the State in declaring invalid a marriage in which they have been disregarded."[8]

From the above it follows that the Church possesses an *indirect* power in temporal matters over the State, that is, she has the right to judge whether any civil law is pernicious or harmful to the spiritual welfare of her subjects; in such cases she has the right to demand that harmful laws be changed or abrogated. On the other hand, there is no parallel argument to give the State indirectly jurisdiction over the Church in matters purely temporal. The Church is higher in the order of divine providence than the State. She is nobler because of its nobler origin and sublime end. The Church therefore is in no way subject to the State. Although independent of the Church in purely temporal matters, the State is nevertheless subject to the Church *directly* in spiritual affairs, and *indirectly* in temporal matters in so far as they are related to spiritual concerns.

"Whatever, therefore, in things human is of a sacred character, whatever belongs either of its own nature or by reason of the

---

[8] Ryan and Millar, *The State and the Church* (New York: The Macmillan Co. 1922), pp. 50, 51.

end to which it is referred, to the salvation of souls, or to the worship of God, is subject to the power and judgment of the Church. Whatever is to be ranged under the civil and political order is rightly subject to civil authority."[9]

4. CHURCH AND STATE EACH SUPREME IN ITS OWN SPHERE

The independence of Church and State has always been considered a fundamental principle by the most renowned theologians and jurists of the Christian world. Thus St. Thomas maintains that spiritual as well as temporal power comes from God, that secular power depends on spiritual power only in so far as God has subordinated temporal matters to the salvation of souls. He, moreover, holds that in whatever concerns the material well-being of the community, secular power is independent of spiritual authority, according to the evangelical precept: "Render to Caesar the things that are Caesar's and to God the things that are God's." St. Robert Bellarmine declares that the Pope is not the sole ruler of the world and not even of the Christian world, as he does not possess the divine right to any such direct civil jurisdiction. Christ Himself, the Founder of the Church, was not a conquerer of earthly kingdoms. Much less should the Pope be one. Hence civil power has its own purposes and functions, its own tribunals, laws, etc., and the Church also has her own specific goal, her own tribunals, laws, etc. The spiritual power must not interfere in purely civil matters, but must allow civil affairs to follow their course freely, provided they are not detrimental to the welfare of souls and to the general well-being of all.

The mutual independence of the Church and the State in their respective spheres is held by Molina, Suarez, and other eminent theologians; it is confirmed by the immortal words of Leo XIII: "The Almighty, therefore, has appointed the charge of the human race between two powers, the ecclesiastical and the civil, the one being set over divine and the other over human things, Each in its kind is supreme, each has fixed limits

---

[9] Leo XIII, *op. cit.*

within which it is contained, limits which are defined by nature and the special object of the province of each, so that there is, we may say, an orbit traced out within which the action of each is brought into play by its own native right. But inasmuch as each of these two powers has authority over the same subjects, and as one and the same thing under different aspects but still remaining identically the same, might chance to fall under the jurisdiction and determination of both, God, who foresees all things and is Author of these two powers, has marked out the course of each in right correlation to the other. 'For the powers that are, are ordained of God'" (Rom. 13:1).[10] Therefore to accuse the Church of teaching doctrines detrimental to the independence and sovereignty of the State, shows either a crass ignorance of what the Church and her outstanding theologians have always upheld as a fundamental principle of political philosophy, or a sectarian hatred which attributes to the Church aims she has never claimed.

THE SEPARATION OF CHURCH AND STATE

The theory explained in the preceding section, although so logical and unbiased, does not satisfy those who would make the Church subservient to the State. These attribute to the State the right to watch over Church activities; they scrupulously insist that civil authorities should be prepared against her attacks, and ready to repress ecclesiastical abuses. This in general is the attitude of liberalism, an attitude which with its false principles and prejudices, has poisoned the mind and heart of modern nations, and has too often been destructive of the best interests of the State itself.

---

[10] Leo XIII, *op. cit.*

Liberalism advocates a total separation of Church and State. It regards the Church not as a supreme society but as a mere human association depending for its rights upon the State. Liberalism contends that the Church should not be accorded greater freedom or privileges than those accorded to other private associations; it glories in the formula: A free Church in a free State. In the words of Leo XIII: "Many wish the State to be separated from the Church wholly and entirely, so that regard to every right of human society, in institutions, customs, and laws, the offices of the State, and the education of youth, they would pay no more regard to the Church than if she did not exist; and, at most, would allow the citizens individually to attend to their religion in private if so minded."[11]

Liberalism considers the separation of Church and State as necessary in order to prevent the former from overthrowing civil authority. Such reasoning is nonsense. The civil and religious powers have distinct ends and distinct means. The subjects of the two powers are confined within the limits of the same territory, but the relations of dependence are different. Since the object of order and dependence is distinct, no serious difficulties can arise from the fact that in a given territory two powers are vested with a proper jurisdiction over the same subjects. When any problems present themselves, there are ample means to rectify them according to the principles of justice and equity. History is not wanting in examples of this conciliatory spirit of the Church, of the eagerness and charity with which she has always sought to satisfy the legitimate aspirations of the civil powers. In this connection it is well to remember that the Church does not forcibly thrust her faith and laws on any one. "In fact the Church is wont to take earnest heed that no one shall be forced to embrace the Catholic faith against his will, for, as St. Augustine wisely reminds us 'Man cannot believe otherwise than of his own free will.' "[12]

The statement that the Church and State are two societies

---

[11] Leo XIII, *Libertas Humana* (Human Liberty).
[12] Leo XIII, *Immortale Dei.*

perfect and supreme in their respective field of action does not entail division or separation. An actual separation of Church and State instead of solving the problem of interrelation, is only a lesser evil which under certain circumstances is permissible and at times even desirable. Such a separation is clearly preferable to a continuous intervention on the part of the civil authorities in ecclesiastical matters or, what is worse, a servile dependence of the Church on the State. Any unwarranted surrender of Church rights, any servitude on the part of the Church to civil power would hinder the spread of the gospel and would detract from the high ideals which Christian peoples have always entertained of the Church. Indeed wherever there is a vast number of religious sects, each claiming supremacy and rendering a dignified accord and agreement between the two powers impossible, separation of Church and State is to be tolerated as a lesser evil. Thus when the State is confronted by two or three hundred religious denominations as in the United States, it is impossible to establish a regular plan of relations with one Church only. In like cases, a separation, provided that such a separation is not detrimental to either Church or State, is the only solution.

A complete separation, however, cannot practically be of long duration, because of the many points of contact between the two powers, contacts which cannot be simply set aside or ignored. The Church and State have for their subjects the same persons who under different aspects are members of civil and ecclesiastical society. A complete separation, therefore, is both theoretically and practically impossible. Furthermore, whenever the Church is in fullness of vigor and life, she cannot but imbue her members with her own vivifying spirit; and once convinced of the truth of her doctrines, those members follow them. This fact is bound to have a repercussion in the social and political life. Hence the fact that Catholics and Protestants are often diametrically opposed in their political views may be traced to their different religious tenets. Inspired by her divine mission, the Church has always made every effort to instruct and inform her members on her basic principles and sooner or later the influence of these principles have been felt in civic life. As a consequence the State must, "willy-nilly," become exposed to the influence of the Church in proportion to the zeal and number of the faithful.

On the other hand, the State in its turn exercises its influence on the religious life of the individual; its powerful arm is ubiquitous and accompanies man from the cradle to the grave. Thus the newly born comes into existence under the influence of civil legislation; as soon as he reaches the use of reason he is summoned to the classroom; later on he is inducted into military service. The State exercises its influence on public morality, on the press, on theaters, etc.; it can either inculcate respect for well-established customs and religious liberty, or violate sacred personal rights. In a word, public prosperity and happiness depend greatly on statal influence.

It is sometimes objected that when the State does not profess any religious belief, it has no right to concede to the Church a treatment different from that accorded to individuals and other private associations. But this is obviously a sophism. The rights of the Church exist, and as such they possess full efficacy both in regard to individuals and in regard to the State, even though individuals and the State should obstinately refuse to recognize them. Just as the rights of the State do not depend on caprice nor on public or private approval, neither do the rights of the Church. Whether the State likes it or not, the Church has a right to her existence and to the exercise of her proper activities; she possesses sacred and inalienable rights which the State cannot ignore. On the contrary the State has a positive duty to protect the rights of the Church, because the Church is not an intruder, but has a right to be there; and whoever and whatever has a right to be there has a consequent right to be guarded by the State against molestation. This is more obviously true when the right to be there comes from a higher authority, as in the case of the Church.

Again, a complete separation of the two powers would open the doors to religious indifference, and logically lead to an atheistic and materialistic State. We have already shown that indifference in religion is intrinsically immoral. In addition, religious indifference could not but give rise to devastating consequences in the political and social order. Therefore every attempt at a systematic separation of Church and State must be rejected.

The State must have at heart the common well-being of all its citizens. It must see to it that personal rights are respected; that justice actuate the reciprocal relations of individuals and society; that the spirit of sacrifice and temperance take root in the public conscience; that the great law of human brotherhood and Christian charity be not a mere empty phrase, but a sure token of peace for all classes without distinction; that, finally, laws be observed and constituted authorities obeyed. But all this in the absence of morality and religion would be a chimera. The State, then, cannot ignore the Church but must recognize her true status not merely halfway, but fully and unreservedly. It is not true that a complete liberty of the Church is equivalent to slavery of the State, that the Church's independence entails statal servitude, or that there must be a perennial dualism in the exercise of Church and State sovereignty. From what has been said it is clear that the independence of the Church is not irreconcilable with the dignity of the State or with the principle of its sovereignty. This would be the case only if these two powers regarded man from the same point of view; for example either from the exclusively temporal or the exclusively spiritual point of view. But it has already been shown that the end of the Church is essentially distinct from the end of the State. Therefore there is no justification for a complete separation of these two powers.

Furthermore, separation of Church and State must inevitably engender reciprocal hatred and contempt. By its very nature and purpose the State is in constant and intimate contact with the Church, hence while the latter aims at the sanctification and spiritual betterment of her members, the State must simultaneously aim at the temporal well-being of the same persons. As a

consequence, any friction between these two powers will naturally disparage respect for both.

How difficult and troublesome is the separation of the two
powers is evidenced by the situation prevailing in the United
States. The Constitution of September 17, 1787, states expressly
the principle that Congress "shall make no laws respecting an
establishment of religion or prohibiting the free exercise thereof."
This separation has led to a series of difficulties with the manifold religious denominations, as for instance concerning private
education of youth, marriage, etc. These, and numerous other
problems, when not regulated by common accord between
Church and State, lead inevitably to intestine conflicts, wherein
might often prevails over right. From the Catholic point of view,
a complete separation cannot be justified. Such a separation can
have no other meaning than the emancipation of civil society
from God, of creature from the Creator; the perversion of the
ultimate end of man; and a violent separation of man into two
personalities — the citizen and the believer. Hence follow the
numerous contrasts between the duties of man as citizen and
man as believer. The separation itself tolerated by the Church
in some exceptional cases, and only to avoid a greater evil, cannot be regarded as a normal solution of the problem. Such a
separation always implies a precarious condition of things — a
condition that is tolerated only because of necessity, a condition
harmful no less to the State than to the Church. Even though
religious conditions in the United States are in general better
and more favorable than in many Catholic countries, yet we
must not forget the genuine Catholic teaching on this subject
embodied in an encyclical letter of Leo XIII addressed on January
6, 1895, to the people of the United States: "The Church among
you, unopposed by the Constitution and government of your nation, fettered by no hostile legislation, protected against violence
by the common laws and the impartiality of the tribunals, is
free to live and act without hindrance. Yet, though all this is
true, it would be very erroneous to draw the conclusion that
in America is to be sought the type of the most desirable status

of the Church, or that it would be universally lawful and expedient for the State and Church to be, as in America, dissevered and divorced. The fact that Catholicity with you is in good condition, nay, is even enjoying a prosperous growth, is by all means to be attributed to the fecundity with which God has endowed His Church, in virtue of which unless men or circumstances interfere, she spontaneously expands and propagates herself; but she would bring forth more abundant fruits if, in addition to liberty, she enjoyed the favor of the laws and the patronage of public authority."[13]

Mutual and friendly cooperation is the ideal solution of the relations between Church and State. Naturally, no true friendship can exist without the spirit of sacrifice and forbearance. Of course, the situation confronting Church and State, will never be smooth, easy, and devoid of difficulties; these difficulties however can be ironed out and settled by mutual accord and in conformity with the principles of justice and equity. The resulting advantages would be immense for Church and State, both in enhancing respect for one another and in avoiding misunderstanding. Thus on the one hand, the State will expedite the task of the Church; on the other, the Church by her teaching and example will certainly consolidate the foundations of the State, by insuring obedience to legitimate authority, respect for law and social order. Leo XIII has solemnly and justly reminded the States that, by the very nature of things as well as by divine dispensation, an absolute separation, and much less a conflict between Church and State cannot be admitted, but "there must, accordingly, exists, between the two powers, a certain orderly connexion, which may be compared to the union of soul and body in man."[14]

The great benefits of such a union are thus described by Ivo of Chatres, "When kingdom and priesthood are at one, in complete accord, the world is well ruled, and the Church flourishes and brings forth abundant fruit. But when they are at variance,

---

[13] Leo XIII, *Catholicity in the United States.*
[14] Leo XIII, *Immortale Dei.*

not only smaller interests prosper not, but even things of the greatest moment fall into deplorable decay."[15] Leo XIII enumerates the great achievements of the Christian State in the past: "Christian Europe has subdued barbarous nations, and changed them from a savage to a civilized condition, from superstition to true worship. It victoriously rolled back the tide of Mohammedan conquest; retained the leadership of civilization; stood forth in the front rank as the leader and teacher of all, in every branch of national culture; bestowed on the world the gift of true and many-sided liberty; and most wisely founded very numerous institutions for the solace of human suffering. And if we inquire how it was able to bring about so altered a condition of things, the answer is: Beyond all question, in large measure, through Religion; under whose auspices so many great undertakings were set on foot, through whose aid they were brought to completion. A similar state of things would certainly have continued had the agreement of the two powers been lasting."[16]

Is it not strange that in spite of these luminous facts the Church should still be regarded as an enemy of progress and culture? To show the groundlessness of this allegation, it may be well to consider briefly the following pertinent facts.

In the field of speculation the Church has produced the greatest intellectual lights, a St. Augustine, a St. Thomas of Aquin, a Scotus, a Dante, Suarez, and a host of others. As in the past, the Church today blesses all true progress and condemns the false systems of philosophy which have brought about the present intellectual, moral, economic, and political chaos. She not only preaches full freedom, but encourages and cherishes by all means at her disposal the study of the sciences, of chemistry, physics, mathematics, astronomy, biology, medicine, etc. No wonder then that so many of the leaders in the various scientific fields belong to her fold, since she encourages their best endeavors. She remonstrates only when scientists transgress their

[15] *Ibid.*
[16] *Ibid.*

proper limits and invade the field of metaphysics, or when they advocate absurd hypotheses opposed to reason and to divine revelation. History bears solemn witness to what the Church has accomplished for culture, progress, and civilization. If it is true that progress does consist not so much in worldly possessions and material goods as in spiritual and intellectual riches, the Church has unquestionably been the greatest benefactor of the human race. How could it be otherwise? She was the first to proclaim equality among men, abolishing all distinctions of caste; she alone fearlessly affirmed the dignity of man, the nobility of work; she alone taught true obedience to legitimate authority, loyalty, purity of morals, temperance; she raised matrimony to a dignity formerly unknown, thus cementing its indissolubility; she stood up against every kind of tyranny, showing by word and example that all men are children of the same heavenly Father. And what she has done in the past, she is continuing to do single-handed in the present maelstrom of unbridled passions and rugged individualism.

The momentous problems of life regarding the nature and destiny of man, the origin and supreme purpose of things, have been philosophically and theologically solved by the Church to the great advantage of speculative sciences. In view of these facts, how can the Church be an enemy to progress? She has also been the inspiration for masterpieces of art, poetry, music, and literature. Is not this a wonderful help for the well-being of all and of the State?

PART IV

PRE-EMINENCE OF THE CHURCH

It was shown that the Church and the State are free in their proper function; that the members of both make up one and the same community. Now, just as the State has no right to in-

terfere in the spiritual government of the Church, so the latter
has no right to infringe upon State prerogatives. This is fundamental; but practically speaking, the two powers form a unique
"togetherness," inasmuch as the same individuals constitute the
one as well as the other. An absolute segregation of the two is
impossible without rending the very soul of the nation. Hence
for a harmonious maintenance of the two elements, a mutual
and loyal understanding should prevail between the spiritual
and civil authorities. These two powers must, in virtue of an
internal natural law, recognize their reciprocal rights, and each
in its own peculiar way strive for a common goal — the happiness of humanity and the well-being of the community.

However, since the less perfect must be subordinate to the
more perfect, it follows that the place of pre-eminence must be
assigned to the Church. Obviously, the goal of the Church which
is the eternal happiness of man, is higher than the goal of the
State. The latter embraces all men in their natural relations and
from a purely natural viewpoint; the Church embraces them
from a supernatural viewpoint. Now, just as the supernatural
order is higher than the natural order, so the Church is higher
than the State. Yet, there is a close correlation between the ends
of these two powers. The individual man cannot have two antagonistic ends, one for the present and another for future life;
such a situation would clearly engender discord and unhappi-
ness. Hence, although Church and State are supreme each in its
own sphere, fully independent and sovereign, yet the Church is
higher in the plan of divine providence. The fear that such a
pre-eminence might lead to abuses is without foundation. The
Church has always respected the rights of the State and acted
equitably in examining and settling controversies with States.
The history of twenty centuries bears testimony to this.

This pre-eminence of the Church has been recognized even by
her adversaries. And rightly so. For, as heaven is above the
earth so the salvation of human souls is above and immensely
more precious and noble than any temporal well-being; the
majesty and sublimity of holiness exceeds and surpasses any ma-

terial value. This is the true conception of the hierarchy of values, a conception which is not subject to change or modification or alteration of its efficacy, as long as Christianity lasts.

Neither can it be said that the State is an end unto itself. From the Christian viewpoint neither the State nor the Church can be the ultimate end of man; they are only a means to that end which is God. In the light of Christian teaching the pre-eminence of the Church over the State, of the priesthood over the empire is incontrovertible; ecclesiastical power is higher than civil power, just as divine and spiritual things are on a higher level than material and temporal. Such a pre-eminence from the philosophical-Christian point of view is fully justified, for in no other way can we have well-regulated and lasting relations between the two orders — natural and supernatural.

Although the State, as a natural institution is ultimately of divine origin, yet its proximate origin rests upon historical and conventional factors. The Church, on the contrary, has been directly established by Jesus Christ. She alone can boast of the undeniable prerogatives of unity, stability, and immutability. Like a star in the firmament which has seen countless meteors come and pass by, the Church has witnessed the rise and fall of numberless political organizations. She soars on high, undisturbed by the whirlpool of human opinions.

Irrespective of race and nationality, the Church regards all men as brethren, as members of the same human family; she is by her very nature, catholic or universal, and in her divine work of leading men to eternal happiness she embraces the entire human race under her unique scepter. Christ has founded the Church visible and universal, entrusting to her the mission of directing all, rich and poor, rulers and subjects, princes and servants, in the same way as a shepherd is entrusted to guide and feed his master's sheep. This is not all: Christ has given to His Church the power of binding and loosing, without any reservation. Now, when the divine legislator has given full powers in such an absolute form, it is not permissible to make distinctions or reservations concerning those powers. These prerogatives clearly entitle the Church to a place of pre-eminence and superiority over all other institutions.

On the contrary, if the State were to have pre-eminence over the Church, it would destroy the religio-social union of men, and bring about separation and subdivision of Christian people into at least as many churches, as there are States. Throughout the Middle Ages, when the relations between Church and State were regulated by fairly equitable principles, there prevailed not only religious unity, but also a superb social organization. On the other hand, one of the results of Oriental schism has been the subordination of the Church to the State. The ultimate outcome of this fact, was not merely a Greek church distinct from the Roman Church, but a variety of Greek churches, small and large, as the Russian, the Ottoman, the Bulgarian, etc. On its part, Protestantism also contributed toward making the Church subservient to civil power. The consequences were the same; there were more Protestant churches or denominations than were Protestant countries, and today hardly any reference is made to the unity of the Protestant Church except in reference to the negation of Catholicism. Hence, just as it is certain that Christ has founded the visible Church on earth, depository of the true Christian doctrine; just as it is certain and undeniable that the Church is one, holy, catholic, and apostolic, so too is it certain that the Church is superior to the State. And since a perfect equality between these two powers is impossible, we are forced to conclude that the Church possesses the right of pre-eminence over the State.

The status of pre-eminence of the Church over the State has always contributed to public prosperity and social happiness; while schism and heresy has invariably given rise to ancient and modern Caesaro-Papism. We hear much of the alleged abuses committed by the Popes during the Middle Ages, to the detriment of States, but not a word of what the Church has done for the triumph of right over might. The Church reminded the rich and the poor, subjects and princes of their duties. But in the opinion of her enemies no greater misfortune can befall the human race than to have someone courageous enough to teach men the observance of the moral law, someone who will fearlessly raise his voice against tyrants, someone who will not quail before the haughty and overbearing ways of dictators, kings, and prime ministers. But in spite of the judgment of the world, the Church of Christ is ever ready to combat all moral and social evils, and to defend mankind against oppression and to protect it from the calamities which revolutions bring.

The Church has no other weapon than moral force. Her power does not rest on mighty armies and navies, but on her moral strength, veracity, and holiness. This is why she is inflexible in whatever concerns her dogmas and moral code, although in other respects she is the very personification of mildness and tolerance. This also explains why so many Protestant churches lean toward Caesaro-Papism. In fact, all other religious sects not possessing in themselves any stable and unitive basis are compelled to seek strength either in free thought or in the power of the State. The Catholic Church finds her strength in her unity and stability. Hence all other religions, yielding to fear, or from want of experience and lack of conviction have submitted to lay authority on the condition that they be allowed to live. The Catholic Church alone replies: "I give to Caesar the things that are Caesar's, but first of all, I give to God the things that are God's. I obey you in all things, as long as the rights of God are not invaded, but when these are transgressed, I cannot, I will not, I must not obey." The Catholic Church prays for and respects all those in authority; she acknowledges all legitimate forms of government. But she has never surrendered and never will surrender a single iota of her doctrine; she has never betrayed and never will betray the trust committed to her by Christ.

The Church is always well-disposed toward civil authority. She does not pretend to dominate the State, but neither does she bow her head to statal whims and arbitrariness. The various Protestant sects, are generally small and very often depend for their existence upon the good will of civil power. The Catholic Church, on the contrary, represented from the very beginning a universal monarchy. Christ has not founded an American, or English, German, Italian, or French church, but a Church catholic and universal. What therefore Christ has joined together let no State put asunder.

It follows then, that within the range of possibility, Church and State should cooperate in such a manner as to bring about the realization of the divine plan in the world. Just as the earth has nothing to be ashamed of, for being destined to revolve around the sun, so the State must not be ashamed to have God for the centripetal point of its activity. As the sun is the center in the planetary system, so God and His kingdom the Church are the central points in the moral order. Coming social upheavals themselves will prove once more the immutability of this order, since what has been placed at the periphery cannot one day arrogate to itself a place in the center. On the contrary, whatever detaches itself from the center must necessarily lapse into nothingness. No matter how great the difficulties, the Church will continue calm and undisturbed in her course, carrying on her work of moral and social regeneration. All her combined adversaries will never be able to arrest her course or to render void the words: "Who is like unto God?" The Church is a divine institution destined to last unto the consummation of the world. She will continue unchanged in her perennial youth, in her adamantine character, as the source of life, of civilization, and of human happiness.

SELECT READINGS

Alter, K. J., "Church and State," in the *Ecclesiastical Review*, May, 1942.

Catholic Encyclopedia, art. "Church and State."

Dawson, Christopher, *Christian Religion in the Modern State* (New York: Sheed and Ward, 1936).

Hoare, F. J., *The Papacy and the Modern State* (London: Burns, Oates and Washbourne, 1940).

Leo XIII, *Immortale Dei* (Christian Constitution of States); *Libertas Humana* (Human Liberty); *Catholicity in the United States; Graves de Communi* (Christian Democracy).

Marinoff, I., *The Heresy of National Socialism* (New York: P. J. Kenedy & Sons, 1942).

Pius XI, *Mit brennender Sorge* (The Present Position of the Catholic Church in Germany).

Ryan-Millar, *The State and Church* (New York: The Macmillan Co., 1922).

Sturzo, Luigi, *Church and State* (New York: Longmans, Green and Co., 1939).

Winkler, E., *Four Years of Nazi Torture* (New York: Appleton-Century Co., 1942).

BIBLIOGRAPHY

A Catechism of Catholic Education (N.C.W.C.).

Alter, K. J., "Church and State," *Ecclesiastical Review,* May, 1942.

Augustine, St., *Confessions* (New York: G. P. Putman's Sons, 1932); *De Civitate Dei.*

Bellarmine, St. Robert, *De Laicis* (Tr. by K. E. Murphy) (New York: Fordham Press, 1928).

Belloc, H., *The Crisis of Civilization* (New York: Fordham Press, 1937).

Berdyaev, N., *The Fate of Man in the Modern World* (New York: Sheed and Ward, 1935).

Betten, F. S., S.J., "The Morality of Sterilization," *Catholic Mind,* October 22, 1933.

Blackstone, W., *Commentaries on the Law of England* (London: Lippincott, 1879).

Bosanquet, B., *The Philosophical Theory of the State* (London: The Macmillan Co., 1899).

Brennan, R. E., O.P., *Thomistic Psychology* (New York: The Macmillan Co., 1941).

Bruehl, C., *Birth Control Eugenics* (New York: J. F. Wagner, 1928).

Cahill, E., S.J., *The Framework of a Christian State* (Dublin: Gill and Son, 1932).

Catholic Encyclopedia (New York: D. H. Appleton and Co., 1907).

Cicero, Marcus Tullius, *De Republica* (London: Hainemann, 1928).

——— *Select Orations* (New York: Hinds and Noble, 1895).

Coker, F. W., *Readings in Political Philosophy* (New York: The Macmillan Co., 1938).

Committee of the American Neurological Association, *Eugenical Sterilization* (New York: The Macmillan Co., 1936).

Cox, I. W., S.J., "The Folly of Human Sterilization," *Scientific American,* October, 1934.

Cronin, M., *The Science of Ethics* (New York: Benziger, 1922).

Cuthbert, Fr., O.S.F.C., *Catholic Ideals in Social Life* (New York: Benziger, 1910).

Dante, Alighieri, *Divine Comedy* (Tr. by H. F. Carry) (London: Dent, 1908).

Darwin, C., *The Descent of Man* (New York: D. H. Appleton and Co., 1903).

Dawson, Christopher, *Religion and the Modern State* (New York: Sheed and Ward, 1936).

De Luca, F., *La Dinamica delle Forze Sociali* (Napoli, 1906).

Devas, C. S., *Studies of Family Life* (London, 1908).

De Wulf, M., *Mediaeval Philosophy* (Cambridge: Harvard Press, 1922).

Donat, Joseph, S.J., *The Freedom of Science* (New York: J. F. Wagner, 1914).

Dubray, C. A., *Introductory Philosophy* (New York: Longmans, Green and Co., 1928).

Durant, W., *The Mansions of Philosophy* (New York: Simon and Schuster, 1929).

Encyclopedia of the Social Sciences (New York: The Macmillan Co., 1937).

Farrell, W., O.P., *A Companion of the Summa* (New York: Sheed and Ward, 1941).

Gilson, Etienne, *God and Philosophy* (New Haven: Yale Press, 1941).

Gosney, E. S., "Eugenic Sterilization," *Scientific American,* July, 1934.

Groppali, A., *Filosofia del Diritto* (Milano, 1906).

Guchteneere (de), Raoul, *Judgment on Birth Control* (New York: Sheed and Ward, 1933).

Gurian, W., "The Philosophy of the Totalitarian State," *Proceedings of the American Catholic Philosophical Association,* Vol. XV, 1939.

Haas, F. J., *Man and Society* (New York: Century, 1930).

Hettinger-Bowden, *Natural Religion* (New York: Benziger, 1900).

Hildebrand (von) D., *Marriage* (New York: Longmans, Green and Co., 1942).

Hoare, F. J., *The Papacy and the Modern State* (London: Burns, Oates and Washbourne, 1940).

Hoffman, R. J. S., *The Will to Freedom* (London: Sheed and Ward, 1935).

Holaind, R. I., S.J., *Natural Law and Legal Practice* (New York: Benziger, 1899).

Husslein, Joseph, S.J., *The Christian Social Manifesto* (Milwaukee: The Bruce Publishing Co., 1931).

Ireland, J., *The Church and Modern Society* (Chicago: McBride, 1896).

Jennings, H. S., *Scientific Aspects of the Race Problem* (New York: Longmans, Green and Co., 1942).

Jerrold, D., *The Future of Freedom* (Oxford: Sheed and Ward, 1938).

Kohn, H., *World Order in Historical Perspective* (Cambridge: Harvard Press, 1942).

Kologriwof-Ambruzzi, *God, Man and the Universe* (London: Coldwell, 1937).

Krzesinski, A. J., *Is Modern Culture Doomed?* (New York: The Devin-Adair Co., 1942).

Lacordaire, H., *Conferences on God* (New York: O'Shea, 1871).

La Farge, J., S.J., "Racism and Social Unity," *Catholic Mind,* Jan. 8, 1939.

Leclercq, J. J., *Marriage and the Family* (Tr. by Thomas R. Hanley, O.S.B.) (New York: Pustet, 1941).

Leibell, J. F., *Reading in Ethics* (Chicago: Loyola Press, 1926).

Leo XIII, *Immortale Dei* (Christian Constitution of States); *Libertas Humana* (Human Liberty); *Rerum Novarum* (The Condition of Labor); *Arcanum* (Christian Marriage); *Catholicity in the United States.*

Lilly, W., *First Principles in Politics* (New York: G. P. Putman's Sons, 1909).

Manion, C., *Lessons in Liberty* (South Bend: Notre Dame Press, 1939).

Manning, H. E., *The Fourfold Sovereignty of God* (New York: Benziger).

Marinoff, I., *The Heresy of National Socialism* (New York: P. J. Kenedy & Sons, 1942).

Maritain, Jacques, *Freedom in the Modern World* (New York: Scribners and Sons, 1936).

––– *The Natural Law and Human Rights* (Ontario: Christian Culture Press, 1942).

Mayer, Joseph, *Gesetzliche Unfruchtbarmachung Geisteskranker* (Freiburg, 1931).

McNamara, S.J., *American Democracy and Catholic Doctrine* (Brooklyn: I.C.T.S., 1925).

Mercier, D., *A Manual of Modern Scholastic Philosophy* (London: Kegan, 1919).

Michel, V., O.S.B., *Christian Social Reconstruction* (Milwaukee: The Bruce Publishing Co., 1937).

―― *Philosophy of Human Conduct* (Minneapolis: Burgess, 1936).

Montesquieu, C., *De l'esprit des lois* (Genève, 1749).

Moore, Thomas V.,"The Heredity of Feeblemindedness," *Thought*, Vol. IX.

Muench, A. J., "Sterilization By Law" (St. Louis: Central-Verein Bureau, 1929).

Murray-Flynn, *Social Problems* (New York: F. S. Crofts Co., 1938).

"Nazi Decree," *Literary Digest*, Jan. 13, 1934.

Nell-Bruening, *Reorganization of Social Economy* (Milwaukee: The Bruce Publishing Co., 1936).

Neumann, F. L., *Anatomy of Nazism* (New York: Oxford Press, 1942).

Noll, J. F., *Our National Enemy No. I: Education Without Religion* (Huntington: Our Sunday Visitor Press, 1942).

O'Brien, M. C., *Christian Social Principles* (New York: P. J. Kenedy & Sons, 1941).

O'Toole, G. B., *The Case Against Evolution* (New York: The Macmillan Co., 1925).

Parsons, W., S.J., *Which Way, Democracy?* (New York: The Macmillan Co., 1939).

Pastoral Letter of the Bishops of the United States, 1919

Pearl, R., *The Present Status of Eugenics* (Hanover, N. H.: Sociological Press, 1928).

Petrone, L., *La Fase Recentissima della Filosofia del Diritto in Germania* (Pisa, 1895).

Pius XI, *Quadragesimo Anno* (Reconstruction of the Social Order); *Casti Connubii* (Christian Marriage); *Providentissimus Deus* (Christian Education of Youth); *Divini Redemptoris* (Atheistic Communism); *Non Abbiamo Bisogno; Mit Brennender Sorge.*

Pius XII, *Darkness Over the Earth.*

Rauschning, H., *Totalitarianism or the Revolution of Nihilism* (New York: Alliance Book Co., 1940).

Rickaby, Joseph, S.J., *Moral Philosophy* (London: Longmans, Green and Co., 1918).

―― *Political and Moral Essays* (New York: Benziger, 1902).

Rosmini, A., *Filosofia del Diritto* (Milano, 1841).

Ross, E. J., *A Survey of Sociology* (Milwaukee: The Bruce Publishing Co., 1932).

—— *The Catholic Church and the Citizen* (New York: The Macmillan Co., 1928).

—— *Questions of the Day* (Boston: Stratford Press, 1931).

—— *Distributive Justice* (New York: The Macmillan Co., 1940).

—— *American Democracy vs. Racism and Communism* (New York: The Paulist Press), pamphlet.

Rousseau, J. J., *Social Contract* (Tr. by R. M. Harrington) (New York: G. P. Putman's Sons).

Ryan, J. A., *Catholic Doctrine on the Right of Self-Government* (New York: The Paulist Press).

Ryan-Boland, *Catholic Principles of Politics* (New York: The Macmillan Co., 1940).

Ryan-Millar, *The State and the Church* (New York: The Macmillan Co., 1922).

Schanz, P., *A Christian Apology* (New York: Pustet, 1902).

Sheed, F., *Communism and Man* (New York: Sheed and Ward, 1938).

Sheen, Fulton J., *Freedom Under God* (Milwaukee: The Bruce Publishing Co., 1940).

—— *Liberty, Equality and Fraternity* (New York: The Macmillan Co., 1938).

—— *The Moral Universe* (Milwaukee: The Bruce Publishing Co., 1936).

Sieber-Mueller, *The Social Life of Primitive Man* (St. Louis: B. Herder, 1941).

Spencer, Herbert, *Social Statics* (New York: D. H. Appleton and Co., 1892).

—— *The Principles of Sociology* (New York: D. H. Appleton and Co., 1903).

—— *The Principles of Ethics* (New York: D. H. Appleton and Co., 1903).

—— *The Principles of Psychology* (New York: D. H. Appleton and Co., 1903).

—— *The Science of Ethics* (London, 1882).

Sturzo, L., *The Totalitarian State*, Dublin Review, July, 1935.

Suarez, F., *De Defensione Fidei.*

Sullivan, J. F., S.J., *Special Ethics* (Boston: Holy Cross Press, 1931).

Tawney, R. H., *Equality* (London: Allen and Unwin, 1931).

The New Testament (Revised Edition) (Paterson, N. J.: St. Anthony Guild Press, 1941).

Thomas, St., *Summa Theologica* (Rome: Desclée et Socii).

—— *In Libros Politicorum* (Taurinii: Marietti, 1924).

Tolomei, J., *Diritto Naturale* (Rome, 1899).

Westermarck, E., *History of Human Marriage* (London: The Macmillan Co., 1925).

—— *The Origin and Development of the Moral Ideas* (London: The Macmillan Co., 1906).

Willigan-O'Connor, *Sociology* (New York: The Macmillan Co., 1940).

Willoughby, W. W., *The Ethical Basis of Political Authority* (New York: The Macmillan Co., 1930).

Wilson, W., *The State* (Boston: Heath, 1898).

Winkler, E., *Four Years of Nazi Torture* (New York: Appleton-Century, 1942).

APPENDIX

LEGAL STERILIZATION OF MENTAL DEFECTIVES

WE DISTINGUISH three kinds of sterilization: (1) therapeutic which seeks to repair or restore a person's health; (2) punitive which is performed as a punishment for offenses; (3) eugenic[1] which tries to eliminate from the racial stock the unfit and undesirable.

As this appendix is confined to the eugenic sterilization, we shall dismiss the others with a word here. Indirect therapeutic sterilization is permitted, if it is reasonably sure that such is necessary for the welfare of the whole body since the body is more important than any of its members. Punitive sterilization is a moot question. That theoretically the state has the right to mutilate the body as it has the right to execute for crime, is conceded by St. Thomas and modern theologians. Formerly criminals guilty of social crimes were castrated; being a harsh practice it had a deterrent effect. But the modern painless process of vasectomy causes criminals no pain and far from being a deterrent it acts as an incentive to sex crimes and gratification. The sterilized criminal can indulge his passion without fear of the inconvenience of children. From this it appears hard to justify punitive sterilization in practice, since for those who value the right to progeny it is an excessive and unreasonable punishment, while those who value fecundity lightly will not be deterred by its deprivation.

---

[1] A. J. Muench, "Sterilization by Law" (Central-Verein, St. Louis), p. 16.

1. HISTORY OF STERILIZATION

Sterilization is nothing new. It was practiced by all nations at all times. In former times it was generally the fate of conquered enemies, whom the conquerors wished to exterminate: sometimes it was used as a punishment; sometimes out of religious motives. The old Egyptians and Lydians sterilized weaklings lest they give rise to more weaklings.[2] Aristotle advocated sterilization of those who were likely to generate weak offspring.[3] Hippocrates, the Father of Medicine, and Theophrastes, the Father of Botany and noted disciple of Aristotle, both knew of plants, herbs, roots, etc., which would cause sterility, as did Homer.[4] The Church set herself against the practice from the beginning. Jerome[5] and Augustine[6] inveighed against it. St. Thomas[7] held that an intention of using means to procure sterility was a diriment impediment to matrimony.

In our day and especially in our country it is much more in vogue than we are inclined to suspect. "The United States is the land of legislative experiment and seems anxious to become the social laboratory of the world."[8] It is the great melting pot of the world; the land of the Negro problem, the Indian problem, the Chinese and Japanese problem. It is not surprising that the United States should have been the first nation of modern times to make use of sterilization. Already in 1855 Kansas had a law providing for castration of Negroes convicted of rape. In 1899 Dr. Harry Sharp, physician for the reformatory at Jeffersonville. Indiana, performed vasectomy on a young man who asked for it. Dr. Sharp claimed such benefits from the operation that it became the starting point of a widespread movement toward sterilization. Indiana was the first state to provide for sterilization of

---

[2] Mayer, J., *Gesetzliche Unfruchtbarmachung Geisteskranker*, p. 165.
[3] *Polit.* 7, 5.
[4] *Odyssey* 10, 510.
[5] *Ep. ad Eustochium* c. 13.
[6] *De nupt. et concup.* L. I., c. 15.
[7] *LV Sent.* dist. 27, q. 2, ad 1.
[8] Bruehl, *Birth Control* (New York, 1928).

defectives. Other states fell in line so that by January 1, 1932, twenty-seven of the forty-eight states had legal birth control[9] of which in 1926 eight enforced their laws, viz., Wisconsin, Iowa, California, Nebraska, Michigan, Connecticut, Montana, and Ohio. Close to 20,000 individuals have been sterilized in this country. California claims 10,000 of these.

In 1927, the Supreme Court of the United States, in a decision read by the late justice, Oliver Wendell Holmes, upheld the sterilization law of Virginia. The facts in the case are: Carrie Buck, the daughter of a feeble-minded mother and mother of an illegitimate, feeble-minded child, had been committed to the state colony for the feeble-minded. She was ordered sterilized as provided for by the state, and J. H. Bell was deputed to perform the operation, salpingectomy. Her guardian appealed to the Supreme Court of Virginia and lost; he carried it to the Supreme Court of the United States where the decision of the lower court was upheld. The court overruled the plaintiff's argument, that the due process clause of Amendment 14 of the Constitution had not been observed and that the police power of the State was not wide enough to include sterilization. "The principle," says the Court, "that sustains compulsory vaccination is broad enough to cover cutting the Fallopian tubes."[10] But a little thought should have shown Mr. Holmes the fundamental difference between the two. Vaccination deprives a man of no vital function, but sterilization deprives him of a natural power, the power to continue himself into the future.

On January 2, 1934, the German human sterilization law went into effect. This is the most systematic, thoroughgoing, and ruthless application of sterilization so far devised. Every physician must report those subject to the law, and through a comprehensive legal system, these will be ordered sterilized. The diseases which make a man eligible for sterilization are nine: Hereditary

---

[9] Alabama, Arizona, California, Connecticut, Delaware, Idaho, Indiana, Iowa, Kansas, Maine, Michigan, Minnesota, Mississippi, Montana, Nebraska, New Hampshire, North and South Dakota, Utah, Vermont, Virginia, North Carolina, Oklahoma, Oregon, Washington, West Virginia, Wisconsin.

[10] J. A. Ryan, *Questions of the Day*, p. 297.

feeble-mindedness; split personality; manic-depressive insanity; epilepsy; St. Vitus dance; hereditary deafness and blindness; bodily deformity; and alcoholism. According to semiofficial reports 400,000 persons are to be sterilized in this radical scheme to purify the Nordic strain in the German people. It is feared that the Jews may soon come to be classed with those afflicted with hereditary diseases.[11]

2. NATURE OF STERILIZATION

Sterilization may be defined as the surgical operation by which the subject is rendered incapable of procreation. This effect may be accomplished in males either by castration or by vasectomy, which consists in cutting the vas deferens, or sperm duct, thus preventing the emission of the fertile spermatozoa and rendering the seminal discharge infertile. Vasectomy unlike castration does not destroy the urge for indulgence, nor render a person incapable of sex gratification. Similar operations are used in the case of female. In ancient times the ovaries were cut out, but this dangerous operation has been replaced by salpingectomy, which consists in cutting the Fallopian tubes, through which the ovum passes from the ovaries to the womb. Another means has recently been discovered to sterilize both men and women. The X-ray is used to burn or singe the cells so that they die. The advantage of this is that the individual can be sterilized for any length of time desired. What about eventual effects of X-ray on the body?

3. THE PURPOSE OF EUGENICS

In 1865, Gregor Mendel discovered his famous laws of inheritance. The rediscovery of these laws in 1900 gave the starting impetus to a new sociological idea. Studies and experimentations upon mice, rats, etc., showed that they held for animals as well as for plants. If for other animals why not for men also. However, men could not be experimented on for obvious reasons, so scientists did the next best thing: looked up geneologies.

---

[11] "Nazi Decree," *Literary Digest,* Jan. 13, 1934, p. 17.

They uncovered the famous Kallikak family. Martin Kallikak, the first of the Kallikaks, had during the American Revolution relations with a feeble-minded woman, who begot him an illegitimate son. This son was the ancestor of 480 descendants, of whom 143 were feeble-minded, 36 illegitimate, 71 immoral, leaving 46 normal; the remaining 82 died in infancy. But Martin after his affair married respectably. From this second union descended 489 persons all normal.

On the other hand, eugenists found another family, the Edwards. Richard Edwards married Elizabeth Tuthill. This union gave rise to 13 college presidents; 295 college graduates; 65 college professors; 100 clergymen; 100 lawyers; 80 public officers; 75 army officers; 60 prominent authors; 60 physicians; 30 judges; some governors and congressmen; 3 United States senators; 2 United States Presidents, and a chief justice of the United States Supreme Court. Richard Edwards later married Mary Talcott from which union only ordinary persons descended. From these and similar cases the eugenists concluded that feeble-mindedness and intelligence are hereditary and cast about for a means of preventing further cases of feeble-mindedness. Says E. S. Gosney, of the Human Betterment foundation of California:

"Nature's method for insuring the survival of mankind and for promoting a certain amount of progress, was to kill off, by severe conditions of life, the weak and unfit while the children of the strong, able, and intelligent had a better chance to survive, reach maturity, and become the parents of the next generation.

"The progress of civilization has made many changes in this primitive and ruthless but effective program of natural eugenics. The increasing complexity of culture and science has resulted in the failure of the more intelligent part of the population to produce enough children even to replace their own numbers.

"On the other hand, these factors have not made themselves felt to the same degree among the feebleminded, the unstable, the restless, the alcoholic, and the chronically dependent paupers. Not only has the birth rate in these groups continued relatively high, but the progress of civilization, human sympathy, and charity have intervened in nature's plan, rescued these weak and defective children, nursed them to maturity, and allowed them to reproduce children who often perpetuated their own type and weakness."[12]

Consideration of the present widespread misery of a feeble-minded population presents indeed a dark picture to the eugenists; but the future, according to them, is still more terrible. The abnormal population reproduces itself twice as fast as the normal. This is but natural, because while sound people often limit by fair means or foul, the number of their offspring, defectives in mind or body have neither moral nor social reasons for regulating their sexual intercourse. Because they cannot confine themselves within the bounds of matrimony, they multiply themselves indefinitely through illegitimate births. It is well known that the great army of prostitutes is largely recruited from the ranks of the feeble-minded.

From the qualitative viewpoint the outlook, it seems, is still more tragic. If a farmer were to sell his best corn every year and plant only the poorest, not only would the amount of good corn be soon reduced to a minimum but the poor corn would become poorer, till finally its whole substance would be dissipated. That a racial qualitative degeneration is possible may be learned from a study of the Assyrians, the Persians, the Greeks, or the Romans.[13] Every civilized country faces this problem, and the past two or three decades have seen an attempt to meet it on a scale not used since Augustus tried in vain to prevent the disappearance of the Roman people 1900 years ago.[14]

"No one will deny that there is in each generation some degree of inheritance of physical and mental fitness. Therefore, on any theory of heredity it is clear that under existing conditions the average level of intelligence and of physical and mental fitness in the American population is declining steadily. The exact rate of this decline is debatable. The fact that the decline exists is

---

[12] E. S. Gosney, "Eugenical Sterilization," *Scientific American*, 151:18.
[13] Mayer, *op. cit.*, p. 6.
[14] Gosney, *op. cit.*, p. 18.

not debatable (in the opinion of the author, quite debatable)."[15]

Sterilization is described as an act of neighborly love and of provision for future generations. Dr. Adolf Lorenz, famous Viennese surgeon, says that it will eventually come to all civilized countries as a means of getting rid of the scum of humanity.[16] "In short, advocates of sterilization seek 'the elimination of undesirable elements in society, along with the burden so long imposed upon it by their weakness and helplessness.' "[17] Many current factors tend to accentuate the problem. The depression has made it more difficult to maintain asylums; and a reduction of the population seems an easy solution to the unemployment problem.

4. STERILIZATION IS IMPRACTICAL

Before we discuss the morality of sterilization from the strictly ethical standpoint, it will be well to examine the purely pragmatic considerations that alone condemn it as a policy.

In the first place, conditions are not as dreary as alarmists paint them. We must remember that those who cite staggering increases in the feeble-minded population since 1880, must be reminded that in those days the feeble-minded were not taken care of in State institutions, and that the majority of them were overlooked. Therefore, there is something wrong in Mr. Gosney's calculations that there are 1,000,000 insane and feeble-minded people in this country.[18] It is a well-known rule of biology that nature tends to a golden mean. When insanity or feeble-mindedness attack a stock they will either kill the stock off within three generations, or will themselves be eradicated.

Furthermore, environment often plays the major part in the making of a feeble-minded person. Members of the Kallikak family who moved out of the poor Adirondack region were all normal. Our highly mechanized industrial system with its fright-

---

[15] *Loc. cit.*

[16] Adolf Lorenz, *Scientific American*, Vol. 151, p. 17.

[17] Cox, Ig. W., S.J., "The Folly of Human Sterilization," *Scientific American*, Vol. 151, p. 188.

[18] *Literary Digest*, Vol. 114, p. 16.

ful monotony for the laborer has caused more mental derange-
ment, perhaps than Nature herself. For this reason Fr. Ignatius
Cox excoriates the humanitarians who instead of working to
correct our perverted and immoral economic system at its source
are proposing palliatives and pseudo-remedies such as birth
control and sterilization.[19]

In the second place sterilization is ineffective. "The eugenic
purpose of sterilization is based on the possibility of eliminating
from the race all the defective genes. (A gene is an element in
the chromosome of the parents which determines the physical
characteristics of the offspring.) The sterilizers simply propose
to find out all the male and female defectives in the country
and make it impossible for them to transmit these genes. Their
proposal is based on a complete misconception of biology, as
Dr. Fraser has no difficulty in showing. There is not one, but
there are two ways, by which defects are inherited: the person
may be feebleminded, and thus be easily recognized; but on the
other hand, he may be entirely normal himself, but a carrier of
a defective gene. You could eliminate all the known feeble-
minded, but how are you going to find the carriers, that is those
normal persons who have a single defective gene in their chromosomes, and who, to produce an individual with the defect indi-
cated, would have to meet another individual, defective or normal who has a defective gene in the same order. (NOTE: there
are millions of genes in each chromosome any one of which may
unite with any one of the millions in the other chromosome.)
Two feeble-minded persons, on the other hand, can generate a
perfectly normal, even superior, child, because their defection
genes are in different positions in the chromosomes."[20]

"Hence, Dr. A. F. Tredglod, a leading English authority on
mental deficiency, declares that 'in order to produce any marked
decrease in the total number of mental defectives a generation
hence, it would be necessary to sterilize or otherwise prevent the
propagation of not merely those who are in themselves defec-

[19] *Daily American Tribune*, Apr. 22, 1935.
[20] Wilfrid Parsons, "Sterilization Is Criminal Folly," *America*, 44:445.

tives, but all those who are carriers, that is to say, every person suffering from germ vitiation.' What proportion of those who are capable of transmitting mental deficiencies are themselves defective and what proportion are carriers? Dr. H. S. Jennings cites the estimate of R. A. Fisher that about 11 per cent of the feeble-minded are derived from feeble-minded parents, while the other 89 per cent have carriers as their parents. It is estimated that 'by entirely excluding the feeble-minded from propagation in the present and future generations, the number of feeble-minded is reduced at the first generation by about 11 per cent; thereafter very little progress is made in reducing their number.' To decrease the proportion of inherited feeble-minded in the population by only 10 per cent *would* require about 68 generations or about 3000 years. With this it must be remembered that only about half of the cases are inherited. The other half would continue.

"And to make the demonstration simply crushing, Dr. Fraser recalls that a gene is not 'something that gives rise to a unit characteristic,' but 'something that in a given environment gives rise to a certain characteristic.' Thus a child may be the offspring of two parents each with a defective gene in the same position and yet not be defective himself at all, unless he develops in an environment favorable to the cultivation of the effects of that gene. Finally and worst of all, Dr. Fraser tells us, 'We have abundant evidence that they (defective genes) are being manufactured in normal individuals as fast as we could possible get rid of them.' "[21]

Parsons commenting on this continues, "From this demonstration taken from facts developed by experiments under Abbot Mendel's law, it is perfectly clear that eugenics, and particularly that form of it which demands sterilization of the 'unfit' is probably the most gigantic and cruel hoax that has ever been foisted on a credulous people."[22]

---

[21] J. A. Ryan, *op. cit.,* pp. 286, 287.

[22] Parsons, *op. cit.,* p. 446.

In the third place sterilization is unsure. We have shown that sterilizing defectives will not prevent the birth of more. The theory that superior individuals come only from superior people is likewise untenable. As a matter of fact, if Germany's sterilization bill had been in effect all the time, many of the world's greatest geniuses would never been born, because their parents would have been sterilized. Raymond Pearl says that 95 per cent of the world's greatest philosophers, poets, and scientists would have been lost to the world if the eugenists could have gotten at their parents.[23]

Elizabeth Tuthill, wife of Richard Edwards and mother of the famous Edwards family spoken of before, was divorced by her husband on the ground of adultery and gross immorality. Seemingly it was in her blood, for her sister killed her own child, and a brother his sister. Surely if any one should have been sterilized it was she. And yet if the eugenists had had their way the famous line of authors, officials, and university graduates, would have remained in the realm of potential essences. Are we going to trust our future geniuses to the *nutum* of a few half-crazed eugenists?

5. Morality of Sterlization

Until 1931, theologians were divided on the morality of sterilization. Some such as Mayer argued that since the defective has no right to reproduction, the State would not be depriving him of anything in removing the faculty. Laboure, Donovan, and others also defended the proposition that the State could sterilize. They held that as an individual may remove any of his members to preserve the body, so the State may cut off some of the parts of its members for the welfare of the body politic.

But all controversy was settled when on Jan. 1, 1931, Pius XI stated: "Public magistrates have no direct power over the bodies of their subject, therefore, where no crime has taken place and there is no cause present for grave punishment, they can never

---

[23] Raymond Pearl, *Present status of Eugenics* (Hanover, N. H.: Sociological Press, 1928).

directly harm, or tamper with the integrity of the body, either for the reasons of eugenics or for any other reason."[24] *Roma locuta, causa finita.*

Sterilization subverts the natural law for while it frees the individual from all danger of possible children, it leaves with him the old urges and passions. "The moral law obliges man to use his faculties in accordance with the finality written in their nature. To use a faculty and positively to frustrate its finality is to use that faculty to abuse it. To say that sterilization leaves the faculty unimpaired, as not a few have done, is absurd. Its primary purpose is defeated. One may legitimately refrain from the use of a faculty as of speech or of sex. It is quite another thing to use such faculties and in their abuse to provide positive means for frustration of their primary purpose as happens in the case of lying and sterilization."[25]

Has the State the right to deprive a citizen of the procreative faculty? State sterilization implies State absolutism, namely, that the citizen exists for the State and not the State for the citizen. But as has been shown, "the individual with his personality and all his original rights exists antecedently to the State. Wherever there is a multitude of men, a State will arise either by force of circumstances or by the deliberate action of the people. The first purpose of the State is to safeguard the community and its members against injuries in all those things and on those occasions where the individual would be too weak. It is therefore evident that the public authority must respect individuals as it finds them, that is, as endowed with all the rights with which they have been invested by their Creator. Among the foremost of these rights is the right to the physical integrity of their person. The right of man to himself is one of those rights which man possesses independently of any created power or agency, or of any other man or combination of men. He enters life as a person, that is, as one of the most definite beings possible which by its very existence must be endowed with the most definite right to

---

[24] Pius XI, *Casti Connubii* (Christian Marriage).
[25] Cox, Ig., S.J., *op. cit.*, p. 188.

itself such as it is, body and soul; a right which cannot be more closely defined or limited or rectified or modified. Man's right to himself and all parts of himself originates with every individual and is essentially inseparable from him.

"This right of man to all the parts of his physical personality includes a sacred and serious duty toward God. As man is owner of the things he produces, so the Maker of man is man's superior owner. Man holds his own physical personality in trust from Him who created him, and he is responsible for it to his Creator. He must respect God's higher ownership."[26] In a very real sense sterilization involves a degradation of man's personality and degrades him to the barrenness of unorganized matter. The State is bound not only to respect but also to protect in every reasonable manner this right of its subjects.

But it will be objected, are not these defectives a menace to the commonwealth? Has not the State the right of self-defense? Cannot the State demand this sacrifice from its weaker members, as Justice Holmes expresses it, "We have seen more than once that the public welfare may call upon the best citizens for their lives (e.g., in war). It would be strange, if it could not call upon those who already sap the strength of the State for these lesser sacrifices, often not felt so much by those concerned, in order to prevent our being swamped with incompetency?" We must distinguish here with F. R. Betten, between direct and indirect action. "In the case of direct action the State is responsible for the thing that is done. When the State sends out soldiers, it has by no means the will that they shall be killed. It does not order them to be shot or wounded. On the contrary it takes every possible precaution to protect them from any injury. It is the enemy who kills them. This is indirect action. The death of the soldiers is not intended but merely permitted, because under the circumstances it simply cannot be helped.

"In the case of sterilization the State is the actor. The State expresses its will that the imbecile be subjected to treatment.

---

[26] Betten, "The Morality of Sterilization," *Catholic Mind*, 1933.

The State takes every step necessary to bring that mutilation about. The State positively wants the unfortunate person to leave the operating room a cripple in one of his natural rights. Hence the State itself directly attacks the victim in one of his inviolable and most sacred rights. The State is responsible for sterilization in the fullest sense of the word. It is impossible to plead for the State the necessity of self-defense. If I know that someone is going to attack me next year, I may not take his life now. It is indeed very thoughtless to speak of the procreation of imbecile children as an attack upon the welfare of the State or the public treasury. Neither the feeble-minded parents nor the imbecile children are burglars. At any rate if there were an attack it is not actual, it does not happen right now. It would take place after a considerable lapse of time, if at all."[27]

However, the State has the right to rid itself of persons who are a continual danger. It may exile them; it may confine them. Of course, in so doing it takes away their right of free intercourse with their fellow men, but they remain full men, they retain all their integral parts. Proponents of legal sterilization hold that sterilization would mean an immense saving for the taxpayer inasmuch as many feeble-minded could be released from institutions. But the State could not turn them loose even if they were sterile. For a sterile woman knowing that she had no consequences to fear in the form of children might be the prey of vicious men, and the costs of immorality and social diseases would in the end be higher than the cost of institutional care.

There are two classes of defectives, the one of those so socially incompetent that custodial care is necessary, and the other composed of such as could be allowed to live in society. With respect to the first, since they would have to be kept in institutions there is not reason for sterilization. The other class composed of the higher grade of morons can be employed under the supervision of trained attendants. They should be placed in colonies. These are practically self-supporting, since the inmates contribute sub-

---

[27] Betten, *op. cit.*

stantially to their support. After a period of training in these places, they may be returned to society. Dr. Fernald head of the school for feeble-minded at Waverly, Massachusetts, says that a surprisingly small number of the women released become mothers.[28]

Thomas Verner Moore sums up his study on the heredity of feeble-mindedness with the following remarks:

1. "We don't know how mentality is inherited.

2. "We don't know the contribution of the total environment to the mentality of the individual.

3. "We don't know how many persons of very high grade intelligence our present society could stand.

4. "We don't know how we should distribute the degrees of mentality in the general population for the greatest welfare of society."[29]

SELECT READINGS

Betten, S.J., "The Morality of Sterilization, *Catholic Mind.*

Bruehl, Charles, "Eugenical Sterilization," *Homiletical and Pastoral Review,* Vol. 26:1235.

——— "Moral Aspects of Sterilization," *Homiletic and Pastoral Review,* 26:1123.

Cox, Ig., S.J., "The Folly of Human Sterilization," *Scientific American,* 151:188.

Gest, "Legal Status of Sterilization," *Ecclesiastical Review,* Vol. 91.

Gosney, E. S., "Eugenical Sterilization," *Scientific American,* Vol. 151, p. 18 f.

Landman, "Human Sterilization," *Scientific American,* Vol. 151.

Mayer, J., *Gesetzliche Unfruchtbarmachung Geisteskranker,* '31 Freiburg.

Moore, Thomas V., "The Heredity of Feeblemindedness," *Thought,* Vol. IX, 560 ff.

Muench, A. J., "Sterilization by Law" (St. Louis: Central-Verein Bureau, 1929).

"Nazi Decree," *Literary Digest,* Jan. 13, 1934, p. 17 f.

---

[28] A. J. Muench, *op. cit.*

[29] "The Heredity of Feeblemindedness," *Thought,* Vol. IX, p. 562.

Parsons, Wilfrid, S.J., "Sterilization Is Criminal Folly," *America*, 44:445 f.

Ryan, J. A., *Questions of the Day* (Boston: Stratford Press, 1931), Ch. 20.

See also *Ecclesiastical Review*, Vol. 42–47, *passim*, for a thorough discussion of the morality of vasectomy.

Siegfrid, Andre, *The Epic of America*, "Race Consciousness."

INDEX

Absolutism, and divine origin of power, 59; democratic, 45–50; Hobbesian, see Hobbes; monarchic, 4, 47; State, 1

Act and potency, and Aristotle, 194 f.

Aggression, unjust, and force, 153

Agnosticism, 19

American Declaration of Independence, and rights, 206

Anarchy, 253; and absolute liberty, 17; and authority, 14, 16; and autonomy, 18; and common good, 14; and human rights, 18; and modern educators, 19; and new social order, 18; and private property, 18; and scholastic contractualism, 74; and self-realization, 15; and theory of might, 17; critical analysis of, 16 ff.; impracticability of, 18 f.; social, absurdities of, 16; social, theory of, 14 ff.; struggle against, 19; see also Social anarchy

Anti-Semitism, 202

Arbitrariness, and natural right, 164

Aristotle, on act and potency, 194; on extra-social man, 29; on family, 20; on purpose of State, 99; on slavery, 99; on specific qualities, 5 f.; on State, 99; on sterilization, 331

Artificial birth control, see Birth control

Aspinas, organic view of State, 119

Association, right of, and common good, 237 f.

Atheism, consequences of, 305

Atomistic theory of State, 26

Authority, and anarchy, 14, 16; and natural law, 168; and naturalism, 42; and State, 24; divine origin of, 56; limitation of, 57; necessity of, 16; social, definition of, 25; see also Civil authority; Civil power

Autonomy, among ancients, 99 f.;

and anarchy, 18; of human reason, 92; State, 92

Bakounine, M., on civil society, 16

Bañez, on rebellion, 73

Beccario, on society, 25

Bellarmine, on civil power, 66; on equality, 69 f.; on papal authority, 308

Biogenetical law, 190

Birth control, 280 ff.; and individual, 281; and Malthus, 280; and Pius XI, 281; and State, 282 f.; intrinsically bad, 281; see also Contraceptives

Blackstone, on natural law, 158

Bluntschli, and end of State, 35; on civil power, 33 ff.; on State, 119

Bodin, 119

Bosanquet, identification of State with real will of individual, 37

Buck, Carrie, 332

Caesaro-Papism, 320

Capital, and labor, 258

Capital punishment, 214; and individual rights, 44; and St. Thomas, 214

Cardinal Bellarmine, see Bellarmine

Casti Connubii, 231

Categorial imperative, 123, 154

Catholic church, see Church

Causality, 185 f.

Cause, definition of, 185; efficient, 185; final, 185; formal, 185; intelligent, existence of, 196; material, 185

Choice of profession, and collectivism, 234 f.; and parents, 234; and State, 233 ff.; importance of, 234

Christianity, and equality, 256, 263; and family, 102; and human personality, 100, 127; and individual, 102; and racism, 203 f.; and State, 102; and totalitarian State, 133 f.; apostasy from, 19

345

and communism, 254 ff., 295 f.; and education, 293 f.; and morality, 247, 305; influence of on society, 304 f.; State attitude toward, 303 ff.
Rerum Novarum, 109, 114, 220, 258
Revolution, and Rousseau, 67
Riches, use of, Leo XIII, 224 f.
Rickaby, on right, 178
Right, and coercion, 143 f.; and custom, 146; and enforcement, 147 ff.; and evolutionism, 13; and God, 163; and human welfare, 81; and Kant, 153 ff.; and law, 164; and might, 130 f.; and moral law, 158 f.; and moral obligation, 145; and morality, 171 ff.; and obligation, 18; and positivism, 136 f.; and statal will, 127 f.; and State, 136–177; and subjective norm, 18; and theism, 156 ff.; defined, 158; essentially distinct from wrong, 146; natural, and Cicero, 167; natural, and State, 167; obligatory character of, 170; of association and common good, 237 f.; of self-determination, and Ryan, J. A., 81; of self-determination, and savages, 81; source of, and Rosmini, A., 145; to education, 283 f.; to liberty, 232 ff.; to life, 208–215; to marry, 271; to private property, 215–225; to work, *see* Right to work; ultimate basis of, 156 ff.
Right to work, 228 ff.; and distributive justice, 229; and St. Thomas, 228 f.; and socialism, 230; and State, 229 f.; meaning of, 229
Rights, and American Declaration of Independence, 206; and human personality, 183; and materialism, 181; and morality, Kant on, 154 f.; and positivism, 184; and Rickaby, 178; and Rousseau, 153 ff.; and social sanction, 155; and socialism, 260; inalienable, 1
Robespierre, on despotism, 103
Rosmini, A., on source of right, 145
Rousseau, 119; and civil obedience, 49; and contractualist hypothesis, 45–50; and equality, 45; and government, 47; and law, 47; and rebellion, 67; and theory of social contract, 5 f.; criticism of his theory, 50; his state of nature, 5; Ireland on, 50; on civil power, 5, 33; on civil society and free contract, 5; on general will, 5; on

personal liberty, 89; on rights, 153; on society, 25
Rugged individualism, 93
Rule of might, 55
Russia, 18
Russian Revolution, and naturalism, 42
Ryan, J. A., on origin of authority, 82 f.; on right of self-determination, 81

St. Augustine, 331; *Confessions,* 30; on Catholic belief, 310; on State, 30
St. Jerome, 331
St. Paul, on man's end, 199 f.
St. Thomas, and necessity of ownership, 218 ff.; and punitive sterilization, 330; and social contractualism, 74 f.; and teleology, 196; on capital punishment, 214; on common good, 97, 108 f.; on derivation of positive law, 114; on distributive justice, 114; on eternal law, 157 f.; on family, 20; on instinct, 191; on law, 75; on legal justice, 68; on ownership, 216; on natural law, 157 f.; on the nature of civil society, 30; on origin of power, 308; on purpose of material goods, 260; on right to work, 228 f.; on social aspect of ownership, 224; on sterilization, 331; on unjust laws, 175 f.
Salpingectomy, 332
Salus populi suprema lex esto, 99
Santayana, 187
Schaeffle, on social organism, 119
Scholastic contractualism, 64–76; and anarchy, 74; and faith, 75; and Hobbes and Rousseau, 66 f.; and St. Thomas, 75 f.; arguments against, 69–76; criticism of, 68 ff.
Secret societies, and State, 237 f.
Self-defense, and unjust aggression, 208 f.
Self-development, and private property, 218 f.
Self-preservation impulse, 11
Self-protectionism, and statal end, 88 f.
Self-realization, and anarchy, 15; and egoism, 15
Self-reflection, power of, 12
Separation of Church and State, 309–317; and United States, 314; complete, evil consequences of, 312 ff.; Leo XIII, 310

356 INDEX

State absolutism, 1; and Christianity, 100; and Hegel, 101; and individualism, 95 f.; and liberalism, 98; and Plato, 98 f.; and sterilization, 340 ff.; *see also* Totalitarianism
State autonomy, 92
State totalitarianism, *see* Totalitarianism
Statolatry, and Pius XI, 134; and statal end, 101 ff.
Sterilization, 330–343; and biology, 337; and Egyptians, 331; and Lydians, 331; and man's personality, 341; and natural law, 340 ff.; and Pius XI, 339 f.; and State, 340 ff.; and theologians, 339; and United States, 331 ff.; and United States Supreme Court decision, 332; and world's greatest geniuses, 339; eugenic, 330; German law of 1934 for, 332; history of, 331 ff.; impractical, 336 ff.; ineffective, 337; morality of, 339 ff.; nature of, 333; punitive, 330; therapeutic, 330; unsure, 338 f.
Stirner, Max, and civil society, 15
Struggle for existence, 6, 89, 93
Struggle for life, 11
Suarez, on civil power, 63; on equality, 69 f.; on patriarchal power, 71 f.; on social contract, 63, 65; on tyranny, 73 f.
Subhuman, prehistoric, and anthropology, 10
Subjectivism, Kantian, 195
Subjective right, and coercion, 150 ff.; defined, 150
Suicide, 209 f.
Summa Theologica, 176
Superman, Nietzsche's, 15

Teaching, a natural right, 285; and Leo XIII, 285; and socialism, 286; and State, 286; parental right, 286
Teleology, 184–197; and Kant, 195 f.; and mechanism, 190 f.; and pantheism, 196; and private ownership, 217; and St. Thomas, 196; cosmic, 187
Theism, and man's goal, 160; and right, 156 ff.
Theophobia, 187
Theories of State, erroneous, 3–19

Theory of economics, 89 f.
Tolomei, on coercion, 149
Totalitarian State, 116–135; and Christianity, 133 f.; and Church, 296 f.; and democracy, 134 f.; and education, 284; and equality, 257; and family, 265; and individual rights, 206 ff.; and international law, 124 ff.; and liberty, 239 f.; criticism of, 121–135; defined, 120; *see also* Totalitarianism
Totalitarianism, 116; and distributive justice, 131 f.; and family right, 128 ff.; and Hoffman, R. J. S., 120; and individual rights, 128 ff.; and liberalism, 117 f.; and Maritain, 127; condemned by Catholic bishops, 133; ideologies of, 118; philosophical sources of, 119; *see also* State absolutism, Totalitarian State
Truth and liberty, 242
Tyranny, and Hobbesian absolutism, 45; and Suarez, 73 f.

United States, and Church, 297; and separation of Church and State, 314; and sterilization, 331 ff.; religious policy of, 311
Unitive principle, necessity of, 52
Universe, Christian concept of and Spencer, 13 f.
Unjust aggression, and self-defense, 208 f.
Unjust laws, and Aquinas, 175 f.; and obedience, 174 f.
Utilitarians, on human nature, 159
Utopia, communistic, 15

Vasectomy, 330
Verner Moore, on heredity of feeble-mindedness, 343
Volitions, and instincts, 14
Von Galen, Bishop, on Euthanasia, 212 f.

War of every man against every man, 17
Westermarck, E., on group marriages, 270; on promiscuity, 269; on promiscuity hypothesis, 8
Will, defined, 182
Wilson, Woodrow, on origin of civil power, 32